The Surprising Election and Confirmation of King David

HARVARD THEOLOGICAL STUDIES
63

CAMBRIDGE, MASSACHUSETTS

The Surprising Election and Confirmation of King David

J. Randall Short

DISTRIBUTED BY

HARVARD UNIVERSITY PRESS

FOR

HARVARD THEOLOGICAL STUDIES
HARVARD DIVINITY SCHOOL

The Surprising Election and Confirmation of King David

Harvard Theological Studies 63

Series Editors:

François Bovon

Francis Schüssler Fiorenza

Peter B. Machinist

The foreign language font (New Jerusalem) and transliteration fonts used in this book are available from Linguist's Software, Inc., PO Box 580, Edmonds, WA 98020-0580; tel: (425) 775-1130. Website: www.linguistsoftware.com

Short, John Randall, 1970-
    The surprising election and confirmation of King David / John Randall Short.
        p. cm. -- (Harvard theological studies ; 63)
    Includes bibliographical references (p.   ) and index.
    ISBN 978-0-674-05341-0 (alk. paper)
    1. David, King of Israel. 2. Bible. O.T. Samuel, 1st, XVI-Samuel, 2nd, V--Criticism, interpretation, etc. I. Title.
    BS1325.52.S56 2010
    222'.406--dc22
                                                                    2010022427

For My Wife,
Atsuko

My Daughters,
Cana, Emmy, Mana

and

Our Parents,
Melton and Linda Short
Tadashi and Hatsue Tsunemi

Table of Contents

Acknowledgments

I sometimes imagine a version of this book with embedded videos and pop-up texts that tell some of the many life stories behind its making. Perhaps we will soon see digital books come to resemble DVD movies in that way, with special features that include stories from and about the author's family, friends, mentors, and others who played some direct or indirect role in its production. Though most readers might take little interest in my own book's special features menu, they must know that I could offer them little of substance were it not for the many behind-the-scenes stories, both big and small, that gave meaning and purpose to the research, writing, and editing of every page. Though I cannot tell those stories here, I am happy to acknowledge some of the many who played leading and supporting roles in the making of this book.

I completed most of my work on this book while writing my Th.D. dissertation at Harvard Divinity School. I am especially grateful to Professors Jon D. Levenson, Gary A. Anderson, and Paul D. Hanson for serving on my dissertation committee and extending to me their guidance, patience, and encouragement. Professor Levenson's direction and sage advice was always timely, deeply insightful, and seasoned with his good humor. He assisted me in leaping over many a wall (to use an expression from 2 Sam 22). Professor Anderson inspired me to concentrate on the story of David's rise in an independent study with him, and he, too, offered me invaluable guidance and feedback, both before and after his move from Harvard to Notre Dame. Professor Hanson steered me away from more than one dead end through stimulating discussions both in and outside of the classroom. I would also like to extend my special thanks to Professors Peter B. Machinist and Annewies van den Hoek for their invaluable instruction and encouragement.

The editorial and production staff at Harvard Theological Studies has been astounding. I would like to thank managing editor Margaret Studier, who expertly and graciously guided me (and her staff) throughout the entire process. This included her mediation on behalf of two anonymous reviewers, who stimulated my rethinking of numerous points, and her timely encouragement that made every stage of this publication enjoyable and educational. I am also grateful to Rebecca Hancock, who meticulously proofread and painstakingly typeset my manuscript, Hebrew and all; and I am thankful to Eve Feinstein, Richard Jude Thompson, and Keith Stone for their editorial contributions. Though I found the image for the cover, Eric Mulder must receive all credit for the beautiful cover design. Finally, I extend my sincere thanks to HTS series editors François Bovon, Francis Schüssler Fiorenza, and Peter B. Machinist.

There are many others at Harvard who deserve special recognition. In particular, I wish to thank Steven Beardsley, Michelle Gauthier, Renata Kalnins, Gloria Korsman, Bernadette Perrault, Clifford Wunderlich, and especially Laura Whitney at Harvard-Andover Theological Library for helping me on too many occasions to count. And I would like to acknowledge Barbara Boles, Julie Field, Debbie Gronback, Kathryn Kunkel, Sarah Lefebvre, and Margaret Studier for their assistance in many practical matters that made it possible for me to complete my doctoral work while supporting my family.

I have benefited enormously from the work of many scholars, as my footnotes on nearly every page amply testify. I would like to make special mention here, however, of my respect for P. Kyle McCarter and his work, which figures significantly in my own. I wish to thank the Society of Biblical Literature for permission to quote numerous excerpts from: P. Kyle McCarter, "The Apology of David," *Journal of Biblical Literature* 99 (1980): 489–504. I also thank Koninklijke Brill NV for permission to re-publish quotations from Th. P. J. van den Hout, "Apology of Ḫattušili III" in *The Context of Scripture, Vol. 1: Canonical Compositions from the Biblical World* (ed. William W. Hallo and K. Lawson Younger, Jr.; Leiden: Brill, 1997), 199–204. All Hebrew quotations— minus the Masoretic markings—are from *Biblia Hebraica Stuttgartensia*, 4th corrected ed. (Stuttgart: Deutsche Bibelgesellschaft, 1990), and all translations of the biblical text, unless otherwise indicated, are my own.

Generous funding from the following sources made it possible for me to concentrate my energies upon my research and writing of the bulk of my manuscript: the Harvard Divinity School Dean's Dissertation Fellowship; Tokyo Christian Institute Foreign Research Fellowship (Chiba, Japan); Nagakute Presbyterian Church (Aichi, Japan); the International Junior Fellowship from Korea Institute for Advanced Theological Studies and Boondang Central House (Seoul, Korea); and Lamp Presbyterian Church

(Seoul, Korea). At the risk of failing to mention some, I extend mine and my family's deeply felt gratitude to the following individuals from these institutions (titles omitted): in Japan, Tatsushi and Hiromi Abe, Stephen Franklin, Akio Ito, Nobuyoshi Kiuchi, Takanori and Miyako Kobayashi, Masato Kuno, Masanori Kurasawa, Tadataka Maruyama, Akihiko and Chizuru Ogoshi, Tomoya Shimokawa, and Yoichi Yamaguchi; and in Korea, Jong-Cheon Choi, Jae-Hyun Kim, Young-Sun Park, and Young-Tark Yune.

Many dear friends encouraged my family and me while I worked on this book. I wish to thank, in particular, Eric and Jen Baldwin, Todd and Rachel Billings, Rick and T Downs, Ming and Emi Fong, Michael and Abby Legaspi, Mark McKinnon, John and Bea Orfanidis, Joseph Poulshock, John Rhee and Young-A Park, and Genzo and Ellen Yamamoto. Early on, unbeknownst to them, I designated Michael Legaspi and Genzo Yamamoto as two of several "virtual readers"—I stand in deep admiration of these two men as they broadly and critically engage the world of ideas in fruitful and stimulating ways.

My wife Atsuko and I grew up in different worlds—she in the East, I in the West—but the both of us were raised by loving and nurturing parents to whom we are immeasurably indebted. I thank Tadashi and Hatsue Tsunemi for accepting and supporting me as their own, and for patiently waiting for us to bring their grandchildren back to Japan. As for my own parents, Melton and Linda Short, they must be partly credited for anything good and worthwhile that I have accomplished. I owe my early interest in the Bible to my father above all (though, where I tend to make it difficult, he has "made it simple"). I also thank our siblings—Dwayne Short, Lachelle Koon, Teresa Wilson, Delaine Crim, and Naoko Hojo (together with their families)—for their love and encouragement.

My final words of thanks go to my family. I am thankful to and grateful for my daughters, Cana, Emmy, and Mana. They have amazed me by their level of enthusiasm for, and understanding of, my work. The many opportunities to set my work aside for softball and soccer games, piano and recorder lessons, Japanese Saturday school sports festivals and trips to visit family down South, or just a good tickle-session in the living room—all this has kept me well-grounded, basically sane, and deeply happy. Finally, I thank my wife Atsuko. She made many sacrifices as I worked towards this book's completion, and yet she accepted every challenge with strong purpose and resolve. Day after day, through her steadfast love and dedication, Atsuko surpassed all, as she "strengthened my hand in God."

Abbreviations

BibInt	*Biblical Interpretation*
BRev	*Bible Review*
CBQ	*Catholic Biblical Quarterly*
CurBS	*Currents in Research: Biblical Studies*
HUCA	*Hebrew Union College Annual*
JAOS	*Journal of the American Oriental Society*
JBL	*Journal of Biblical Literature*
JPJ	*Journal of Progressive Judaism*
JSOT	*Journal for the Study of the Old Testament*
VT	*Vetus Testamentum*
ZAW	*Zeitschrift für die alttestamentliche Wissenschaft*
DtrH	Deuteronomistic History
DtrP	Prophetic Deuteronomist

Introduction

King David, in the view of some biblical scholars, was a serial killer, an Israelite terrorist-turned-dictator comparable to Saddam Hussein. Consider, for example, these recent evaluations of King David based on historical reconstructions of the biblical account of Samuel, in particular:

> The real David was not someone whom it would be wise to invite to dinner. And you certainly would not be happy to discover he was marrying your daughter, or even a casual acquaintance. But he did have one virtue. His achievement in creating Judah and conquering Israel left, through his wife and through his successor, if not his son, a legacy of hope and of aspiration. If that legacy has little to do with the real David, if later imaginings of his empire magnify a small, sanitize a corrupt, and beautify an ugly reality, a reality there nevertheless was. The biblical story of David is indeed mythic in nature. But the myth was made necessary, though not by his glory, by his gore.[1]

> [David] could also be compared to other, more recent and more infamous Middle Eastern dictators, like Saddam Hussein. Both were clever politicians and military commanders. Both led outlaw bands that rivaled the ruling family. Both eventually replaced their rivals, leaving a trail of dead bodies behind. Both gained and retained power through military force.[2]

---

[1] Halpern, *David's Secret Demons*, 479–80. Halpern's fourth chapter is titled "King David, Serial Killer" (73).

[2] McKenzie, *King David*, 22. Elsewhere, McKenzie characterizes David as a "terrorist" (88–110, in his chapter, "Holy Terrorist: David and His Outlaw Band") and "a Middle Eastern tyrant" (188). McKenzie concludes his biography of David with this statement: "In a sense, this biography is truer to the Bible than the more traditional images of David that have been formed along the trajectory begun by the apology. The Bible never denies or downplays David's humanity. Critical scholars have simply explored what a human being of David's

Another scholar concludes that, in contrast to biblical texts that "narrate fundamental theological rules . . . to all Israel," the account of "David as Proper King" in 1 Sam 14:52–2 Sam 8:15 "offers no such religiously ideological lessons; instead it is interested in secular, political ideology, namely fostering Davidic kingship."[3] How have these and other contemporary scholars arrived at assessments of David and the biblical account that depart so radically from previous interpretations spanning more than two millennia.

First, in the course of analyzing the books of Samuel, scholars have postulated numerous historical contexts and life-settings, or *Sitze im Leben,* in which various segments of the text seem to have originated and in light of which they seem to make the best sense. "The History of David's Rise" (HDR), or "the Apology of David," is identified by many scholars as an originally independent and unified literary source underlying the present biblical account in 1 Samuel 16–2 Samuel 5. This original source has been dated to a number of periods, including the lifetimes of Solomon and other descendants of David, when it presumably served the function of legitimizing Davidic kingship. Some scholars,[4] however, understand HDR as a personal[5] apology that originated in the Davidic court in Jerusalem during David's own lifetime for the purpose of legitimizing his ascension to, or usurpation of, Saul's throne. These scholars have arrived at this interpretation of HDR — and, in many cases, have constructed the image of David reflected in the quotations above — based, to varying degrees, on a number of factors: a critical examination of selected details and themes within the text; a comparison of HDR with the thirteenth century B.C.E. Hittite apology of Ḫattušili III's

---

social rank in the Middle East three hundred years ago would have been like. The image that I have constructed in this biography is a composite of the results of those scholarly explorations. We can probably never know the *real* David. This image is at least a *realistic* likeness of David" (189) [emphasis in original].

[3] Brettler, *The Creation of History,* 99. Brettler is contrasting the History of David's Rise, or "David as Proper King," as he designates the narrative, with 2 Samuel 9–20, which he characterizes as "a theological unit, interested in showing the severe ramifications of serious sins, even when committed by David."

[4] That is, some among those who accept an originally independent HDR, or who, while opposing or remaining agnostic regarding the existence of an originally independent source, view the biblical text as a more or less historically reliable testimony to David's life and times.

[5] In characterizations of the "Apology of David" here and below, "personal," "individual," and similar modifiers should not be taken to mean "private," "secret," or "unofficial." By these terms, rather, I mean to emphasize how some scholars make sense of the reconstructed original source — and, in some cases, even the final biblical narrative — as directly pertaining to, and intended chiefly for the sake of, a particular historical individual, namely, King David.

seizure of the throne; and general knowledge of how Middle Eastern despots, from ancient to modern times, conduct themselves.[6]

My initial interest in the biblical account of David's rise to kingship stemmed from the recognition of a tendency of many readers to conflate the supposed meaning and significance of the putatively original and independent HDR with that of the present biblical account in 1 Samuel 16–2 Samuel 5. This is largely due to the determination by scholars, beginning with Leonhard Rost, that what we now have in 1 Samuel 16–2 Samuel 5 is essentially the same as an originally independent History of David's Rise.[7] But even if one believes that the two are "essentially" the same, or verbatim equivalents, one must account for how the establishment of new contexts of reading—in this case, the larger biblical narrative of 1 and 2 Samuel and beyond—can subtly, and sometimes dramatically, affect the narrative's meaning.

In the course of my reconsideration of these potential differences in meaning occasioned by new contexts, however, there arose a new set of questions concerning the soundness of arguments for reading even the reconstructed HDR as an originally independent, personal apology of the historical David, not to mention questions about contingent arguments supporting gossamer construals of David as a Saddam Hussein-like tyrant. The present work is my attempt to answer these and other related questions about the significance and meaning of the account of David's rise to kingship.

In chapters 1–3, I shall examine many of the assumptions and conclusions that lead to the interpretation of the biblical account of David's rise to kingship along the above lines. Chapter 1 will provide the necessary background for my discussions in chapters 2 and 3 by considering, at some length, one

---

[6] Interpretation based on the principle of realism is not a modern innovation. See, for instance, Simon, "Religious Significance," 47–48, where Simon explains how medieval Jewish exegetes, intent on discovering the straightforward meaning of the text, base their interpretations on philology and realism: "Just as the *peshat* exegete assumes that the Bible's language is subordinated to the rules of grammar and the manner of discourse of 'ordinary language' [*leshon benei adam*], so does he relate to the personalities of the Bible as to ordinary people, examining that which is related in it in light of his own familiarity with reality and life experience. This realism the Rashbam calls 'expertise in how people conduct themselves' [*beki'ut derekh erets shel benei adam*] (commentary to Lev. 13:2)" [bracketed transliterations are Simon's]. Simon goes on to distinguish between medieval and modern approaches to *peshat*: "Whereas the *peshat* of the Medieval savants was merely philological (that is, tied to the text), scientific *peshat* is philological-historical (that is, tied to the text in its historical framework)" (51).

[7] I shall discuss this in more detail in ch. 1.

particular reconstruction of an original History of David's Rise and how some scholars identify and interpret HDR as an apology of the historical David that is preserved essentially unchanged in the biblical text of 1 Samuel 16–2 Samuel 5.[8] My secondary aim in this chapter will be to highlight the historical rootedness or particularity that this interpretation of HDR assumes and, indeed, requires. These observations will prepare the way for challenging the common assumption that this particular historical-critical framework provides the best means for interpreting 1 Samuel 16–2 Samuel 5.

In chapter 2, I shall reassess the nature and degree of similarity between the reconstructed HDR and the Hittite Apology of Ḫattušili. As I compare and contrast these texts, I shall argue that, thematically and functionally speaking, HDR has less in common with the Apology of Ḫattušili than scholars have asserted. While similarities between the two are generally held up more as confirmation of the view that HDR is an apologetic text than as the primary basis for this view, scholars often regard the parallels as highly significant evidence for dating HDR to David's own lifetime and for proving that, consequently, HDR must have meant to David what the Hittite text meant to Ḫattušili: personal vindication, or self-justification, vis-à-vis charges of lese-majesty. Inasmuch, then, as my study significantly erodes the common ground between the two texts, the hypothesis that an originally independent History of David's Rise was composed as essentially personal self-justification for David himself merits a fundamental reconsideration. It thus becomes necessary to reexamine the bases for detecting in the biblical account (in any of its literary stages) the sort of "rhetorical posture" that some have proposed.

Chapter 3, therefore, attends more directly to the rhetorical posturing that some discern in HDR and interpret as having been evoked by several underlying charges against the historical David. I shall demonstrate that this interpretation is persuasive only to the degree to which the reader assumes the particular historical situation and motives that certain scholars have reconstructed and proposed as the impetus for the composition. While this interpretation may be based upon a close reading of the text, as scholars claim, it is also based heavily upon extra-textual determinations of "what really happened." As chapter 2 also demonstrates, the basis for these assumptions

---

[8] Though I will touch upon other reconstructions of HDR, the reasons for focusing on that of Kyle McCarter will become clear in the course of my discussion.

with regard to HDR read in isolation from the surrounding biblical account is weaker than many have acknowledged.

In the first three chapters, then, my aim is to challenge the assumption that the biblical account of David's rise to kingship was originally composed, and is thus best understood, as an independent work of religio-political propaganda designed to serve the personal exigencies of David himself. Attempts at reconstructing the putative original apology, and arguments attributing its genesis or evocation to individual, propagandistic needs, rely as heavily on hypotheses of "what really happened" in the life of the historical David as on a "close reading of the text."

Still more problematic than this hypothetical, historically particularized reading of HDR is the tendency of scholars to regard it as determining the meaning of the full account found in the present biblical narrative, which I examine in chapters 4 and 5. As noted above, some scholars have conflated the meanings of the reconstructed and final forms of the account at least partly because of the assumption that the original HDR has been transmitted essentially unchanged in form and thematic thrust into its present shape in 1 and 2 Samuel. I shall contend, however, that Samuel's story of David's replacement of Saul as Israel's king should not be read chiefly as a personal apology exonerating an individual king—whether David or one of his descendants—from charges that he usurped the throne illegitimately. The biblical narrative is best understood, rather, as dramatically representing to YHWH's covenant-community His mysteriously and wonderfully surprising election and confirmation of "the least" as YHWH's beloved. I shall demonstrate this in chapters 4 and 5 while concentrating chiefly upon the biblical account leading up to Saul's death. First, in chapter 4, I shall argue that YHWH's initial election of David is helpfully understood in terms of His "finding," "choosing," and "providing" Himself a new king. Then, in chapter 5, I shall demonstrate how YHWH's election of David is confirmed—with great surprise and wonder—through the gradual emergence of David as the beloved son of Jesse, the beloved son of Saul, and the beloved son of YHWH and the people of Israel.

My Approach to the Hebrew Biblical Text

It is complicated enough to interpret any Hebrew text from antiquity. This complication is compounded when the discussion must encompass one or more hypothetical sources thought to underlie the biblical text. Consider, too, that the text of the books of Samuel is riddled with many textual difficulties, and the prospect of establishing a common ground for the sake of discussion—not to mention agreement—can seem rather bleak. Such is our dilemma in the present study of the biblical account and putative sources of David's rise to kingship. The following questions, in particular, need to be addressed. Should one boldly reconstruct an "original" text (or texts, if positing multiple literary stages) despite the inevitability that many will regard this reconstruction with guarded skepticism? Or should one work primarily with the Masoretic Text (MT)[9] despite the fact that it does not fully represent a singular pristine form of the biblical account (a point on which all can agree, even if not on the details)? There are no easy answers to these questions, but it is important here at the outset to comment on my approach to the Hebrew text, and to note briefly the primary advantages and limitations that accompany this approach.[10]

I have selected *Biblia Hebraica Stuttgartensia* (*BHS*) as my base text for reading and interpreting the story of David's rise to kingship—both in the "abridged" version of HDR (especially in chapters 1–3) and the "unabridged" version familiar to modern Bible readers (especially in chapters 4 and 5). *BHS* has much in its favor. In its various editions, *BHS* is, by far, the most widely disseminated and interpreted text of the Hebrew Bible among modern biblical scholars and translators.[11] This wide acceptance is a result of *BHS*'s

[9] All references to the "Masoretic Text" or "MT" in the present study are, in fact, to one particular Masoretic tradition among others—the Tiberian Masoretic Text attributed to the ben Asher family during the Middle Ages—whether explicitly identified as "Tiberian" or not. My reasons for following the Tiberian tradition shall become clear in the ensuing discussion.

[10] For introductory treatments of the text of Samuel by relatively recent commentators, including brief discussions on the "received" Masoretic Text and other Hebrew texts, as well as Greek, Aramaic, Syriac, Latin, and other versions that have been preserved from antiquity, see the following: McCarter, *I Samuel*, esp. 5–11; idem., *II Samuel*, esp. 3; Klein, *1 Samuel*, esp. xxv–xxviii; Anderson, *2 Samuel*, esp. xxi–xxiii; Tsumura, *First Book of Samuel*, esp. 2–10.

[11] The most recent edition of *BHS* was published in 1997; the previous single-volume editions were published in 1977, 1984, 1987, and 1990. *BHS* was the successor to the 1937 edition of *Biblia Hebraica* (*BH*), which was the first to use the Leningrad Codex, and it will

attempt to reproduce the codex Leningrad B19a,[12] which is important for
several related reasons. First, dating to the early eleventh century C.E., the
Leningrad Codex is the oldest extant complete manuscript of the Hebrew
Bible. Second, it adheres closely to the vocalization system established by
Aaron ben Moses ben Asher in Tiberias in the tenth century, which is most
accurately preserved in the Aleppo Codex.[13] This is significant because it is
the Tiberian Masoretic manuscript tradition that eventually emerged among
others as the authoritative tradition in Judaism and Christianity (except
among Orthodox Christians, for whom the Septuagint and/or translations
thereof are authoritative).[14]

The Tiberian MT's pedigree and contemporary authoritative status alone,
however, do not constitute sufficient grounds for its adoption by scholars
whose main focus is the significance of the biblical text for its earliest
readers.[15] Such scholars must base their analyses on a text or texts that can
be reasonably presumed to have attained an authoritative claim among the

eventually be succeeded by *Biblia Hebraica Quinta* (*BHQ*), which is currently being published
in fascicles by the United Bible Societies with the German Bible Society's sponsorship. The
Leningrad Codex is also represented in *Biblia Hebraica Leningradensia* (*BHL*) and in most
Bible software applications, as well as in *The Leningrad Codex: A Facsimile Edition*. On
the importance of the Leningrad Codex see, in particular, the introductory essays in *The
Leningrad Codex* by Beck ("Introduction to the Leningrad Codex," ix–xx), Lebedev ("The
Oldest Complete Codex of the Hebrew Bible," xxi–xxviii), and Revell ("The Leningrad
Codex as a Representative of the Masoretic Text," xxix–xlvi).

[12] One can recognize, however, some differences between the Leningrad manuscript
and *BHS* in, e.g., the sequence of the biblical books; *BHS*'s style of presenting "poetry";
the notes of the Masorah; and even a few typographical mistakes in *BHS*, at least up to the
1984 edition. On these and other minor differences, see, e.g., Tov, *Textual Criticism*, 2–8.
Dotan's brief discussion about the difficulty of accurately reproducing the original manuscript
is instructive in this regard (*BHL*, xi–xxi).

[13] Aaron ben Moses ben Asher himself vocalized and accented the Aleppo Codex in or
around 925 C.E. Unfortunately, approximately one-fourth of the codex, including most of the
Torah, was lost or destroyed when the Great Synagogue of Aleppo was burned by rioters in
1947. Goshen-Gottstein published a facsimile edition of the remainder in *The Aleppo Codex*.
The extant manuscript is the base text of the *Hebrew University Bible* (*HUB*), which thus
far includes the books of Isaiah, Jeremiah, and Ezekiel.

[14] For helpful discussions on the Tiberian and other Masoretic traditions, the emergence
of the Tiberian tradition as authoritative, and modern editions based on the accurate Tiberian
manuscripts, see, e.g., Mulder, "Transmission," 104–32; Sáenz-Badillos, *Hebrew Language*
76–111; Tov, *Textual Criticism*, 22–79, 371–78; idem., "The Masoretic Text," 234–36, 239–43;
and Penkower, "The Masoretic Bible."

[15] Some, in fact, see the MT's authoritative status as a major obstacle to recovering the
"original" text of the Hebrew Bible. See, in particular, Tov, "The Masoretic Text."

earliest readers of the completed biblical composition. This is the major limitation of any study based upon the MT.

On the one hand, comparisons with the manuscripts discovered at Qumran, as well as with the Septuagint, indicate that the consonantal Tiberian MT—and therefore the modern editions that represent it, such as *BHS*, *BHL*, *BHQ*, and *HUB* (see notes 11 and 13)—closely approximates a version of the biblical text that was authoritative, and thus relatively stable, as early as the third century B.C.E. The proto-MT of Samuel—that is, the consonantal text largely corresponding to that of the Tiberian MT—probably dates to an earlier period, but unfortunately the extant evidence from Qumran takes us no further back than the third century B.C.E.[16] On the other hand, regarding practically every other aspect of the MT—the vocalization system, which helps to indicate the grammatical forms and meanings of words; the para-textual elements such as verse and paragraph divisions; the cantillation signs, which indicate syntactical relationships between words, among other things; and the Masoretic apparatuses, which functioned as an aid to scribes seeking to make accurate copies by focusing on orthography and other textual details[17]—confidence in its value as an attestation to the original or earliest biblical compositions must be tempered with humility and caution. Even if the MT is rooted in a tradition reaching back to the end of the biblical text's compositional history and the beginning of its transmission history, there is no getting around the fact that the Masoretic tradition amounts to an "interpretation" of the consonantal text that, in places, reflects the interests, biases, and misunderstandings of the Masoretes.[18]

Instead of focusing on the MT, some readers would undoubtedly prefer to base studies such as this upon an eclectically reconstructed text that replaces numerous Masoretic readings with alternate Hebrew readings now attested in the Samuel scrolls from Qumran—especially 4QSam[a],[19] which predates the accurate Tiberian manuscripts by about a thousand years—and/or reflected in Septuagint manuscripts (which frequently agree with the Qumran texts against the MT, and also disagree with both groups in places), as well as with alternate readings from other ancient versions, and some emendations based

---

[16] See, e.g., Tov, *Textual Criticism*, 23.

[17] See ibid., 22–76, where Tov surveys these and other features of the proto-Masoretic and Masoretic texts.

[18] See e.g., ibid.; Mulder, "Transmission," 104–15; Revell, "Massoretic Punctuation."

[19] Now fully published in DJD 17.

on simple conjecture. Let us briefly consider the primary problem with the common approach of emending the MT in light of alternate readings from the Dead Sea Scrolls and the Septuagint, in particular.

There is a considerable degree of uncertainty about the precise nature of the relationship between the so-called proto-MT (i.e., the early consonantal text or texts presumed to underlie the Masoretic manuscripts) and the Samuel texts found at Qumran, as well as between the proto-MT and the LXX. If one could conclude definitively that the variants in the texts represent what might be described as solely a text-critical problem—that is, if the variants arose during the transmission of a single, original composition—then the MT, the Qumran manuscripts, and the LXX might reasonably be eclipsed in the hope of reconstructing that elusive original composition, however non-definitive the results. But we now know that the problem presented by many of the variants is, at least in part, one of a literary-critical, or source-critical, nature. The Samuel scrolls discovered near the Dead Sea have proven what could previously only be conjectured based upon the Septuagint and other ancient versions: There were multiple versions of Samuel during the Second Temple period (the extant evidence takes us back no further than the third century B.C.E). This raises the question as to whether any given variant reading in the MT reflects some "late Masoretic interpretation," or whether it stems from the different textual traditions that, apparently, had reached some level of authoritative status in their respective communities near the end of the first millennium B.C.E.[20] Though there are numerous exceptions, generally speaking, scholars cannot identify with absolute confidence where the Masoretic Text accurately reflects "original" or early readings and where it has become "corrupt."[21]

---

[20] This statement is not meant as a decision against "the *Urtext* theory of de Lagarde" in favor of Kahle's theory of multiple original texts. Rather, I am addressing the general shape of the books of Samuel by around the third century B.C.E., regardless of the shape of the original text(s), which must date to a much earlier period. For a nuanced discussion of the original shape and subsequent development of the biblical text, including treatment of the many issues surrounding this unsettled "de Lagarde–Kahle debate" (though the majority of scholars hold to some articulation of the former), see Tov, *Textual Criticism*, 164–97.

[21] One need only compare, for instance, the 1 Samuel commentaries by McCarter (*I Samuel*) and Tsumura (*First Book of Samuel*) on MT texts that have frequently been identified by modern scholars as corrupt or otherwise problematic. Whereas McCarter tends to distrust the MT and suggests, instead, well-reasoned solutions based on other (non-MT) readings and conjectures, Tsumura tends to trust the MT and suggests well-reasoned solutions based on linguistic analyses (especially see Tsumura, *First Book of Samuel*, 7–10).

My intent here is not to deny the potential value of presuming the existence of—and attempting to reconstruct—a single, original text that was directly related to the proto-MT, the Qumran scrolls, and the LXX, among other ancient attestations. I maintain, however, that this approach is not the only valid option, especially given the possibility that textual variants, whether large or small, may represent different textual traditions and not merely different versions of the same tradition. Particularly if this is so, the potential disadvantages of basing one's arguments on a systematically eclectic text—a reconstruction of one's own composition, so to speak, that may have never existed in any stage—outweigh those of working with a text that certainly existed at some stage, and that, in many if not most cases, likely existed from the point of its original composition, that is, the point that its compositional or literary history ended and its transmission history began.[22]

In sum, while I appreciate the value of exegetical work based on the Dead Sea Scrolls, the Septuagint, and other ancient versions on their own merits, my interests here are in the biblical textual tradition that is preeminent among interpreters within both academic and religious reading communities today, and which stands in close continuity with one or more of the earliest reading communities. Among other merits of the *BHS*, it offers that elusive but important common ground. Of course, we must keep in mind the limitations of the Tiberian MT, and thus of *BHS*, especially for assertions concerning historical meanings of the biblical account (i.e., the proto-MT) at the time of its composition and in subsequent periods of its transmission. And there remain numerous other difficulties in the MT that continue to frustrate readers; it will be necessary in the present study, too, to consider alternative readings in the course of translating and discussing the biblical text. Generally speaking, however, where I judge a text-critical issue to have no real bearing on my discussion, which is usually the case, I follow the Masoretic Text of *BHS* without comment.

In the end, I must bypass the question of whether the story of David's rise to kingship had an original form that was either different from or the same as its form within the larger narrative of the MT. This is because I see no certain way of dealing with that original form that is not compromised by prior assumptions about the nature of the historical context from which the original form is supposed to have emerged. In the latter chapters, therefore,

---

[22] See Tov's balanced discussion of various issues and problems surrounding the definition of the "original text" (*Textual Criticism*, 164–80).

I will focus on the story of David's rise in its present MT form and as part of the larger MT narrative of 1–2 Samuel. Whether any or all of this reflects the intent of the composer of an early form of the Samuel narrative ultimately remains a matter of speculation.

CHAPTER 1

1 Samuel 16–2 Samuel 5 as "the History of David's Rise"/"the Apology of David" in Modern Scholarship

Overview of HDR in Modern Scholarship

Many Hebrew Bible scholars agree that centuries before the story of David's ascendancy to the throne reached its final form[1] in the biblical books of 1 and 2 Samuel, there existed an independent and unified account identified primarily by its "overarching unity of theme and purpose."[2] In scholarly literature this account is called "the History of David's Rise" (HDR). Until the early twentieth century, most scholars believed that Pentateuchal sources continued into the book of Joshua, and many maintained that they continued through Judges and Samuel, where they were thought to have been interwoven by early redactors in much the same way as scholars had postulated for the Pentateuch.[3] Leonhard Rost broke from this view, however, when he proposed that lying behind 1 Samuel 16–2 Samuel 5 was an originally independent, single source that was later taken up and incorporated into a larger history of the monarchy's establishment in Judah / Israel. Rost's identification of an independent and unified "History of David's Rise" (HDR) dating back to the early days of Israel's monarchical period was precipitated by his prior identification of the so-called "Succession Narrative" (SN) and "Ark Narrative" (AN). This left the stories of Samuel (1 Samuel 1–3), Saul's anointing and rejection (1 Samuel 7–15), and David's rise (1 Samuel 16–2 Samuel 5) for independent treatment along similar lines.[4] Alt's adoption of this approach[5] was influential, and it eventually became the majority view.

---

[1] The question of the final form of the books of Samuel is quite complicated; see my discussion in the introduction.

[2] McCarter, "The Apology of David," 490.

[3] See esp. Budde, *Richter und Samuel*; idem, *Die Bücher Samuel*; Eissfeldt, *Die Komposition der Samuelisbücher*.

[4] Rost, *Succession*, esp. 109–12.

[5] Dietrich and Naumann, "The David-Saul Narrative," 294, citing Alt, *Die Staatenbildung der Israeliten*.

Since Rost, HDR has been delineated variously. (In fact, the earlier view of the narrative as a composite of interwoven strands connected to Pentateuchal sources and/or certain cultic centers was never completely abandoned,[6] and a two-source theory for HDR and the surrounding narratives is even making something of a comeback.[7]) Numerous studies provide nuanced treatment of the "theme and purpose" of HDR, disagreeing primarily over its dating and original provenance.[8] Differences notwithstanding, many scholars agree that HDR was originally composed for the propagandistic purposes of an individual monarch, that is, as a personal royal apology akin to those from Anatolia and Mesopotamia dating from the latter part of the second millennium B.C.E. to around the middle of the first millennium B.C.E.[9] While they differ over whether the work was composed in service of David himself,[10] Solomon,[11] or one of the later Davidic kings,[12] these interpreters

[6] Besides those cited above in n. 3, see, e.g., Hölscher, *Geschichtsschreibung in Israel*; Schulte, *Entstehung der Geschichtsschreibung*; North, "David's Rise."

[7] See, e.g., Halpern, *Constitution of the Monarchy*; Friedman, *Hidden Book*; Hutton, "The Transjordanian Palimpsest." Terminology varies, especially among those who maintain a two-source theory. For example, Hutton (194–234) distinguishes between "HDR$_1$," the "original apology of David's reign," which was appended to "the Narratives of Saul's Rise," and "HDR$_2$," which was composed later and appended to "the Court History / Succession Narrative." In his view, the two HDR's were combined at some point after these two complexes had been composed.

[8] A representative sampling of these includes Nübel, "Davids Aufstieg"; Ward, "David's Rise"; Grønbæk, *Geschichte*; Ishida, *Royal Dynasties*; Lemche, "David's Rise"; McCarter, *I Samuel*; idem, "The Apology of David"; Dietrich and Naumann, "The David-Saul Narrative"; McKenzie, *King David*; Halpern, *David's Secret Demons*; and Hutton, "The Transjordanian Palimpsest." Dietrich and Naumann provide a concise yet remarkably comprehensive survey of historical-critical treatment of "the Rise of David Narrative" in "The David-Saul Narrative."

[9] E.g., Wolf, "The Apology of Hattušiliš"; Hoffner, "Hittite Analogue"; idem, "Propaganda and Political Justification"; McCarter, "The Apology of David"; Stott, "Herodotus"; Dick, "David's Rise to Power." For related studies, see, e.g., Machinist, "Literature as Politics"; Perdue, "The Testament of David"; Tadmor, "Autobiographical Apology"; Ishida, "The Succession Narrative."

[10] E.g., Alt, *Die Staatenbildung der Israeliten*; Bentzen, *Introduction to the Old Testament*; Weiser, "Legitimation"; Ward, "David's Rise"; McCarter, "The Apology of David"; McKenzie, *King David*; Halpern, *David's Secret Demons*; Hutton, "The Transjordanian Palimpsest" (HDR$_1$).

[11] E.g., Hutton's HDR$_2$ (see n. 7, above).

[12] E.g., Grønbæk, *Geschichte*; Schicklberger, "Die Davididen"; Mettinger, *King and Messiah*. These scholars date HDR to the early period of the divided kingdom, when Israel (i.e., the northern kingdom) rejected the legitimacy of Davidic rule. Conrad ("Zum geschichtlichen Hintergrund") attributes the work to southern writers living in the days of Jehu's usurpation of the throne in the north.

agree that HDR was written for the purpose of "political self-justification."[13] The aim of this Israelite apology was to legitimize "David's" succession to the Saulide throne by exonerating him from various charges, including treason and murder, and showing that he ascended to the throne by lawful means and was therefore the rightful king over the southern and northern tribes of Israel.

Furthermore, the majority of these scholars have maintained—or simply accepted the conclusion of Rost and others following him—that this original History of David's Rise was transmitted through numerous redactions, eventually leading to the present biblical text, essentially unchanged. With regard to its historicity, earlier critics were fairly optimistic about HDR's representation of historical events, and a sizable majority still believe that an historical David succeeded an historical Saul as king over Israel, even if this succession did not occur exactly as the existing and reconstructed records depict. These conclusions taken together have resulted in a certain amount of confusion in discussions about "the history of David's rise." In both scholarly and popular writings on the books of Samuel, "the history of David's rise" can refer to a) the actual historical events surrounding David's rise to kingship; b) the putative source behind 1 Samuel 16–2 Samuel 5; and/or c) the biblical text of 1 Samuel 16–2 Samuel 5. In the latter two cases, "the History of David's Rise" (HDR), constitutes the title of the reconstructed text (b) or the actual biblical text (c).

Historical and literary (i.e., synchronically-oriented) critics alike, as well as many traditional interpreters, frequently use the various designations for the biblical text throughout its literary history almost interchangeably. For example, in addition to designating the putative source as "a/the History of David's Rise," "an/the Apology of David," and the like (using both uppercase and lowercase), scholars often use these designations in reference to the present biblical text as well. Conversely, critics typically refer to the hypothetically reconstructed source(s), as well as the biblical text, by means of biblical chapter-and-verse references (e.g., the first part of HDR is referenced

---

[13] McCarter, "The Apology of David," 498. McCarter does not use this phrase directly in relation to HDR, though that is the implication given the context: "Surely there is nothing distinctively Hittite or even ancient Near Eastern about the literary category of political self-justification with its accompanying claims for the legitimacy of the usurper, his ability to rule, his moral rectitude, and his divine election to office. . . . [T]he apology of Hattushilish demonstrates the potential for an elaborate development of this genre in the general cultural milieu in which the history of David's rise was composed."

as "1 Samuel 16–19," as opposed to, say, "1 Samuel 16–19[HDR]"), or more generally by designations such as "the biblical text" or "the biblical history." I have attempted to avoid this sort of conflation in my own analysis. Unless I am quoting or speaking in the terms of another scholar, I use designations such as "the books of Samuel," "the biblical text," "1 Samuel 16–2 Samuel 5," and the like only to refer to the present biblical text. When referring to the source document that many scholars believe to underlie the biblical text, I use designations such as "(the) History of David's Rise" / "HDR," "(the) Apology of David," "the biblical source," and "1 Samuel 16–19[HDR]." (I use the superscripted siglum only when the text in question contains sections that the source critic under discussion does not attribute to the original HDR. So, for example, "1 Samuel 16–19[HDR]" refers to these chapters minus texts that the source critic thinks were added later, such as 1 Sam 16:1–13.) An exception to this distinction between putative source and final text is my use of the phrase "the biblical account," which may, depending on the context, refer to any stage or stages in an episode's literary history, incuding the extant Masoretic version.

Some scholars make no real distinction between the biblical text and its putative original source (not to mention any intermediate redactions or literary stages), rendering the aforementioned considerations moot. Such a lack of distinction can be seen, for example, in Michael Dick's essay comparing the "History of David's Rise to Power" with certain "Neo-Babylonian Succession Apologies."[14] In the opening paragraph, where he briefly notes the differing views of several scholars regarding the parameters of HDR, it is already clear that in Dick's view the biblical text and HDR (wherever it begins and ends) are nearly identical.[15] After asserting that HDR's purpose "is to portray David as the legitimate successor of the Northern king Saul and to justify the usurpation of Saulide rule by the Judahite David,"[16] Dick states:

---

[14] Dick, "David's Rise to Power."

[15] Ibid., 3. Dick notes the views of Rost, Mettinger, and Weiser, and only in one instance — with regard to Mettinger's view that a few verses in 1 Samuel 15–16 were inserted by DtrP — does Dick acknowledge any possible differences between HDR and the biblical text (ibid., n. 2), though it is hard to imagine that he is not aware that the source analysis of HDR is more complicated than a mere discussion of its parameters suggests.

[16] Ibid., 3–4. With regard to its provenance, Dick adds, "Since David's family is portrayed as having legitimate claim to both Israel and Judah, the work might well have been a polemic dating back to the beginning of the divided monarchy."

For the thesis of this essay, it is not really germane whether the HDR is a discrete literary unit, where it begins or ends, or even when it may have been written. I am solely interested in the content of the apology in HDR defending the Davidic claim to legitimate succession of Saul's kingship. . . . David's challenge is clear: What right does he have to usurp the throne? The HDR represents that political apology. The rhetoric of the HDR has a twofold goal: (1) to discredit Saul; (2) to raise David in his stead while exonerating him from complicity in regicide (2 Sam 1:1–16).[17]

Because Dick treats "the content of the apology" as a given irrespective of historical or literary context, he does not distinguish between the form, content, or meaning of HDR and the biblical text. Other scholars, such as Kyle McCarter, are more careful than Dick on this point, however, and recognize the need to delineate sources and postulate historical settings in order to discuss the apology's content.

Approach and Aims

Below, I present in considerable detail a particular reconstruction and interpretation of HDR as David's personal[18] apology, namely, that of Kyle McCarter as found in his essay "The Apology of David" and his commentaries on the books of Samuel. While McCarter's work does not represent a consensus in all, or even most, of its details—indeed, as I have already indicated in the discussion and notes above, even scholars who agree over HDR's original independence from the larger biblical account disagree over numerous details regarding its contours, provenance, and related issues—many among the wide range of scholars who interpret the narrative as an exoneration of an individual king and his "house" cite McCarter's work as representative of this view. For instance, John Van Seters cites McCarter as a chief representative of the "fairly broad consensus that the Story of David's rise expresses the theme of David's legitimate and rightful succession to the throne of Saul," and numerous other works quite varied in their scope and aims indicate the prominence of McCarter's "Apology" essay and Samuel commentaries in their acceptance of this view.[19] More importantly, several recent monographs

---

[17] Ibid., 4.

[18] See n. 5 in the introduction.

[19] Van Seters, *In Search of History*, 265. Consider this sampling of works: Kang, *Divine War*, 214; Chavalas, "Genealogical History as 'Charter,'" 125–26; Matthews, *Brief History*,

by prominent scholars lean heavily upon McCarter's work.[20] Another reason for this focus on McCarter's analysis is that it offers us an accessible and concise—yet quite thorough—argument supporting the popular view that the biblical account of David's rise to kingship should be interpreted fundamentally as the self-justification, or vindication, of David himself.[21] By reviewing and analyzing his source-critical analysis of 1 Samuel 16–2 Samuel 5, together with his comparison of HDR and the Hittite Apology of

41; White, "Saul and Jonathan," 129–30. Also see nn. 9–12, above, and the related discussion on pp. 14–15.

[20] For instance, in the notes on his chapter "Ideology in the Book of Samuel," Brettler states that he has "based much of [his] analysis" on McCarter's "Apology" article and Samuel commentaries, together with Weiser's "Legitimation" (*The Creation of History*, 202 n. 67); McKenzie identifies McCarter's "Apology" essay as his inspiration at an important point in his discussion (*King David*, 32–33 and 197 nn. 13 and 14); and Halpern describes McCarter's Second Samuel commentary and his "Apology" article as "the definitive approach" to questions about the book of Samuel's origin, nature, and purpose ("Text and Artifact," 315; this section has been incorporated into his more recent *David's Secret Demons*, 75–76).

[21] See the previous two notes. McCarter popularized the designation "the Apology of David" among biblical scholars as an alternate title for HDR, but he is preceded in its usage at least by Wolf in his "The Apology of Hattušiliš" and by Wolf's teacher, Hoffner, in "Propaganda and Political Justification," which I shall discuss further below. As evidence of the popularity of interpreting not only an originally independent "History of David's Rise" but, in many cases, the present biblical account as an individual king's apology, one need only pick up a recent survey of the Old Testament / Hebrew Bible. Consider, for instance, the following textbooks, each of which was apparently designed for undergraduate and graduate students. In *The Old Testament*, Matthews and Moyer describe the "story of David's rise to power" as a "Davidic apology narrative, which is designed to show David's worthiness to rule by portraying him as a sympathetic character" (108). Similarly, in their *Survey of the Old Testament*, Hill and Walton treat "the history of David's rise" as "vindication of David" (210, 214–16; they make reference to McCarter's 1980 essay on p. 215 n. 3). The authors conclude that the narrator "was presenting evidence by which he intended to legitimize David's claim to the throne," and that "this material had propagandistic value" (216). Neither textbook differentiates between the present biblical account of David's rise to kingship and the presumed underlying source. I do not mean to suggest that the above authors ought to present a detailed source-critical analysis of the text—that would be unreasonable for entry-level textbooks such as theirs. I think it is highly significant, however, that an interpretation based initially on numerous assumptions and conclusions about an originally independent source has been applied to the present biblical account. Somewhat more nuanced in this regard is Coogan's *The Old Testament*. Coogan refers to "the Deuteronomistic Historians' principal source for David" in 1 and 2 Samuel (up to 2 Samuel 5; see 248), which he describes as "a propagandistic presentation of David as the legitimate successor to the divinely rejected Saul" (237). He parenthetically notes that HDR is "*embedded*" in 1 Sam 16–2 Sam 5" (233 [emphasis added]), thus maintaining a distinction between the putative source and the present biblical account.

Ḫattušili, we can better understand and evaluate the sorts of assumptions and conclusions about historical and ideological forces that many scholars think lie behind the genesis of the account. For many such scholars, moreover, these assumptions and conclusions about what really happened inform their interpretation not only of HDR but of the present biblical account in 1 Samuel 16–2 Samuel 5 as well.[22]

My ultimate purpose in examining McCarter's and, along the way, other studies of HDR is not to prepare the way for yet another set of hypotheses surrounding the source analysis, dating, provenance, function, and genre of the "original History of David's Rise." In my view, the story of David's rise to kingship should not be extracted and interpreted independently of the preceding biblical account of Saul's election and reign, or of the following account of David's reign. On the one hand, I find the working assumptions and propositions that figure into the isolation of an originally independent HDR to be highly questionable, if not untenable. Demonstrating this is one of my primary aims, in particular, in chapters 2 and 3 though I also point out a number of problems and uncertainties surrounding the delineation of sources elsewhere, including the present chapter. On the other hand, the account identified as HDR below is so thoroughly embedded in, or interwoven with, the surrounding narrative that it is irrecoverable without the very assumptions and propositions that I find to be problematic. I address this issue directly at numerous points throughout my work, and my entire discussion in chapters 4 and 5 indirectly supports this integrated view of the account. Nevertheless, though I ultimately approach and interpret the biblical account quite differently from McCarter, it is useful for the sake of my argument in the first three chapters to adopt and work with his particular reconstruction.

First, I shall outline the general hermeneutical rationale and assumptions behind the source-critical project of reconstructing one or more historical sources of the biblical text on David's rise to kingship (and particularly an original "History of David's Rise"). Then, for the reasons given above, I shall

---

[22] To the examples of this conflation in the previous note, one might add the discussion by Gordon in *I & II Samuel*. Gordon recommends dispensing with source-critical discussions in order to concentrate on the theme of 1 Samuel 16–2 Samuel 5, and he approvingly cites Hoffner and McCarter for corroboration that " 'David's Rise' is therefore in the business of defending David against charges destructive of his credibility and potentially subversive of his throne" (38, 327 n. 63). "That this is a fair reading of these chapters," he later asserts, "can scarcely be questioned, even if the independent status of the narrative, and its allegedly early date, are points in need of more substantiation" (149).

focus my attention primarily on McCarter's work. I am especially interested in understanding the historically particular nature of McCarter's own reading of HDR by analyzing how he roots the account of David's rise to kingship in the specific historical context that he has reconstructed, in which attendant circumstances occasioned the need for David's personal self-justification and defense. My treatment of these various issues in chapter 1 will also prepare the way for my discussions in chapters 2 and 3. In chapter 2, I shall reconsider the extent of thematic similarities between HDR and the Hittite "Apology of Ḫattušili," the extra-biblical text with which HDR is most often compared. Then, in chapter 3, I shall revisit the question of the "rhetorical posture" that McCarter and some others detect in HDR and attribute to unstated accusations against David. This will allow me to accomplish the aims outlined above, and to clear the ground for a fresh appreciation in chapters 4 and 5 of features of the biblical account that have been largely eclipsed by readings based upon particular construals of what really happened to evoke the account and render it meaningful in the first place. It is first necessary, therefore, to gain a solid understanding of how and to what degree readings that construe the meaning of the account—an original HDR for McCarter, but also the present biblical account of 1 Samuel 16–2 Samuel 5 for Dick and others—in terms of the exigencies of usurpation have resulted from "exegesis" of history and Hittite literature of royal apology as well as of the biblical text. This will be the chief aim of the following discussions in chapters 1–3.

Basic Assumptions and Rationale Underlying the Identification of HDR

Let us briefly consider the basic hermeneutical rationale or logic behind the supposition that the biblical text in 1 Samuel 16–2 Samuel 5 stems from one or more source documents predating by many centuries the edition reflected in the present Masoretic Text. In the first place, historical critics recognize that the biblical text of 1 Samuel 16–2 Samuel 5 received its present form (roughly speaking, of course, given the many text-critical problems in Samuel) some time in the post-exilic period. As a part of the larger story of YHWH's dealings with Israel in the pre-exilic period, it recounts how YHWH elected the shepherd-boy David as Israel's new king and providentially guided him as he supplanted King Saul, a rejected and hostile predecessor who lost his grip on both his sanity and his kingdom. But secondly, most scholars believe that there was, in fact, a historical David. Despite recent attempts to rewrite Israel's history and history-writing as an almost entirely post-exilic enterprise,[23] the majority of biblical scholars still agree that 1 Samuel 16–2 Samuel 5 and its larger context, as well as the archaeological record,[24] point to an actual historical David and actual historical events or circumstances in early Iron Age Israel. If so, then thirdly, most likely the biblical account (and any intermediate stages in the account's literary history) somehow depended upon and incorporated a historical or historiographical source(s) of some kind. Let me elaborate on the second and third points.

Scholars point to the preservation of details and larger accounts that they conclude would have been irrelevant or superfluous in later periods as evidence that the biblical editors did not simply make things up, but rather were driven, in part, by some basic historical impulse. For instance, in a discussion of David's life leading up to his ascent to Saul's throne, Israel Finkelstein and Neil Silberman argue that "[d]etailed descriptions of environment and settlement patterns are perhaps the most important evidence for dating the Bible's historical texts."[25] They view these details as "fossils embedded in the rock of biblical tradition" that "can be placed in quite specific historical periods."[26] With regard to the story of David in 1 Samuel 16–2 Samuel 5, they find that these "fossils" date back to the days of David and Solomon themselves. Scholars are able to conclude, then, that although the biblical editors' work certainly differs in character from modern historiographies, their transmission of the sort of details that would have been difficult to appreciate in a post-exilic context suggests that they attempted to base their account on

[23] E.g., Davies, *Ancient Israel*; Lemche, *The Israelites*; Thompson, *The Mythic Past*; and idem., *The Messiah Myth*. For various perspectives on the issues at stake, see Long, *Israel's Past*; and Day, *Pre-Exilic Israel*.

[24] There is extensive literature on the debates surrounding the range and use of archaeological evidence in arguments about the historical David, in particular, and the early monarchy, in general. These and related issues, however, fall outside the purview of the present discussion. On this subject, and for helpful bibliographies of more technical treatments, interested readers might consult, among others, Mazar, *Archaeology*, esp. chs. 9 and 11; Meyers, "Kinship and Kingship," esp. 232–56; Halpern, *David's Secret Demons*, 427–78; Provan, Long, and Longman, *A Biblical History*, esp. 193–238; Finkelstein and Silberman, *David and Solomon*.

[25] Finkelstein and Silberman, *David and Solomon*, 33. For other examples, see Edelman, "Tel Masos." Scholars also point to other kinds of evidence, such as historical linguistics, in tracing and dating the biblical text's literary history. See, e.g., Freedman, "Early Israelite History"; Hurvitz, "Biblical Texts."

[26] Finkelstein and Silberman, *David and Solomon*, 35.

historical reality, or at least on what they thought really happened.[27] So, too, did the editors of the Deuteronomistic History, the editors of the Prophetic Record before them, and the editors at any other intermediary stage in the text's literary history.[28] Therefore, even if the original account suffered from prophetic, deuteronomistic, and any later tendencies to idealize David and to refine his story for other purposes in later centuries, many biblical scholars are generally confident that they can "excavate the tell in the text"[29] and uncover various literary stages, going back to the original composition and even beyond. Even if the biblical text is not (entirely) "true history," it is of some use in the work of historical reconstruction because it is driven by true historical or historiographical interests and impulses. Already we can see how the argument necessarily becomes at least somewhat circular. Conclusions about the historical significance of the biblical text are informed by many underlying presuppositions and assumptions. Some of these are acknowledged and articulated by some exegetes, others are not. They include, for example, background presuppositions or assumptions about the realms of possibility for, or character of, ancient Near Eastern kings in general, ancient Israelite kings in general, and King David in particular. All this is informed, to one degree or another, by the biblical text and assumptions about its nature and history; interpretations of other ancient Near Eastern texts and inscriptions, few of which are without controversy; the archaeological record; and a variety of other considerations. I shall discuss all this further below.

I say that scholars regard the Bible as having only some historical utility because even the so-called "maximalists" cast a skeptical eye toward any and all "historical" claims of the biblical text. Their positive assessment of the historical interests reflected in and behind the biblical text (at least in comparison to the "minimalists") does not mean that they treat the biblical text as in fact transparent or trustworthy with regard to "what really happened." Most modern scholars therefore tend to be cautious about accepting the

---

[27] See, e.g., Halpern, *The First Historians*, where he argues "that the historians of DtrH could and did consciously differentiate myth and history, evidence from confection, and reconstruction from dramatization; that they set out from the conviction that history vindicated their partisan biases to set down what they could learn of the events; that their antiquarian curiosity balanced the urge to censorship; that they subdued whatever was ideologically troubling more by metahistorical, editorial discourse than by falsifying concrete political developments" (277).

[28] I shall discuss these various stages in more detail below.

[29] As expressed by Eugene McGarry, a colleague at Harvard University.

historical elements and details—those that they think must date back to contemporaneous sources—at face value. In fact, as we will see, McCarter and many other critics think that such elements of HDR are quite misleading with regard to what really happened. They maintain, rather, that the historical or historiographical impulses are offset or conditioned to varying degrees by various ideological[30] impulses (not to mention the demands inherent to any literary representation[31]). In other words, scholars recognize that every composition or re-composition of David's story throughout its literary growth and development, however slight the revision, owes its impetus and nature not simply to a "historical impulse," but also in large part to ideological interests of the authors and/or editors. That is to say, the authors' and/or editors' understandings of why certain things happened (which must have developed and changed throughout Israel's history, and would have differed quite significantly, say, from pre-exilic Josianic times to post-exilic Persian times) framed and colored their descriptions of what happened and how. Like any other ancient or modern historiographical work, then, the "History of David's Rise" was not history for the sake of history—far from it. Rather, critics argue, it served particular ideological interests or agendas from its earliest stage during or soon after David's own reign, down to its post-exilic literary setting (i.e., its place in the *Nebiim*, or "Prophets") many centuries after the events that it recounts. In other words, at each stage or edition throughout the course of the biblical narrative's literary growth and development, leading up to and including the biblical text itself, the story of David's rise was redacted to address the needs and concerns of each period, not merely to narrate "what really happened."[32]

The next step for scholars primarily interested in investigating the scope and nature of the source(s), and in using this as a window into "what really

[30] The scholarly works reviewed in this chapter appear not to differentiate between "ideology"/"ideological" and "theology"/"theological."

[31] On this, see the helpful discussions in Provan, Long, and Longman, *A Biblical History*, esp. "Narrative and History: Stories about the Past" (ch. 4).

[32] This discussion raises a distinction between two kinds of historical knowledge that we might gain from historical-critical analyses: historical knowledge about the actual people and events depicted in the text, and historical knowledge about the people and events of the time at which a given edition was composed. Whereas most traditional readers and some early critical scholars were chiefly interested in the theology or ideology of the characters in the story (such as Saul and David), most scholars today primarily concern themselves with analyzing the theology or ideology of the authors and editors of the text and its source(s), whether their aim is to reconstruct ancient Israelite history or to exposit the meaning of the text.

happened," is to attempt to identify the parameters, content, genre, and provenance of the underlying source or sources in any and each of its prior stages of transmission. They accomplish this by means of highly complex analyses requiring the development of theories or hypotheses regarding historical events and actors, genre, provenance, and purpose, which account for how the text (given hypothetical pluses and/or minuses) made sense to readers in different historical situations. This requires the identification and bracketing of redactional additions, later accretions, and other signs of editorial activity so as to reconstruct prior sources, eventually going all the way back to the "original source," if possible. Identification of these additions or accretions is enabled, in part, by prior determinations (or unspoken assumptions) regarding the nature, genre, historicity, and ideological interests of this or that literary stage. For instance, having determined that there is a source dating to David's own day that has certain apologetic tendencies, the critic attempts to identify epigenetic material that does not accord with or fit that particular historical context. We will see how this plays out below. But first, it is important to be clear about the general aim behind historical critics' attempts to identify and explicate original sources underlying the present biblical text. In an excellent survey of modern scholarship on 1 Samuel 16–2 Samuel 5 and its antecedent literary and pre-literary stages, Dietrich and Naumann describe these efforts as attempts to uncover the "truth" about David:

> The question arises, however, whether what the latest editors of the biblical text—sometime between the exile and the period of canon formation—thought they could recognize as the truth about David and Saul is the only or even the entire truth. . . .
>
> Scholarship has the task, and very likely also the means, of ascertaining as exactly as possible the various facets of the truth about David and Saul that were recorded as they were perceived during the course of Israelite-Judahite (intellectual) history. It is methodologically sensible to begin by carefully distinguishing the respective stages— diachronically—from each other, to describe each by itself, and then to observe—synchronically—their biblical juxtaposition and interpenetration and to reflect on the whole.[33]

---

[33] Dietrich and Naumann, "The David-Saul Narrative," 292–93. For more general discussions on the aims and purposes of source criticism, see, e.g., Tigay, "Stylistic Criterion"; Viviano, "Source Criticism"; Hughes, "Compositional History."

With regard to 1 Samuel 16–2 Samuel 5, then, the assumption behind attempts to "go back to the source" is that by doing so we can go a long way to uncovering both the historical truth about David and the Davidic ideology, that is, how court writers spun his story (or his personal and court "history") to consolidate his control. Who was he? How did he really rise to power? What originally generated this "history" of David's rise to kingship in 1 Samuel 16–2 Samuel 5? That is, what is it really about? Let us now review the reconstruction of HDR and see how scholars have attended to these questions. Again, for the reasons given above, under "Approach and Aims," I shall center my review of the identification and interpretation of HDR around McCarter's important proposal regarding the independence, contours, nature, and function of HDR as self-justification for the historical David.

Source Analysis and the Identification of 1 Samuel 16–2 Samuel's Earlier Editions

Most reconstructions of HDR since Rost have been relatively uncomplicated, at least in comparison to critical reconstructions of Pentateuchal sources.[34] McCarter, along with most scholars, concludes that after HDR itself was composed from yet earlier sources, traditions, and legends, it underwent few changes throughout its literary history. In McCarter's view, these changes are limited to a handful of prophetic, deuteronomistic, and other glosses, insertions, or accretions. In summary form in his highly significant essay, "The Apology of David," and in more detail throughout his commentaries on 1 and 2 Samuel, McCarter identifies HDR by detecting additions that he attributes to two major redactional stages—the "prophetic history" and the "Deuteronomistic History"—as well as numerous "accretions" that date to various stages throughout the text's literary history. In the following presentation of McCarter's source analysis, I shall begin with his identification of deuteronomistic elements and work backwards to demonstrate the process of "peeling away" later additions in order to discover the narrative core.[35] I shall then reverse that order in my summary of the consensus view represented

---

[34] For a brief overview of scholarship on the text's literary history, see Dietrich and Naumann, "The David-Saul Narrative," 296–98.

[35] It is sound practice to begin with elements about which there is the widest scholarly agreement. This is Carr's approach, for example, in *Fractures of Genesis*, in which he works "from the later, easier-to-reconstruct stages to the earlier, more difficult ones" (39). Source analyses of the books of Samuel, similarly, show the greatest agreement over later stages of

by McCarter's work to highlight, instead, the chronological growth and development of the account. In practice, of course, the source-critical process is more circular than linear (in either direction) because the identification of later elements presumes some conception of the form and content of the earlier elements or stages from which they are distinguished, and vice versa, even if their detection stems initially from perceived or real tensions in the text. In the course of presenting McCarter's source analysis of 1 Samuel 16–2 Samuel 5, I shall selectively point out ways in which his assumptions and conclusions about these various literary stages — and how he supposes they necessarily relate to the historical events, figures, and ideologies reflected in and by the various editions — have informed his identification and interpretation of HDR and its subsequent stages or redactions.

Deuteronomistic Edition (Dtr¹) of HDR

McCarter accepts Frank Moore Cross's theory that the Deuteronomistic History was redacted in two stages or editions.[36] According to this view, the first deuteronomist, a Josianic historian, assembled the bulk of the material that is now found in the books of Deuteronomy, Joshua, Judges, 1 and 2 Samuel, and 1 and 2 Kings "to support the reform of Josiah with its emphasis upon the priority of the Jerusalem temple and allegiance to the Davidic king."[37] That the reforms ultimately failed, however, was evidenced by the destruction of the temple, the fall of Jerusalem, and the Babylonian exile that followed. A second deuteronomist, an exilic historian, then added the remainder of 2 Kings (beginning with Josiah's unexpected death) and made a number of insertions or revisions throughout the Deuteronomistic History. McCarter agrees with most biblical scholars that the sources underlying the books of Samuel required relatively minor revisions by the deuteronomistic historians because they received them "already arranged in accordance

---

composition, i.e., the deuteronomistic elements, though there are also points of considerable disagreement, as we will see below.

[36] See Cross, *Canaanite Myth*, 274–89. For a broader overview and more in-depth discussion of the issues surrounding scholarly reconstructions and evaluations of the Deuteronomistic History, see esp. Campbell and O'Brien, *Unfolding the Deuteronomistic History*; Knoppers and McConville, *Reconsidering Israel and Judah*; Römer and Pury, "Deuteronomistic Historiography," as well as other essays in Pury, Römer, and Macchi, *Israel Constructs its History*.

[37] McCarter, *I Samuel*, 15.

with a 'proto-Deuteronomic' viewpoint."[38] With regard to the source behind 1 Samuel 16–2 Samuel 5, McCarter attributes all of the deuteronomistic additions or revisions to the first edition of the Deuteronomistic History "because they display the peculiar concerns and devices of the Josianic historian."[39] McCarter sums up his criteria for the identification of these supplementations and revisions as follows:

> Secondary material produced by this [Josianic] redactional activity can be recognized by its characteristic themes and language and/or its editorial function (i.e., linkage of material to other parts of the deuteronomistic history).[40]

On these grounds, then, McCarter identifies the following passages as deuteronomistic:[41]

1 Sam 17:1–11, 32–40, 42–48a, 49, 51–54. Following Jakob H. Grønbæk, McCarter concludes that the deuteronomistic historian replaced or "overlaid" an older battle account in which David contributed to Saul's military success with "a highly idealized and symbolic form" of what must have been a well known legend: the lone David's victory over the Philistine war hero.[42] This newer version—to which McCarter attributes a "Jerusalemite and probably Josianic origin"—more effectively presents David as "the type of the Israelite king, doing battle with an enemy who is the very embodiment of threatening, destructive power," and supports the theme that YHWH displays His power through the weak.[43]

1 Sam 20:11–17, 23, 40–42. McCarter thinks that the deuteronomistic editor inserted these "intrusive" verses in anticipation of 2 Samuel 9, in which David cares for Jonathan's son. The Josianic historian intended, by this insertion, "to show that the survival of the house of Saul was the

---

[38] Ibid.

[39] Ibid., 16. The only verse in 1 Samuel that McCarter (following Cross) attributes to Dtr² (the exilic deuteronomist) is 1 Sam 12:25, but this lies outside of HDR (*I Samuel*, 15).

[40] McCarter, "The Apology of David," 492.

[41] The following are enumerated concisely in ibid., 492–93; and McCarter, *I Samuel*, 14–17. For more extended discussions, see the relevant sections of McCarter's commentaries on 1 and 2 Samuel.

[42] McCarter, *I Samuel*, 295–96. McCarter's citation of Grønbæk (296 n. 2) is to *Geschichte*, 90–92.

[43] McCarter, *I Samuel*, 296–97.

direct consequence of an act of 'loyalty' (חסד) by David, stemming from his old attachment to Jonathan."[44]

1 Sam 23:14–24:23. According to McCarter, the deuteronomistic historian drew on "older material" to give this "tendentious retelling" of David's sparing of Saul in 1 Samuel 26. It thereby "presents David as a model of Yahwistic piety (cf. 24:6–7) and places in Saul's mouth an explicit acknowledgment of David's future kingship (24:21–22)."[45]

1 Sam 25:28–31. McCarter assumes that the deuteronomistic historian anticipated with Abigail's speech the Davidic dynastic promise in 2 Samuel 7.[46]

2 Sam 2:10a + 11; 3:9–10, 18b; 5:1–2, 4–5. McCarter thinks that the deuteronomistic historian suited his editorial and thematic developmental needs with these "chronological formulae and thematic interpolations."[47]

2 Sam 5:11–6:23. McCarter suggests that the deuteronomistic historian "gathered" and added here "certain other materials pertinent to David's establishment of his capital at Jerusalem."[48]

2 Samuel 7. Finally, McCarter says that the deuteronomistic historian "appended" this account of YHWH's dynastic promise to David "as a capstone for the entire story of David's rise to power."[49]

Allow me to touch upon two points.

[44] Ibid., 344. McKenzie, by contrast, attributes the whole of 1 Samuel 20 to HDR in *King David*, 83.

[45] McCarter, "The Apology of David," 493. Note that McCarter follows the MT in his citations of 1 Samuel 23–24. Because the MT's 1 Sam 24:1 appears as 23:29 in most English versions, 24:1–22 in the latter are the equivalent of 24:2–23 in the former. I also follow the MT, unless otherwise noted.

[46] Ibid. Cf. McKenzie, who attributes these verses to HDR along with the rest of 1 Samuel 25 (*King David*, 33, 96–101). Ward, too, maintains that this passage accords with the ideology of the Davidic court, though he concedes that 1 Sam 25:28b ("YHWH will indeed make for my lord a sure house") may come from Solomon's court. At any rate, he argues that, while Abigail's "speech" "coincides with the teaching of the deuteronomic history," there is insufficient basis to date it as late as that ("David's Rise," 92–93).

[47] McCarter, "The Apology of David," 493.

[48] Ibid.

[49] Ibid. By contrast, Weiser thinks that the original HDR concluded with 2 Samuel 7 ("Legitimation," 342–49).

First, as noted above, McCarter regards 1 Sam 17:1–11, 32–40, 42–48a, 49, 51–54 as a "highly idealized and symbolic" version of David's victory over the Philistine. He explains this as follows:

> The very simplicity that gives the story of David and the Philistine its lasting appeal—the idealizations and absolutes of which it is composed—also calls into question its originality as a part of the oldest narrative of the rise of David. The subtlety and realism of other episodes are missing here.[50]

Following Wellhausen, McCarter argues that characterizations of David elsewhere—most notably as "a powerful man, a warrior, skilled in speech, and handsome" in 1 Sam 16:18, and as slayer of "ten thousands" in 1 Sam 18:7—stand in contrast to his depiction in these verses.[51] McCarter further describes the "highly symbolic form" of this passage thus:

> Here is David, small, apparently defenseless, with none of the bearing or equipment of a trained soldier—the perfect personification of the tiny nation of Judah. And against him stands the gigantic enemy, heavily armed and evidently irresistible, as the enemies of Judah so often seemed. David has no real hope in force of arms, and despite his courage and wit he finally must rely on the one good hope that Judah, too, had in times of danger. 'You come against me with sword and spear and scimitar,' he cries to the Philistine, 'but I come against you with the name of Yahweh Sabaoth, god of the ranks of Israel!' (v 45). He means to win the contest so that 'all the earth will know that there is a god in Israel' (v 46). The theological implications are clear: it is Yahweh who gives victory, and he may give it to the weak (Israel) in order that his power might be known to all.[52]

It is certainly easy to imagine that these verses might have been read in various periods in the "symbolic" way that McCarter suggests. But McCarter's unwillingness to attribute this account to the original HDR on these grounds implies the untenable assumption that other texts which he attributes to HDR were less capable of holding a similar symbolic or typological significance for later readers. In fact, many scholars see no difficulty in attributing these verses to the original HDR, and they argue that the passage presumes and is

[50] McCarter, *1 Samuel*, 295.
[51] Ibid., 295–96; this translation of 1 Sam 16:18 is McCarter's (ibid., 279).
[52] Ibid., 297.

thus connected to the immediately preceding account of David's introduction to Saul's court.[53]

A second example of the problematic nature of McCarter's analysis pertains to 1 Sam 23:14–24:23 and 1 Samuel 26, two accounts in which Saul pursues David in the wilderness and David spares Saul's life. The historical relationship between the two texts is controversial.[54] McCarter follows several others in maintaining that 1 Samuel 26 predates 1 Sam 23:14–24:23, which he assigns to the deuteronomist.[55] However, many critics argue that neither story is the "original," but rather that both grew out of an earlier "campfire" account of sorts.[56] Ward, for example, argues that both accounts were adopted by the Jerusalem court to serve its ideological agenda:

> The dogmatic interests of the court traditions, which are expressed in the final form of the wilderness cycle (xxiii 14–xxvi 25), are shared by the writer of "David's Rise." The two accounts of David's meeting with Saul (xxiv; xxvi) are included in the original writing for ideological reasons and have been set side by side without tying them together.[57]

The point here is that the presence of "doublets" in the books of Samuel does not preclude the possibility that the author of HDR included both versions, because a) he presumably was not concerned with fully smoothing over the "heterogeneous appearance"[58] of his composition, and b) these "doublets" "bear the same thematic concern for legitimizing David's role as successor to Saul and for putting Saul in an unfavorable light." In this respect, they differ from doublets in the Pentateuch, for example, which source critics typically attribute to multiple authors working at cross-purposes.[59]

McCarter concludes that the deuteronomistic historian's "annotations" to the story of David's rise to kingship are "prospective" or anticipations of

---

[53] See, for example, Ward, "David's Rise," 21–26; Halpern, *Constitution of the Monarchy*, 160–65; Hutton, "The Transjordanian Palimpsest," 212–13.

[54] On this question, see Ward, "David's Rise," 66–77.

[55] Among others, see Smith, *The Books of Samuel*, 213, 216; Driver, *Introduction*, 181; Wellhausen, *Prolegomena*, 264–65. Citations from Ward, "David's Rise," 71.

[56] See, e.g., Ward, "David's Rise," 71. Ward also cites Nübel, "Davids Aufstieg," 41; and Koch, *Was ist Formgeschichte?* 157.

[57] Ward, "David's Rise," 76.

[58] McCarter, "The Apology of David," 493, n. 12.

[59] Van Seters, *In Search of History*, 268–69.

"the Deuteronomistic theology of the Books of Kings . . . insofar as these additions associate events in David's early career with his later actions as king and foreshadow, sometimes explicitly, the dynastic promise made in II Samuel 7, the Deuteronomistic capstone of the history of David's rise to power."[60] This, of course, betrays the fundamental assumption that "the History of David's Rise" was originally completely independent from the surrounding narratives in the books of Samuel and was therefore solely concerned with "David's rise."

In any case, McCarter considers these deuteronomistic supplementations to or revisions of HDR to be only "light," and he sees them, if anything, as strengthening HDR's case for David's legitimacy:

> The history of David's rise itself was not significantly reshaped, but, as in the case of the retelling of the story of David's refusal to take Saul's life (1 Samuel 26) in a form that casts the merits of David's case in the best possible light (1 Sam 23:14–24:23 . . .), some of the themes implicit in the history have been made quite explicit by rewriting that may have been deuteronomistic, and there is clear evidence of expansion that anticipates subsequent parts of the deuteronomistic history and of the introduction of the fundamental deuteronomistic motif of the dynastic promise to David.[61]

According to McCarter, then, the identification and peeling away of deuteronomistic passages bring the critic one step closer to the original History of David's Rise.

Prophetic Edition of HDR

Beneath the deuteronomistic stage of HDR lies, according to McCarter, "a pre-deuteronomistic prophetic history of the establishment of monarchy in Israel and the transferral of the royal office from Saul to David."[62] McCarter attributes this "prophetic history" to a northern writer "writing during or

---

[60] McCarter, *I Samuel*, 17.

[61] McCarter, "The Apology of David," 492.

[62] Ibid., 491. For a detailed and comprehensive discussion that is favorable to the reconstruction of the putative "Prophetic Record" (PR), see Campbell, *Of Prophets and Kings*. More recently, see the full-text presentation (with many explanatory notes) of the PR within the larger context of the Deuteronomistic History in Campbell and O'Brien, *Unfolding the Deuteronomistic History*.

shortly after the collapse of the northern kingdom, thus near the end of the eighth century B.C."[63] According to McCarter:

> This history was composed from a prophetic perspective that was suspicious of monarchy in any form, committed to an ideal of prophetically-mediated divine selection of leaders, and thus opposed to hereditary succession and supportive of the prophetic office as an ongoing institution in the age of the monarchy.[64]

And so, he maintains, it was the prophetic historian who "introduced the dominant figure of the prophet Samuel" into the account of HDR, but otherwise incorporated the older account "in more or less unrevised form."[65] According to McCarter, the prophetic historian added the following passages to HDR:

1 Sam 15:35–16:13. McCarter attributes the account of Samuel's anointing of David (together with the last verse of 1 Samuel 15) to the hand of the prophetic historian.[66] He asserts that the northern writer "is prepared to acknowledge the legitimacy of the Davidic throne, at least insofar as he finds in the transfer of kingship from Saul to David a paradigm for the prophetic rejection and election of kings."[67]

1 Sam 25:1a. The prophetic historian made a few minor editorial insertions, such as this brief obituary for Samuel.[68]

---

[63] McCarter, *1 Samuel,* 22. See also Mildenberger, "Die vordeuteronomistische Saul-Davidüberlieferung," 12 and passim; and Birch, *Israelite Monarchy,* 152–54, which McCarter cites here (n. 27).

[64] McCarter, "The Apology of David," 491.

[65] McCarter, *1 Samuel,* 18.

[66] Ibid., 277–78.

[67] Ibid., 22. Von Rad argues that 1 Sam 16:1–13 is "certainly the latest" of three separate introductions (the other two being 1 Sam 16:14–23 and 1 Sam 17). He considers it to be "a late interpretation, one which introduces the Davidic dynasty into a set of concepts which was originally alien to it, namely the antecedent designation of Jahweh's [king] elected by a prophet. Historically, the pious story is therefore in error" (*Historical Traditions,* 309).

[68] McCarter, *1 Samuel,* 388.

1 Samuel 28. The prophetic historian also introduced Samuel in an earlier account of Saul's visit to the medium at Endor. McCarter maintains that Samuel "played no part" in the original version.[69]

I shall comment here only on the assessment that 1 Sam 15:35–16:13 was not part of the original HDR, but was instead inserted by a later prophetic historian. While there are those who argue that Samuel's anointing of David belongs to the original version of HDR,[70] McCarter disagrees on account of Samuel's presence and purportedly central role, as indicated above. Likewise, Campbell and O'Brien assert that 1 Sam 16:1–13 is "the creation of the prophetic circles claiming their mandate to establish and dismiss kings," and that this "illuminates the narrative ahead, without actually playing an explicit role within it":

> At this point the PR [Prophetic Record] has fully delineated the prophetic role in the establishment of David as king. It can leave

[69] Ibid., 422–23. As evidence that the prophetic historian has reworked this account, McCarter reasons: "[T]he introduction of Samuel in v 11 disrupts the natural flow of the narrative and leaves the ghostwife's recognition of Saul in v 12b without explanation. Originally it was Saul's imperious tone in v 10 that alerted the woman that her client was not an ordinary man but the king himself; vv 11–12a are secondary. Similarly the references in vv 17–18 to Saul's Amalekite campaign and the earlier oracle of Samuel, which point back to the thoroughly prophetic account of the rejection of Saul in 15:1–34, are entirely superfluous and out of place here; the original of this speech of the ghost included only the material in vv 16 and 19, the direct answer to Saul's inquiry about the battle. These things suggest that Samuel had no part in this story before it was revised to reflect the prophetic conviction that Saul's death was a direct consequence of his disobedience to the prophetically transmitted word of Yahweh." He concludes, however, that these added themes do not detract from the aim of the original account, which was "to set the tone for the report of the death of Saul and Jonathan in c 31," to show "Saul completely severed from Yahweh," and to set up a stark contrast between Saul and David, who shortly hereafter receives "oracular guidance" in his pursuit of the Amalekites that raided Ziklag in 1 Samuel 30 (*1 Samuel*, 423).

[70] E.g., Weiser, "Legitimation"; Grønbæk, *Geschichte*, 25–27, 37–76 (cited in McCarter, *1 Samuel*, 278 n. 3). McKenzie, by contrast, assigns 1 Sam 15:1–16:13 to a period even later than the Deuteronomistic edition. He explains that the second account of Saul's rejection in 1 Samuel 15 "is unnecessary" and contradictory to other texts in Samuel, particularly in its statement that Samuel did not see Saul again (1 Sam 15:35; see 19:18–24), and in its description of the Amalekites' annihilation (Amalekites still appear in 1 and 2 Samuel). McKenzie does not offer any rationale, however, for dating 1 Sam 16:1–13 later than the DH, but merely cites Van Seters, *In Search of History*, 26–64 (sic; correct pages are 264–65), where Van Seters argues that nearly the entirety of 1 Samuel 15–2 Samuel 5 was composed not independently but together with its surrounding narratives by the deuteronomists (McKenzie, *King David*, 196 n. 7).

the unfolding of the subsequent events substantially to the older Davidic narrative, the Story of David's Rise to power (belonging to both Judah and Israel).[71]

It is difficult to accept this line of argumentation. By the time of McCarter's prophetic writer, the Davidic dynasty has endured for more than two centuries, and it has remained standing while the northern kingdom is falling or has fallen. It seems highly unlikely that any writer (or his audience) would have made a distinction between the divine/prophetic election of the historical David two centuries earlier and the Davidic dynasty as a whole. That is, it would seem counter-productive for a prophetic writer who opposed hereditary succession to provide the strong endorsement of the Davidic dynasty inherent in the account of Samuel's anointing of David and the incorporation of HDR in nearly unrevised form. Furthermore, it might be argued that the seer is cast in a somewhat unfavorable light in 1 Sam 16:1–13 when his "sight" leads him astray.[72] By virtue of this alone, the attribution of this account to a prophetic writer for the reasons McCarter postulates is problematic.

Nevertheless, it is notable that for McCarter the prophetic historian, like the deuteronomistic editor, was content to incorporate HDR into his work largely "as is." The prophetic writer does nothing to detract from the legitimacy of David's rise to kingship but rather supports and enhances it. And it is only an enhancement. As Campbell and O'Brien state, "The prophetic editors do not create fiction [in the claim that YHWH is with David]; they articulate what they see in the unfolding narrative of events."[73]

Other Accretions

Finally, McCarter contends that several accretions entered the biblical account after the two "editions" of the prophetic and deuteronomistic writers were completed.[74] Most significant among these are the following:

> *1 Sam 17:12–31, 41, 48b, 50, 55–58; 18:1–5, 10–11, 17–19, 29b–30.* Proto-MT editors interpolated this from "a full alternative account of David's arrival and early days at court . . . *in toto* into the primary narrative at some

[71] Campbell and O'Brien, *Unfolding the Deuteronomistic History*, 257–58.

[72] See ch. 5, 146–7, 155, below.

[73] Campbell and O'Brien, *Unfolding the Deuteronomistic History*, 257.

[74] See, e.g., McCarter, "The Apology of David," 492 n. 9.

time subsequent to the [fourth century B.C.E.] divergence of the ancestral textual traditions that lie behind MT and LXX."[75]

1 Sam 18:8b, 12b. The MT tradition inserted these phrases after its divergence from LXX[B].[76]

1 Sam 18:21b. "This is a redactional expansion, added to facilitate the interpolation of vv 17–19."[77]

1 Sam 19:18–24. The account of David's escape to Samuel and of the frenzied prophesying by Saul and his men is "a late accretion, written in the spirit of the prophetic history but inconsistent with it in detail (cf. the assertion in 1 Sam 15:35 that Samuel never saw Saul again before he died)."[78]

In McCarter's view, the nature of these accretions is consistent with the rest of the redactional additions that we have seen above: they do not function to recast David in a negative light; if anything, they enhance to varying degrees HDR's *Tendenz* and characterization of David as the lawful and legitimate replacement of King Saul.

Having peeled away the few deuteronomistic, prophetic, and other additions noted above, McCarter finds his original "History of David's Rise," consisting of the following:[79]

1 Samuel 16[HDR] = 1 Sam 16:14–23
1 Samuel 17[HDR] = Earlier battle account that underlies 1 Samuel 17
1 Samuel 18[HDR] = 1 Sam 18:6–8a, 9, 12a, 13–16, 20–21a, 22–29a
1 Samuel 19[HDR] = 1 Sam 19:1–17
1 Samuel 20[HDR] = 1 Sam 20:1–10, 18–22, 24–39
1 Samuel 21[HDR] = 1 Samuel 21
1 Samuel 22[HDR] = 1 Samuel 22
1 Samuel 23[HDR] = 1 Sam 23:1–13

[75] McCarter, *1 Samuel*, 307; also see McCarter, "The Apology of David," 492 n. 11.
[76] McCarter, *1 Samuel*, 311.
[77] Ibid., 316.
[78] McCarter, "The Apology of David," 492 n. 9.
[79] Even this delineation must be qualified, of course, by recognizing the numerous textual emendations of words and phrases that McCarter proposes throughout his commentaries (e.g., "Ishbaal" for "Ishbosheth" in 2 Sam 4:1).

1 Samuel 24[HDR] = Ø
1 Samuel 25[HDR] = 1 Sam 25:1b–27, 32–44
1 Samuel 26[HDR] = 1 Samuel 26
1 Samuel 27[HDR] = 1 Samuel 27
1 Samuel 28[HDR] = 1 Sam 28:1–10, 12b–13, 21–25
1 Samuel 29[HDR] = 1 Samuel 29
1 Samuel 30[HDR] = 1 Samuel 30
1 Samuel 31[HDR] = 1 Samuel 31
2 Samuel 1[HDR] = 2 Samuel 1
2 Samuel 2[HDR] = 2 Sam 2:1–9, 12–32
2 Samuel 3[HDR] = 2 Sam 3:1–8, 11–18a, 19–39
2 Samuel 4[HDR] = 2 Samuel 4
2 Samuel 5[HDR] = 2 Sam 5:3, 6–10
2 Samuel 6[HDR] = Ø
2 Samuel 7[HDR] = Ø

There is the remaining problem for McCarter and others that this history, which he sees as "more or less unified,"[80] retains quite a "heterogeneous appearance," but McCarter explains that this is because HDR was composed from "a variety of materials available during David's lifetime."[81] He does not look for signs of its independence and unity, therefore, primarily in matters of style. Rather, he describes the basis for its independence and unity as follows:

> No one has found in this material the unity and homogeneity generally accorded the succession document or even the ark narrative. As detailed below it betrays the marks of deuteronomistic expansion, and even in its predeuteronomistic form it is somewhat heterogeneous in appearance. Nevertheless it is possible in the opinion of most recent scholars to demonstrate that it has an overarching unity of theme and purpose. This unity is often explained as the consequence of the work of an editor who assembled materials of diverse traditional background and impressed upon them his own point of view. An alternative explanation, which is accepted in the present paper, is that the unity reflects the presence of an underlying, more or less unified

---

[80] McCarter, "The Apology of David," 490.
[81] Ibid., 493 n. 12.

composition by an author with a clear point of view, to which various secondary materials, some of them deuteronomistic, have accrued.[82]

So, although McCarter acknowledges that his own reconstructed HDR retains "some of its heterogeneous appearance," he argues that 1 Sam 16:14–2 Sam 5:10, minus a number of deuteronomistic, prophetic, and other anomalous additions, "is an old, more or less unified composition [i.e., unified by its particular apologetic interests] describing David's rise to power, which can be subjected to independent analysis."[83] This composition is readily identifiable because it has undergone very little revision throughout its literary history.[84]

Summary

Before we proceed to examine McCarter's view of HDR's "overarching unity of theme and purpose," it will be helpful to summarize the literary history of the text chronologically, concentrating this time on the points of major agreement among the majority of scholars. Diachronically-oriented critics, while disagreeing significantly over the parameters of HDR and certain details of its literary history (which I shall note below), widely agree with McCarter on at least the following points:

1) HDR itself was a "composition" of various oral traditions and/or literary sources that were circulating and probably widely known while David (or the Davidide for whom the "history" was composed) was still alive.[85] Even at the stage of its original composition, then, HDR proper would have been marked by *some* degree of unevenness or heterogeneity.[86]

---

[82] Ibid., 490–91.

[83] Ibid., 493.

[84] Ibid., 493–94.

[85] Ibid., 491 n. 6. See also 493 n. 12.

[86] One might consider, as one instance among many, McCarter's treatment of the three episodes in 1 Sam 21:11–22:5 as "narrative scraps" that "seem to reflect unrelated traditions about David's early career that were included at this point for want of a better occasion" (*I Samuel*, 358). It is not surprising, then, that the nature of HDR's pre-literary history alone considerably complicates any attempt at reconstructing the "original" HDR.

2) HDR underwent relatively little change throughout its literary history, though there were a number of recognizable accretions and editorial glossings, interpolations, etc.[87]

3) This sightly revised HDR was incorporated largely intact into a larger "history" that was composed much later to present Israel's history from a deuteronomistic perspective (there is disagreement, however, over the existence and number of intervening compositional stages[88]).

4) The Deuteronomistic History was further edited and redacted into the present biblical text. This post-deuteronomistic stage accounts for the few pluses in 1 Samuel 17–19 that I have noted above.

5) Despite its modest literary history, then, HDR is *essentially* retained unchanged in 1 Samuel 16–2 Samuel 5.[89]

---

[87] Another diachronic problem that complicates reconstruction of HDR is the nature of its *post*-literary history. All scholars who accept the existence of an early HDR agree that there were numerous additions and accretions, and presumably several deletions, as it was transmitted and redacted over the centuries. There is no lack of disagreement, however, over precisely what this entailed, inasmuch as the determination of which words, phrases, or entire passages constitute additions and accretions (as well as the determination of what has been deleted) is largely dependent upon the assumptions and conclusions a scholar makes regarding the nature of HDR and its subsequent redactional stages. The growing support for some version of a two-source theory, such as seen in work by Halpern and, more recently, Hutton, re-introduces a host of problems in this area, as those who accept the two-source theory must account for two HDRs' pre- and post-literary histories (see n. 7, above). Nevertheless, the majority view of the reconstruction of HDR since Rost is relatively uncomplicated, at least in comparison to critical reconstructions of Pentateuchal sources. In McCarter's view, as we have seen, these are limited to a handful of "prophetic," "deuteronomistic," and other glosses or "accretions." On the whole, McCarter and most others conclude that after HDR itself was composed from yet earlier sources, traditions, and legends, it underwent few changes throughout its literary history.

[88] In addition to my own discussion above, see Dietrich and Naumann's review of the scholarship on the existence and extent of the following stages: a history/apology of David's rise; an anti-monarchic prophetic history; a Deuteronomistic revision or revisions; and finally, the biblical edition ("The David-Saul Narrative," 296–98).

[89] The assumption of HDR's originally independent status has generated intense debate over the delineation of its parameters. There is no consensus over HDR's beginning; 1 Sam 15:1, 16:1, and 16:14 are the most commonly proposed. There is even less agreement and more confusion over its end; 2 Sam 5:10, 5:25, 6:23, and 7:29 are among the proposals. We can say, however, that the majority of scholars locate HDR's beginning somewhere in 1 Samuel 16 and its end somewhere in 2 Samuel 5.

Now that we have seen how McCarter reconstructs the History of David's Rise, let us turn our attention from its contours to his and others' conception of HDR's original function as an apology of the historical David.

The History of David's Rise as the Apology of David

Thematic Comparison between HDR and the Hittite Apology of Ḫattušili

In his 1967 dissertation, "*The Apology of Ḫattušiliš* Compared with Other Ancient Near Eastern Political Self-Justifications," Herbert M. Wolf made the first extensive comparison of HDR and a thirteenth-century B.C.E. Hittite account of Ḫattušili III's usurpation of the throne. Wolf draws attention to similarities between the thirteenth-century B.C.E. Hittite text and HDR by analyzing and comparing the form and subject matter of the two, and he concludes that there must have been some direct literary influence between them. Harry Hoffner, Wolf's dissertation adviser and a Hittite scholar, contributed to the discussion with essays of his own. In one of these essays, Hoffner points out a number of parallels between the account of David's contest with Goliath and Ḫattušili's contest with a champion from the "Pišḫuruwian enemy."[90] Hoffner's most important contribution to the discussion, however, came in a study in which he outlines the formal structure and important thematic elements of Hittite "royal apologies."[91] Hoffner describes the "apology" as "a document composed for a king who had usurped the throne, composed in order to defend or justify his assumption of the kingship by force."[92] In this essay, he mentions the "Apology of David," which he understands as the "piece of royal propaganda" that described "the events surrounding the demise of the Saulids and the rise to the throne of David,"[93] but he refrains from drawing any direct parallels between it and the Hittite apologies to which he then turns his attention.[94]

---

[90] Hoffner, "Hittite Analogue."

[91] Hoffner, "Propaganda and Political Justification."

[92] Ibid., 49. This definition appears to be acceptable to most scholars, including McCarter ("The Apology of David," 495–96).

[93] Hoffner, "Propaganda and Political Justification," 50. Hoffner refers to Stefan Heym's *Der König David Bericht*, which he appears to accept as a fair depiction of HDR's propagandistic character.

[94] Hoffner is more cautious than Wolf with regard to the possibility of direct connections between Hittite and Israelite cultures, yet he indicates hope that such a link might eventually

McCarter followed these studies by Wolf and Hoffner with his own comparison of HDR and the Apology of Ḫattušili. His assessment of the Hittite apology's comparative value is evident in the title of his essay: "The Apology of David." It is notable, however, that McCarter describes HDR's character as essentially apologetic before drawing any comparisons between it and the Hittite text. He bases this evaluation primarily on the influential study of Artur Weiser, who argues that HDR emphasizes "the legitimacy of the Davidic claim to the kingship of *all* Israel, north as well as south," and on that of J. H. Grønbæk, who highlights "the importance of the theological undergirding given this legitimation theme in the course of the history of David's rise."[95] McCarter concludes that HDR "must have been composed in the south in pro-Davidic circles, and it must have been promulgated at a time when the throne had just been transferred from one house to another." In other words, it must have been written in "Davidic Jerusalem," and very possibly in David's own day.[96] It is at this point that McCarter looks to the thirteenth-century B.C.E. Hittite "Apology of Ḫattušili" for extra-biblical evidence that HDR functioned as an individual royal apology. His comparative analysis leads him to the conclusion that HDR was to David and the Israelites as the Apology of Ḫattušili was to Ḫattušili and the Hittites.

Like Hoffner, McCarter does not find any direct literary influence of one "apology" on the other. He regards as "prudent" Hoffner's "reluctance to

be proven: "[A]lthough it may be impossible *at present* to prove any formal link between the Apology of Ḫattušili and the royal propaganda of David and Solomon, it is not impossible to speak of a tradition of royal apologies in the Hittite kingdom or even of a certain loose literary form, which several of them seem to assume" ("Propaganda and Political Justification," 50 [emphasis added]). For an extensive bibliography of Hoffner's work, see Haroutunian, "Complete Bibliography." I have found no development of this particular comparative work by Hoffner himself. He notes with apparent approval, however, that McCarter, in "The Apology of David," "was able to build upon Hittite historical materials that were first compared to the stories of Saul and David by Herbert M. Wolf and me" ("Ancient Israel's Literary Heritage," 183).

[95] McCarter, "The Apology of David," 493–94. McCarter's references are to Weiser, "Legitimation," and Grønbæk, *Geschichte*.

[96] McCarter, "The Apology of David," 494. McCarter says elsewhere: "It seems more likely, then, that the HDR is a document from the time of David himself, written before the development of the theology of dynastic promise under Solomon and directed toward those conservative elements in the north, especially Benjamin, who were suspicious of the new king; that is, it was written in the atmosphere illustrated by the accounts of the Shimei incident in II Sam 16:5–14 and Sheba's revolt in II Sam 20:1–22. Its purpose was to justify the succession as a reflection of Yahweh's will and offer rebuttal to charges made against David" (*I Samuel*, 29).

define this 'tradition of royal apologies' too strictly" or to posit any direct literary influence of one on the other, and McCarter states that "[e]fforts to find more than 'a certain loose literary form' shared by the several examples of the category would probably fail."[97] Instead, he generalizes the nature and aims of these documents, such as in the following statement, which provides significant insight into his view of them:

> Surely there is nothing distinctively Hittite or even ancient Near Eastern about the literary category of *political self-justification* with its accompanying claims for the legitimacy of the usurper, his ability to rule, his moral rectitude, and his divine election to office.[98]

Nevertheless, whereas Hoffner limits his scope primarily to an analysis of the Hittite apologies, McCarter regards a comparison between HDR and the Apology of Ḫattušili as potentially fruitful for the following reason:

> [T]he apology of Hattushilish demonstrates the potential for an elaborate development of this genre [of royal apology] in the general cultural milieu in which the history of David's rise was composed, and the striking similarity of themes in the two compositions is a clue to the original character of the Israelite document.[99]

McCarter proceeds to outline the texts' shared themes, demonstrating their "striking similarity," in order to appreciate better HDR's "original" and "apologetic character."[100] It will be helpful to enumerate these themes as McCarter has identified them so that they can serve as a reference point for my discussion below.

First, McCarter recounts the Apology of Ḫattušili. In his retelling, he identifies five major themes that serve to legitimize Ḫattušili's accession to the Hittite throne:

[97] McCarter, "The Apology of David," 498. McCarter thinks that Wolf's conclusion regarding direct literary dependence "seems to go much too far" (ibid, 498 n. 22). In fact, however, McCarter's study is more akin to Wolf's than to Hoffner's, as McCarter goes far beyond Hoffner in pointing out similarities between the two, as we will see below.

[98] McCarter, "The Apology of David," 498 [emphasis added]. Questions regarding the appropriateness of such a generalization vis-à-vis the biblical source will receive considerable attention in ch. 2.

[99] Ibid. McCarter calls the Apology of Ḫattušili "especially instructive for the study of the history of David's rise" ("The Apology of David," 496).

[100] McCarter, "The Apology of David," 498.

First, the ability of Hattushilish to rule is shown by reference to his various administrative accomplishments and military successes. *Second*, it is made clear that he was the favorite of his brother, Murshilish, and his viceregent in the rule of the Hittite dominions. *Third*, he is shown never to have acted out of self-interest though presented with frequent opportunities to advance his own cause, but instead to have conducted himself in accordance with a deep respect for his brother's memory ("... firm in [my] respect for my brother, I did not act selfishly" [3:39, 61; 4:29, 61]). *Fourth*, he is exonerated from all blame in the incessant personal conflict that attended his rise to power, and the source of the antagonism is shown to have been the jealousy of his rivals, especially Armadattash, and the groundless suspicions of Urhi-teshub. *Finally*, as already mentioned, the decisive factor in his ascent at every stage is shown to have been the effective power of Ishtar's favor, by which he was protected from every danger ("Ishtar always rescued me" [1:43, etc.]) and given success in all his undertakings.[101]

Next, McCarter identifies essentially the same five major themes in HDR:

First, David's ability to rule is illustrated by reference to his early military successes, the spontaneous loyalty of the people of Israel and Judah, and the skill and restraint with which he wages the long war with the house of Saul after his accession as king of Judah. *Second*, he is shown to have begun as Saul's trusted lieutenant and to have won the loyalty of the royal family. *Third*, he is depicted as thoroughly loyal to the king, never seeking out the power that steadily comes to him, and indeed refusing at least one opportunity to secure his position by slaying Saul. *Fourth*, he is shown to have been blameless in all his dealings with Saul, whose jealousy and groundless suspicions were responsible for the alienation of David and the conflict that ensued. *Finally*, it is made clear that David's rise to power was made possible, indeed inevitable, by the special favor of the god of Israel, "Yahweh is with him" being, as already noted, the leitmotif of the entire composition.[102]

In McCarter's view, this comparison demonstrates HDR's original apologetic nature in the manner discussed below.

---

[101] Ibid., 497–98 [emphasis added; bracketed insertions are McCarter's]. On the identity of the Hittite usurper's goddess, see p. 56 n. 20, below.

[102] Ibid., 499 [emphasis added].

The transparent aim of Ḫattušili's apology is to convince its readers that Ḫattušili assumed another's throne legitimately, that is, due to his own merit, the wickedness of his predecessors (and his blameless response to it), and the will of the gods, especially "Ištar, My Lady." It supports these claims, in part, by developing the "themes" that McCarter has identified. Though the aim of HDR is not nearly so transparent or overt as that of the Hittite text, it appears to have a number of corresponding themes. According to McCarter's logic, this indicates that HDR must have had the same essential purpose as the Hittite apology — "political self-justification" — and likely originated in a similar historical setting. In other words, the more that the History of David's Rise can be shown to resemble the history of Ḫattušili's rise (which was undoubtedly composed for Ḫattušili during his lifetime), the more assuredly one can identify the original setting of the former as David's own lifetime and appreciate its generic character and purpose as that of royal propaganda, that is, as the "Apology of David." In chapter 2, I shall return to consider this question of thematic similarities between the two texts. First, however, I shall present McCarter's discussion of HDR's "original" or "apologetic character," that is, its "rhetorical posturing."

The Rhetorical Posture of HDR

McCarter sees his thematic analyses of HDR as significant in that they foster the recognition that "[t]he biblical history of David's rise in its original formulation was . . . an apology in the sense defined by Hoffner," that is, "a document composed for a king who had usurped the throne, composed in order to defend or justify his assumption of the kingship by force."[103] If the precise nature and objectives of the account have not always been fully appreciated, this cannot be attributed to heavy-handed redaction of the account itself, for, according to McCarter, HDR has remained essentially unchanged. Whatever the reason that its personal, apologetic character has been overlooked before, once the shared themes and functions of HDR and Ḫattušili's apology are recognized, the discerning reader becomes critically equipped to notice and appreciate HDR's "rhetorical posture" in service of none other than David himself.[104] In turn, proper detection and understanding

---

[103] McCarter, "The Apology of David," 495–96, 499. McCarter cites Hoffner's definition from Hoffner, "Propaganda and Political Justification," 49.

[104] McCarter, "The Apology of David," 499. Similarly, McKenzie (*King David*) speaks of its "apologetic tone" (32, 33), apologetic "overstress" (45), and "apologetic nature" (186).

of this posture leads to informed appreciation of the main significance or meaning of HDR.[105] As McCarter explains:

> A thematic analysis of the history of David's rise that is sensitive to the rhetorical posture of the author reveals the apologetic character of the composition most clearly. Apologetic literature by its very nature assumes a defensive attitude toward its subject matter, addressing itself to issues exposed to actual or possible public censure. This is precisely the posture of the history of David's rise. *A careful reading* leads to the conclusion that the author is speaking to one possible charge of wrongdoing after another in an attempt to demonstrate David's innocence in the series of events that led to his succession. This case for the defense is made by relating the events in question in a way intended to allay all suspicions, and though the author becomes quite explicit at times, as in his report of Abner's death (see below), he does not permit himself to step out from behind his narrative and comment directly on the issue at hand. Nevertheless, the charges against which he defends David are *easily recognized*; the following list shows how they are dealt with in the narrative.[106]

McCarter goes on to present seven "easily recognized" charges that he infers from "a careful reading" of the narrative. The following are the charges or allegations brought against David, according to McCarter, that must have required the responses that we see in HDR:[107]

> Charge 1. *David sought to advance himself at court at Saul's expense.* The extraordinary attainments of the young Judahite at the Benjaminite court, especially in light of his subsequent fall from favor, might suggest that he acted out of a strong and perhaps unscrupulous self-interest while in Saul's service.[108]

McCarter thinks this accusation lies just beneath the surface of the accounts in which David comes to Saul's court only at the latter's request; the accounts

---

[105] Again, in ch. 3, I shall discuss in more detail the nature of this inevitable hermeneutical circle with regard to the reconstruction of HDR as an apology of David.

[106] McCarter, "The Apology of David," 499 [emphasis added]. McKenzie argues, for example, that HDR "goes to great lengths to explain how David was innocent of any wrongdoing" (*King David*, 33, regarding 1 Samuel 25).

[107] McKenzie (*King David*) and Halpern (*David's Secret Demons*), among others, build upon the work of McCarter and develop his suppositions here. It will be sufficient for my purposes, however, to concentrate mostly on McCarter's discussion.

[108] McCarter, "The Apology of David," 499–500.

in which David fulfilled Saul's wishes with complete loyalty while there; and the accounts in which David did not seek advancement through marriage to Saul's daughter, but simply responded to Saul's idea and the encouragement of Saul's servants.

> Charge 2. *David was a deserter.* The circumstances of David's departure from court might lead to the suspicion that he shirked his responsibilities to Saul and deserted.[109]

McCarter reasons that this charge must have evoked the following rhetorical posture: Saul's jealousy and paranoia left David no choice but to flee Saul's court or be killed unjustly. He left reluctantly, and even then, with the support of Saul's own children, Michal and Jonathan.

> Charge 3. *David was an outlaw.* The fact that David was known to have spent part of his life as leader of a band of outlaws—a fact that, we must assume, was too well known to be suppressed—would surely have inspired public disapprobation.[110]

It was necessary, according to McCarter, to cast things in a more positive light: David was driven into the life of an "outlaw" surrounded by "outlaws" because Saul pursued him unjustly. In fact, he preferred reconciliation with Saul over his fugitive lifestyle, and even Saul acknowledged such on a rare occasion.[111]

> Charge 4. *David was a Philistine mercenary.* The public knowledge that David had served in the army of a king of the Philistines, Israel's most hated foe, would certainly have provoked objections. Again this must have been too widely known to be denied.[112]

In order to neutralize the effect of such public knowledge of David's "service" to Achish, McCarter argues that more spin (my term) was called for: David went to the Philistine king only as a last resort. Even then, he achieved semi-

---

[109] Ibid., 500.

[110] Ibid.

[111] McCarter refers to 1 Sam 26:21. The other account similar to this, in 1 Sam 23:14–24:23, McCarter takes to be a "tendentious retelling" of 1 Samuel 26 by the deuteronomists (ibid., 493).

[112] Ibid., 500.

autonomy and used his strategic position and resources to raid the enemies of Israel / Judah and send plunder to Judah.

> Charge 5. *David was implicated in Saul's death.* Some must have suspected, if only on the ground of *cui bono*, that David was involved in the demise of his predecessor, especially since Saul died fighting against the Philistines at a time when David was in the Philistine army. Indeed the forces of Achish were known, it seems, to have participated in the battle of Mount Gilboa (cf. 1 Sam 29:1–2)![113]

As an answer to this, the text takes up the following posture: Though David might have ultimately benefited from Saul's death (and the deaths of his sons), he proved himself time and again to be vehemently against lifting a hand against YHWH's anointed. He was clearly not present when Saul was killed by David's Philistine master (and had he been there, he would have turned on Achish's army and fought with Saul, the text implies).

> Charge 6. *David was implicated in Abner's death.* Suspicion must have fallen on David in regard to the death of Abner, inasmuch as it was he who set Ishbaal on his father's throne (2 Sam 2:8–9) and seemed, therefore, to have been the major obstacle to David's kingship over the northern tribes.[114]

In McCarter's view, the text counters this charge with an elaborate recounting of the events surrounding Abner's death, which makes credible the narrator's threefold assertion that Abner left David "in peace" (2 Sam 3:21, 22, 23) and David's strong declaration of his innocence (3:28). In fact, the text makes clear, Abner left Ishbaal for David of his own volition and even "campaigned" to win Israelite support for David to be king. Abner's blood is not on David, but on Joab, who killed him out of revenge.

> Charge 7. *David was implicated in Ishbaal's death.* As in the cases of the deaths of Saul and Abner, David must have been suspected of treachery in the murder of Ishbaal.[115]

---

[113] Ibid., 500–501.
[114] Ibid., 501.
[115] Ibid., 501–2.

According to McCarter, David's innocence vis-à-vis this last charge is corroborated by the narrative demonstration that David had no prior knowledge of the assassination of Ishbaal ("Ishbosheth" in the biblical text). In fact, he was dismayed at hearing the news, he executed the assassins, and he honored Ishbaal with a proper burial.

I am content for the moment to highlight two points. Firstly, McCarter's analysis is based on the fundamental assumption that the truth of HDR can only be fully appreciated when read within the particular historical context that he has reconstructed. That is, according to McCarter, HDR only makes real sense when read as an answer to "some or all" of the above charges against the historical David in light of his political or ideological need for a defense. McCarter thus concludes:

> Some or all of these charges must actually have been made during David's lifetime. The issues they raise concern his personal behavior and would have been liveliest during his own reign.[116]

McCarter presents the charges above as readily obvious because he is confident about his identification of the correct interpretive context. But it must be recognized that neither the charges nor the "correct" context of reading is so clearly given. As I shall argue in more detail in chapter 3, the allegations against David must be inferred, in large part, from a prior determination about the genre of the text and apparent similarities between HDR and the Apology of Ḫattušili, from assumptions about the actual history behind the text, as well as from assumptions about human nature in general. I shall examine this hermeneutical problem further in chapter 3.

Secondly, the determination leading to McCarter's identification of the above seven "underlying" charges against David rests upon the identification of some themes in HDR that McCarter has selected because they appear to parallel those he has selected in the Hittite apologies. There are important and even central themes in McCarter's HDR, however, that he does not include in his thematic analysis, as we will see in the following chapters. The way in which McCarter has characterized HDR according to what is essentially the

---

[116] Ibid., 502. McKenzie implies his agreement with McCarter that the various accusations "would have been controversial only during David's lifetime or shortly afterward, and an apologetic response would have been unnecessary after he had been dead for several generations and his dynasty firmly established" (*King David*, 35).

sum of the particular themes that he has selected, to the exclusion of others, will become more evident in the following chapter.

In summary, in McCarter's view, HDR—and, thus, by extension, the biblical text of 1 Samuel 16–2 Samuel 5, if HDR has come down to us essentially unchanged—is fundamentally characterized by an "apologetic or rhetorical posture" and, therefore, best understood in these terms. "The History of David's Rise" shared with "the Apology of Ḫattušili" the aim of "political self-justification" for its sponsor: Kings David and Ḫattušili III were both usurpers in need of legitimization. Having correctly understood its character or genre, the critical reader is poised to discern how HDR was composed to answer charges against David too serious to ignore. The author(s) of HDR did not address these directly, but spun their account so cleverly and effectively that, with the passing of time, most of the questions or charges that evoked the account were forgotten. These are "easily recognized," however, when one properly appreciates HDR's rhetorical stance and reads it through the lens of royal apology.

Conclusion

The meaning of a text (or any form of communication, for that matter) is integrally dependent on its context or setting. In the case of an ancient text for which the historical setting is not known with certainty, scholars must engage in a "hermeneutical circle" of informing their reading of the text with educated ideas about its provenance or setting, and, conversely, of informing their ideas about its provenance or setting with an educated reading of the text. One's understanding of the one impacts understanding of the other. Ultimately, to the degree that the reader associates or identifies a text with a particular referential context, that particular referential context plays a determinative role in understanding the text's meaning and significance.

As we have seen, McCarter's interpretation of the History of David's Rise presumes a tenth-century Davidic and Jerusalemite setting in which the king has been charged for certain crimes of lese-majesty. His work begins with his acceptance of the conclusion of Rost, and of many other scholars since, that "an originally independent and unified narrative recounting the early part of David's career," though rather "heterogeneous in appearance," can be detected in the books of Samuel by its "overarching unity of theme and purpose."[117] McCarter unfolds the "theme and purpose" of the original source as that of ancient Near Eastern "political self-justification," or "royal apology," through his source-critical analysis, his form-critical comparison of HDR with the Hittite Apology of Ḫattušili, and his ideological-critical exposition of HDR's "rhetorical posture" in the face of seven unstated charges against David.

One of my major aims in this chapter, in presenting in such detail McCarter's interpretation of HDR, has been to appreciate how, according to this approach, the account's "true meaning" is more or less exhausted in and through reading it as the personal self-justification of an individual king who has been beleaguered by various accusations of illegitimacy by Saulide supporters, insurgents, and other discontents. Having stripped away a few prophetic, deuteronomistic, and other accretions that, at any rate, do not counter but even enhance the narrative's *Tendenz*, we have in this account of David's rise to Saul's throne another example of ancient Near Eastern royal apology serving the pressing needs of an individual monarch to silence any actual and would-be accusers and opponents. Such a setting might explain some features of the biblical account; indeed, if one accepts the assumptions of this reading, it compellingly renders the History of David's Rise intelligible and meaningful in light of an easily imaginable construal of the *res*, or "stuff," of history.

The interpretation of the biblical account of David's rise to kingship as the sort of personal or individual apology that McCarter and others propose, however, is beset with numerous and significant problems. While this particular reading of the biblical account appears to explain some of its themes and features, it is inadequate with regard to many others. Already I have pointed to five problems inherent in McCarter's source-critical analysis of HDR. In the next chapter, I shall take issue primarily with his comparative analysis of HDR and the Apology of Ḫattušili and argue that many of the proposed similarities between the two have been overemphasized, and that practically all of their dissimilarities have been ignored. Then, in chapter 3, I shall revisit the question of HDR's "rhetorical posture." My primary aim there will be to demonstrate in considerably more detail what I have already suggested in the previous section: that McCarter's identification of HDR's "posture" is based as much, if not more, upon extratextually-based assumptions and conclusions as upon a close reading of the text. I present

[117] McCarter, "The Apology of David," 490.

these studies in order to reassess and redirect the assumption that the true meaning of the biblical account, whether in some reconstructed or Masoretic form, can be found in reading and making sense of it first and foremost as an individual king's personal exoneration for ascending to another's throne.

CHAPTER 2

The History of David's Rise and the Apology of Ḫattušili—A Reappraisal

Introduction

As we have seen in chapter 1, McCarter already detects some sort of apologetic meaning and purpose in the History of David's Rise before turning his attention to the Apology of Ḫattušili. He bases this on the conclusion of previous scholars and his own internal analysis of HDR. But this is insufficient for establishing HDR's precise historical context, as the range of scholarly proposals suggests. This is where, for McCarter, the discovery of "thematic similarities" and a shared "rhetorical posture" between his reconstructed HDR and the Apology of Ḫattušili is highly beneficial. It enables him to confirm and clarify the apologetic meaning and purpose of HDR more precisely than had been possible before. The commonalities, in his view, provide corroboration for dating the original HDR to David's own day and, concomitantly, for concluding that "[t]he biblical history of David's rise in its original formulation was, we may suppose, an apology in the sense defined by Hoffner," that is, "a document composed for a king who had usurped the throne, composed in order to defend or justify his assumption of the kingship by force."[1] In short, he concludes that the History of David's Rise is a composition originally and independently created to accomplish for the historical David what the Apology of Ḫattušili accomplished for Ḫattušili: personal self-justification vis-à-vis charges of illegitimate usurpation.

---

[1] McCarter, "The Apology of David," 495–96, at 499, citing Hoffner, "Propaganda and Political Justification," 49.

In the process of detecting and highlighting certain similarities and commonalities, however, McCarter—along with those who have accepted his conclusions—appears to have missed significant formal and thematic differences between HDR and the Apology of Ḫattušili.[2] McCarter's full attention to the "striking similarities" has resulted in a selective representation of the Hittite and Israelite "histories" or "apologies" that obscures the striking dissimilarities. We cannot hope to understand the significance of the biblical source and text if we skirt over important differences and focus only on that which is similar between the Israelite and Hittite texts.

In the following discussion, I shall reconsider the formal structure and thematic elements that Hoffner first identified in the Apology of Ḫattušili and reassess the degree of similarity between this Hittite text and HDR. My analysis will shed light on important themes and aspects in the two texts that are notably dissimilar. In particular, this combined formal and thematic analysis will raise serious questions about the validity of reading HDR—and, thus, the biblical narrative of 1 and 2 Samuel—guided by the presupposition that its "real meaning" has to do primarily with the way in which it answers or refutes certain charges against the historical David. Consequently, this discussion will prepare the way for considering other nuances and possibilities with regard to the nature and function of the biblical source and text.

In the course of my discussion, I shall also include limited reference to one additional text, the Proclamation of Telipinu, because Hoffner includes it in his treatment of the Apology of Ḫattušili. I am principally concerned with the Apology of Ḫattušili, however, because it has figured so prominently in the particular theories about the biblical account of David's rise to kingship with which my study is primarily concerned. I recognize that the present discussion could benefit from expanding my treatment to include numerous other ancient Near Eastern royal apologies and, for that matter, other biblical texts and sources, such as the "Succession Narrative." Do the particular observations and conclusions presented in the present study apply to comparisons of HDR with other personal royal apologies from the ancient Near East? This is an important question to raise, but to attempt an answer that carries any weight would require a far more extensive study than can be offered within the scope

---

[2] In his dissertation, Armington has footnoted some of the significant formal differences between the Apology of Ḫattušili and David's "apology" ("Recurrent Narratives in 1 Samuel," 3–4 n. 9). McCarter does not identify any differences.

of the present work. I hope that my own limited case study, therefore, will spark further comparative work along these lines.

Hoffner's Analysis of the Apology of Ḫattušili III and the Proclamation of Telipinu

It is especially important to revisit Hoffner's essay, "Propaganda and Political Justification in Hittite Historiography," especially because biblical scholars who follow McCarter's lead and treat HDR and/or its derivative account in Samuel as a personal royal apology parallel to those of the Hittites—especially the Apology of Ḫattušili—generally refer to Hoffner's work for corroboration. Hoffner himself makes only passing reference to "the Apology of David." He points to it as another example of ancient "royal propaganda,"[3] but he does not highlight any structural or thematic parallels between the Hittite apologies and HDR in his subsequent analysis.[4] Instead, he presents "the essential structure" and its related thematic elements that he finds in common between two Hittite "royal apologies": the Proclamation of Telipinu and the Apology of Ḫattušili III.[5] Although Hoffner shows interest in drawing some comparison between Hittite and non-Hittite "apologies," such an analysis does not fall within his purview in that essay. Nevertheless, his work on the Hittite apologies offers a valuable framework for comparative analysis. It will be my contention below that HDR bears significantly less resemblance—and thus maintains more distinctiveness by comparison—to the Apology of Ḫattušili than scholars have acknowledged. Revisiting Hoffner's identification and characterization of the formal structure and thematic elements of the Hittite apologies elucidates this best.

Before proceeding further, we should note Hoffner's explanation for his usage of the term "apology":

> The term "apology" as a designation of a formal composition has most frequently been applied to texts from early Christian and pre-

[3] Hoffner, "Propaganda and Political Justification," 50.

[4] On Hoffner's caution with regard to the possibility of there existing any "formal link" between the Apology of Ḫattušili and "the royal propaganda of David and Solomon," see pp. 39–40 n. 94.

[5] Hoffner, "Propaganda and Political Justification," 51–56. He follows this with a brief analysis of a third possible Hittite apology that is preserved only in fragmentary form (ibid., 56–58).

Christian times to denote a detailed defense against false attacks and accusations. The most familiar examples of such apologies are that of Plato and those of the early Christian apologists. The late professor Edgar H. Sturtevant of Yale University, however, employed this term to describe a lengthy text composed in the first person for the Hittite emperor Ḫattušili III. . . . Since Sturtevant's publications on this text the term "apology" has occasionally been employed by other Hittitologists to describe Ḫattušili's remarkable composition, but the prevailing custom has been to call it either an "accession report" (German: *Thronbesteigungsbericht*), an "aretalogy" or an "autobiography." We will use the term "apology" in the ensuing discussion in the specialized sense of *a document composed for a king who had usurped the throne, composed in order to defend or justify his assumption of the kingship by force.*[6]

Because the ancient Hittite texts do not identify themselves by any such term as "apology," Hoffner asserts that "we must identify surviving Hittite examples *by formal criteria alone.*"[7]

It generally goes unnoticed or unmentioned by scholars who depend heavily upon Hoffner's work that he distinguishes these "defenses of usurpations"[8] from other kinds of Hittite royal "defenses." In this latter category, he includes, for example, the "Ten-Year Annals of Muršili." Although Muršili is the rightful heir to the throne, taunts against him from enemy lands are circulating about, saying, for example, "He who now sits on the throne of his father is small and unable to defend the land of Ḫatti and its borders."[9] Hoffner states:

Although the words are attributed to the surrounding enemy lands, they surely reached the king's ears through his own subjects. And the king's concern must surely have been aroused by the possible effect which these words of enemy propaganda might have on the morale, indeed the loyalty, of his own subjects. This lengthy taunt or charge of incompetence was certainly cited for a purpose.[10]

Muršili's ten-year annals, then, were composed not to legitimize his right to the throne, but to recount his personal and extraordinary deeds to prove his

---

[6] Ibid., 49 [emphasis added].

[7] Ibid. [emphasis added].

[8] Ibid., 50.

[9] Ibid.

[10] Ibid.

fitness to be king.[11] Essentially, it is "a defense of the young king's manhood," but Hoffner stresses that "it must be kept distinct from the true apologies, which concern the king's right to the throne."[12] Having made these distinctions, Hoffner proceeds to outline "the essential structure" or "general pattern" that "demonstrates the more or less traditional way in which Hittite usurpers defended their usurpation."[13] He enumerates six elements in both the Proclamation of Telipinu (=T) and the Apology of Ḫattušili III (=H), and gives the citations where they are found in each text:[14]

1. Introduction: T §1, H §§1–2.
2. Historical survey: noble antecedents. T §§1–9, H §§3–10.
3. Historical survey: the unworthy predecessor. T §§10–22a, H §§10–12 [10–11].
4. The coup d'état: T §§22b, H §§12–13 [12].
5. The merciful victor: T §§23 & 26, H §§12–13 [12].
6. The edict: T §§27–50, H §§13–15 [12–14].

Ḫattušili III begins his first-person apology[15] by claiming his right to kingship based on his "remote namesake," Ḫattušili I, and blood-kinship to the royal line, even though he was not the heir-apparent of his predecessor. The first-person proclamation of Telipinu, who also has no claim as the direct heir, begins tersely: "[Thus] the Tabarna, Telipinu, Great King."[16] Next, each

---

[11] See ibid., 50–51, for Hoffner's brief survey of Muršili's defense.

[12] Ibid., 51.

[13] Ibid.

[14] The citations in the following enumeration are Hoffner's (ibid.), following Götze, *Ḫattušiliš*. For my own quotations of the Hittite texts, I have relied on van den Hout, "The Proclamation of Telipinu" and "Apology of Ḫattušili III," in *The Context of Scripture*, 194–204. In Hoffner's enumeration, therefore, I have added bracketed citations to van den Hout's text where it differs from Hoffner's citations to Götze's edition. Van den Hout's translation of "The Proclamation of Telipinu" is based on the Hittite original in Hoffmann, *Der Erlaß Telipinus*; his translation of the "Apology of Ḫattušili III" is based on Otten, *Die Apologie Hattušilis III*. For the sake of comparison, also see translations in Sturtevant and Bechtel, *A Hittite Chrestomathy*.

[15] I shall treat this significant characteristic of the Hittite texts separately below. Hoffner does not discuss the first-person form of the apologies at any length but simply notes the fact that some Hittitologists call the Ḫattušili text an "autobiography," as we have seen above (Hoffner, "Propaganda and Political Justification," 49).

[16] Van den Hout, "The Proclamation of Telipinu," 194 (§1). As an anonymous reviewer of my manuscript at Harvard Theological Studies has noted, "Great King" here functions

apology introduces former righteous kings and their "glorious reigns," and each declares or demonstrates the wickedness of the king whose throne was usurped. The contrast between the two in each case casts the nobility of the former and the wickedness of the latter in relief, and all this together functions to highlight the need for the coup d'état.[17] Both Telipinu and Ḫattušili remove their "unworthy predecessors" from the throne only after those wicked kings have made attempts on their lives. Telipinu justifies his coup based on the murderous plot by his "unworthy predecessor" against him and his wife, and not explicitly based on any divine will, although he has spoken of the gods' punishment of his wicked predecessors in the preceding section. Ḫattušili, too, accuses his predecessor of trying to kill him, but he bases his successful coup on the promise, will, and aid of the gods.[18] Then, both Telipinu and Ḫattušili declare their mercy and leniency over some who had resisted them.[19] And finally, in the Ḫattušili text, there is a brief "edict" in which "the regulations concern only the disposition of royal property to the cult of the goddess Ishtar[20] of Šamuḫa." In the Telipinu text it is a lengthy section in which "the regulations concern the conduct of justice as it affects the royal family."[21]

A Reappraisal of the Formal and Thematic Similarities and Dissimilarities between HDR and the Apology of Ḫattušili

Although McCarter minimizes the relevance of "purely formal elements" and concentrates his analysis on "thematic parallels" between HDR and the Apology of Ḫattušili,[22] formal elements and thematic concerns cannot be so easily divorced. Consideration of the "essential structure" or "formal

---

as a legitimating epithet.

[17] Hoffner, "Propaganda and Political Justification," 52–53.

[18] Ibid., 53–54.

[19] Ibid., 54–55.

[20] Some scholars of Hittite and other ancient Near Eastern studies will be quick to recognize that Ḫattušili did not serve Ištar but the Hurrian goddess Shaushga, an Ištar figure (I thank the reviewer mentioned above for drawing my attention to this point). In order to avoid confusion, however, throughout the present work I shall refer to the goddess as "Ištar" (or "Ishtar," as found in some quotations) in keeping with the reading followed in the essays by Hoffner and McCarter, and that found in van den Hout's translation of the Hittite apology.

[21] Hoffner, "Propaganda and Political Justification," 55.

[22] McCarter, "The Apology of David," 498–99.

elements" that Hoffner has identified—and that McCarter and others who accept his conclusions seem to have missed or overlooked—necessarily engages us in an evaluation of the central "thematic concerns" of any particular text. As the following analysis will show, it is highly beneficial and instructive, then, to compare HDR and the Apology of Ḫattušili in light of Hoffner's important analysis, and not merely based on the comparison of a few selected themes.[23] The more we can recognize and appreciate the formal properties and thematic elements that are both analogous and distinctive, the better we are positioned to understand the nature and significance of the texts. I turn now, therefore, to consider the following questions: To what extent does HDR share any of the formal and thematic elements that Hoffner has identified in the Hittite apologies? What do the differences or dissimilarities—generally overlooked by McCarter and others—suggest about the distinctive nature and function of the biblical source and narrative? While focusing my attention primarily on the Apology of Ḫattušili as McCarter has done, I shall now take each of Hoffner's elements in turn in the interest of answering these questions.

1) Introduction

Ḫattušili begins by listing his credentials as king, that is, his right to the throne based on his natural lineage and namesake:

> Thus Tabarna Ḫattušili, Great King, King of Ḫatti, son of Muršili, Great King, King of Ḫatti, grandson of Šuppiluliuma, Great King, King of Ḫatti, descendant of Ḫattušili, King of Kuššar.[24]

This genealogical list of sorts presents Ḫattušili as the "son" and "grandson" of kings, and thus a direct descendant of the first Ḫattušili, his namesake. One should exercise some caution in attributing too much significance to this genealogical introduction. Indeed, the Hittite king follows a conventional form of self-identification in the opening statement of royal inscriptions that was already well-established in his day.[25] The likelihood that Ḫattušili

---

[23] I am referring here to the five parallel themes that McCarter has enumerated in "The Apology of David," 495–99, and that I have introduced on p. 42, above.

[24] Van den Hout, "Apology of Ḫattušili III," 199 (§1).

[25] Once again I thank a reviewer at HTS—this time for emphasizing this point and leading me to reconsider the degree of overall significance one may reasonably attribute to Ḫattušili's genealogical introduction.

invests this conventional introduction with individual apologetic significance, however, finds strong support in the observation that, throughout the royal document, Ḫattušili explicitly makes numerous asseverations regarding the legitimate and natural course by which he has become the "Great King." He does this as he recounts the following (among other) events: His "brother" the king (Muwatalli) "took [him] back" when Muwatalli recognized Ḫattušili's innocence after envious men caused him "harm" and "were evil" to him;[26] he replaced Armatarḫunta, son of Zida, as ruler of the Upper Country after his brother Muwatalli "gave" it to Ḫattušili "to govern,"[27] and later, his brother the king declared Ḫattušili innocent of a "lawsuit" brought against him by Armatarḫunta;[28] he "di[d] not [do] anything (evil)"[29] after Muwatalli died, but he made Urḫitešub, "son of a concubine," king of Ḫatti because Muwatalli "did not have a [l]egitimate son";[30] when this Urḫitešub, having seen "the benevolence" of Ištar to Ḫattušili, "became envious" and removed Ḫattušili's subjects from him, Ḫattušili "did not react at all" but submitted to him for seven years; only after Urḫitešub started hostilities and tried to destroy him was it that Ḫattušili finally "became hostile to him" and replaced him as "Great King," and this according to the promise and with the help of Ištar.[31]

It is evident that Ḫattušili's "right" was a stretch by ancient standards. Thus, Sturtevant concludes:

> Such action [i.e., that "Ḫattušili declared war upon his titular suzerain, deposed and banished him, and established himself in his place"] was, to say the least, of doubtful legality in what was, after all, a limited monarchy, and it required justification before the *pankus*, the council of the nobility, which we elsewhere call the senate. While the document before us is not ostensibly addressed to this body, it is hard to see what other purpose it could have had.[32]

[26] Ibid., 200 (§§4–5).

[27] Ibid. 200 (§4).

[28] Ibid., 202 (§10a).

[29] Sturtevant and Bechtel translate it as "did not act selfishly" (*A Hittite Chrestomathy*, 75 [§10]).

[30] Van den Hout, "Apology of Ḫattušili III," 202 (§10a).

[31] Ibid., 202–3 (§10c).

[32] Sturtevant and Bechtel, *A Hittite Chrestomathy*, 84. See, though, Beckman, "The Hittite Assembly," 435–42. Beckman argues that the Hittite king's power was not derivative of the *pankus*, whose chief function was "of a judicial character, namely of witnessing agreements and royal proclamations of great importance, and of trying criminal offenders of particularly high status" (442).

In the introduction and elsewhere, the Hittite document points to Ḫattušili's legitimacy by virtue, in part, of his natural lineage and namesake. Of course, Ḫattušili explicitly attributes his preservation and success throughout the document to "Ištar, My Lady," and nowhere more importantly, perhaps, than in the prooemium, where Ḫattušili unequivocally states, "Ištar's divine providence I will proclaim. Let man hear it!"[33] In drawing attention to Ḫattušili's genealogical credentials, one must not under-emphasize the role of the goddess Ištar in Ḫattušili's expression of personal self-justification. Urḫitešub's right to the throne, after all, was based on natural claims even stronger and more legitimate than those of Ḫattušili; Ḫattušili's appeals to natural lineage and namesake, therefore, could not stand by themselves. But contrary to McCarter's observation that "the decisive factor in [Ḫattušili's] ascent at every stage is shown to have been the effective power of Ishtar's favor,"[34] Ḫattušili's natural lineage and namesake are also held up in his defense at critical points, including the opening statement, even if it enjoys this initial position partly by accident of convention. The favor of Ištar is preeminently important, and his brother's (the king's) kind disposition toward him is critical, too; but these are authenticated, to some significant degree, by Ḫattušili's pedigree. How does the introduction to HDR compare?

First, we must be clear about what we mean by HDR's "introduction." One of the relatively few major points of disagreement over the reconstruction of HDR concerns its parameters, that is, the demarcation of its introduction and conclusion, as we have seen in chapter 1. The validity of any comparisons drawn between the introduction to HDR and those of the Hittite apologies is contingent upon the correctness of one's identification of HDR's original introduction. For the sake of the present argument, I shall begin by comparing the introduction of HDR as McCarter has delineated it with that of the Apology of Ḫattušili and see if we might say anything of them beyond, perhaps, "here begins the account of X."

McCarter credits the prophetic historian with the account of the prophet Samuel's seeking out and anointing David in Bethlehem in 1 Sam 16:1–13.[35] His reconstructed HDR begins with the account that follows it in 1 Sam 16:14–23. This tells of the discovery of David "son of Jesse" by Saul's own court in the search for "a man who is skillful at playing the lyre" to bring

---

[33] Van den Hout, "Apology of Ḫattušili III," 199 (§2).

[34] McCarter, "The Apology of David," 498.

[35] See my discussion of this in ch. 1, 31–34.

relief to King Saul, who is bereft of YHWH's spirit only to be tormented by
"an evil spirit from YHWH." David is "seen" as possessing more than his
considerable musical skills:

> And one of the servants answered and said, "See here [הִנֵּה], I have
> seen a son of Jesse the Bethlehemite [רָאִיתִי בֵּן לְיִשַׁי בֵּית הַלַּחְמִי]
> who is skilled at playing, a man of valor, a man of battle, eloquent,
> a comely man, and YHWH is with him [וַיהוָה עִמּוֹ]."[36]

Upon hearing about this man of such skill and character, King Saul sends
for Jesse's son, welcomes him enthusiastically—"And [Saul] loved him very
much" (וַיֶּאֱהָבֵהוּ מְאֹד)—and appoints him to be his armor-bearer and personal
musician in times of personal torment.[37]

McCarter hypothesizes that, at some point during David's lifetime, this
"introduction" of David, together with the subsequent depiction of his
receiving honor and gifts from King Saul, suited apologetic purposes in the
face of charges that David's unlawful usurpation began with aggressive self-
advancement.[38] This account, according to McCarter, would have answered
such charges with a definitive "no." In this view, it would have shown that
David's first important steps toward the throne—as the reader comes to
appreciate these, in retrospect—are inadvertently taken only at Saul's own
invitation. The passage functions, then, to characterize David's ascension to
Saul's throne as both unselfishly motivated and lawful from the very start,[39]
as well as in accordance with the will of YHWH, by whose spirit—or more
precisely, by the presence of which, in David's case, and the lack of which, in
Saul's—each man was marked before the people.[40] I shall return in chapter 3
to consider the logic of, and assumptions behind, McCarter's characterization
of HDR's function at this point. At the present moment, however, I shall limit
my comments to certain important differences between the introductions to
HDR and the Hittite apology.

---

[36] 1 Sam 16:18.

[37] 1 Sam 16:21–23. On the bracketed insertion of "Saul," see p. 178 n. 138, below.

[38] See the first rhetorical posture and charge that McCarter postulates in ch. 1, 44–45.

[39] See McCarter's second, third, and fourth "themes," according to which David "is shown
to have begun as Saul's trusted lieutenant . . ."; "is depicted as thoroughly loyal to the king
. . ."; and "is shown to have been blameless in all his dealings with Saul" (ch. 1, 42).

[40] See McCarter's fifth "theme," according to which "David's rise to power was made
possible, indeed inevitable, by the special favor of the god of Israel" (ch. 1, 42).

In sharp contrast to the Apology of Ḫattušili, the History of David's Rise must be reckoned as not only extremely subtle, but perhaps even subversive of attempts to present David as the reasonable successor to Saul's throne. As McCarter has reconstructed it, not only does it begin without any similar asseveration regarding David's legitimacy by rights of lineage or any other natural means, the account essentially depicts him as an upstart with no prior connection to the royal family, or to any other family of significance.[41] This is underscored even more in the so-called "prophetic" introduction, as I shall demonstrate in chapter 5. And while he certainly has many desirable qualities in the eyes of Saul's court—he is described as "skilled at playing, a man of valor, a man of battle, eloquent, a comely man, and YHWH is with him"—this is a far cry from presuming that this "son of Jesse" retains any natural claim or right to replace Saul as king of Israel. Unlike Ḫattušili, to whom "Ištar, My Lady," explicitly promised the kingship on numerous occasions,[42] David receives no explicit promise from YHWH in McCarter's reconstructed HDR. Furthermore, nothing is said of anything that David may have done specifically to merit YHWH's presence "with him." Even if we were to consider 1 Sam 16:1–13 as the original "introduction," as some others do, and take into account Samuel's anointing of David— presumably accompanied by some pronouncement or promise—and that "the Spirit of YHWH rushed upon David [and stayed with him] from that day on" (וַתִּצְלַח רוּחַ־יְהוָה אֶל־דָּוִד מֵהַיּוֹם הַהוּא וָמָעְלָה), YHWH's election of, and presence with, David remains unexpected, inexplicable, and utterly mysterious.[43] It is all the more so, then, if we begin HDR with 1 Sam 16:14, as McCarter does. David's only right to Saul's throne—if we might call it that, for it is highly subtle at this point, and only the first step in the unfolding of David's destiny—is based not on any presumption of natural desert, but it stands solely on the accident[44] of YHWH's spirit leaving Saul

---

[41] See my discussion (pp. 163–66, below) on the conspicuous absence of any genealogy (beyond the identification of his father) for David in the books of Samuel. While the prominence of David's lineage is highlighted elsewhere, such as in the book of Ruth, it is effectively downplayed, even to the point of denigration, in the books of Samuel.

[42] Van den Hout, "Apology of Ḫattušili III," 203–4 (§§11–12).

[43] 1 Sam 16:13. David's election was so unexpected, it surprised even his own father and brothers, as well as the prophet Samuel. I shall return to discuss this important aspect of David's election on pp. 146–54, 158–63.

[44] I mean this in the following sense: "Anything that happens without foresight or expectation; an unusual event, which proceeds from some unknown cause, or is an unusual

and taking up residence with David, and on the unexplained discovery and acknowledgement of that fact by Saul's own men (and, presumably, Saul himself). David's path to the throne is marked by surprise and wonder from the start and, thus, stands in considerable contrast to the Apology of Ḫattušili, which begins boldly and presumptuously and presents the king as unambiguously standing within and honoring a long line of tradition.

2) Historical Survey of Noble Antecedents

In the Apology of Ḫattušili, Ištar's favor is grounded at least partly in, and made explicable by means of, Ḫattušili's natural claim to the throne through his following in the line of "noble antecedents." These are introduced not only by means of the opening genealogy, which I have discussed above, but also in a relatively lengthy section that tells of his faithful service under two previous kings, namely, his father Muršili and his brother Muwatalli.[45] The Proclamation of Telipinu opens with brief histories of three predecessors— Labarna, Ḫattušili I, and Muršili I—who are characterized as exhibiting strength and maintaining unity.[46]

There is no analogy in HDR to the Hittite apologies' introduction of noble antecedents. Within the scope of McCarter's reconstructed HDR, at least, we might dismiss the necessity for this formal element in David's case based on the common-sense observation that there were no royal antecedents to David besides Saul,[47] and so no royal comparisons could be made. Still, if the sole or primary aim of HDR were to legitimize David's succession to the throne, one would expect the royal apologists to make some explicit connection (at least in some form or another) between David and one or more of Israel's leaders from past ages.[48] Or, perhaps, one would expect the propagandists of HDR to exalt grandiloquently David's family and tribe as the rightful heirs of the throne. The failure to do so, especially in light of the resources almost

---

effect of a known cause." From "accident, *n*." in *The Oxford English Dictionary* (2d ed.; Oxford University Press, Oxford: 2000); also <http://dictionary.oed.com/cgi/entry/50001207>.

[45] Van den Hout, "Apology of Ḫattušili III," 199–202 (§§1–9).

[46] Van den Hout, "The Proclamation of Telipinu," 194–95 (§§1–11). In his discussion of this section, Hoffner states: "The common theme is unity and strength. These three monarchs could easily be called the 'orthodox caliphs' of the Hittite Old Kingdom. Theirs was the golden age of harmony within and unmarred victory abroad" ("Propaganda and Political Justification," 52).

[47] Though Abimelech was declared "king" in Judges 9, it is hardly necessary to consider him as a true antecedent, and certainly not as a "noble" one.

[48] See, e.g., Ruth 4:18–22; 1 Chr 2:1–15; Psalm 78.

certainly available to them, betrays yet another significant difference between the nature and aims of the Israelite and Hittite texts.

Most notably, HDR's author(s) might have explicitly linked David with Israel's great patriarchs, Abraham, Isaac, and Jacob/Israel. These noble antecedents figured prominently in Judah's ancient traditions by virtue of their associations with Hebron/Mamre. After recounting Abraham's personal exodus from Egypt, and how he parted ways with Lot and received YHWH's promise of the land,[49] the biblical text reports: "And Abram moved his tent and came to dwell among the oaks of Mamre, which are in Hebron. And he built there an altar to YHWH."[50] Then, the biblical account records Abraham's purchase of "the field of Machpelah before [coming to] Mamre, that is, Hebron, in the land of Canaan" as a burial ground for Sarah.[51] When Abraham dies, Isaac and Ishmael bury him there as well.[52] Later, the text places Isaac in Mamre/Hebron,[53] as well as Jacob and his sons.[54] Finally, in keeping with Jacob's command, his sons carry his body back to the land of Canaan and bury him with his fathers, Abraham and Isaac.[55] This is all significant, of course, because David, too, has important ties to Hebron. Hebron is included among those cities of Judah to which David sends "the plunder of YHWH's enemies,"[56] and most significantly, according to 2 Samuel 2[HDR], Hebron becomes David's first "capital":

> After this David inquired of YHWH, "Shall I go up to one of the cities of Judah?" And YHWH said to him, "Go up." And David said, "To where shall I go up?" And He said, "Hebron." And David went up there, and also his two wives—Ahinoam the Jezreelitess, and Abigail, the wife of Nabal the Carmelite. And David brought up his men who were with him, each man and his household, and they lived in the towns of Hebron. And the men of Judah came and, there, anointed David as king over the house of Judah. . . . And the time that David

---

[49] Gen 13:1–17.

[50] Gen 13:18.

[51] Gen 23:19.

[52] Gen 25:9.

[53] Gen 35:27.

[54] Gen 37:1, 14.

[55] Gen 49:29–32; 50:13. For other patriarchal associations with Mamre and/or Hebron, see Gen 14:13; 18:1; 23:2, 17–20.

[56] 1 Sam 30:26–31.

was king in Hebron over the house of Judah was seven years and six months.[57]

Ronald E. Clements carefully works out various traditional and literary connections between David and Abraham in his *Abraham and David*. For my purposes here, it is sufficient to note Clements's identification of the geographical link (with some reference to YHWH's promise to Abraham) that is established between the two figures:

> Hebron was the centre from which David negotiated. This was his capital from which he exercised kingship for seven and a half years, and his choice of it must undoubtedly lie in the fact that it was the chief city of Judah. By this close association with Hebron David was brought into a relation with the ancient tradition of Abraham, the ancestor of the Judahite federation. The circumstances arose in which, with David's success against the Philistines and the new eminence that Judah attained, the old promise of land to the patriarch could be regarded as foreshadowing the greatness which Judah was to attain under David. The close geographical link between David and Hebron, and the fact that the shrine of Mamre was the focus of the tradition of the covenant with Abraham, therefore provides a basis for recognizing that a connection was seen in Israel between David and the ancestral figure of Abraham.[58]

Although Clements discusses here the "connection" between David and Abraham, David might also have been connected as easily to Isaac and Jacob/Israel by virtue of their common ties to Hebron, in particular.[59]

There are also unmistakable parallels between David and two other prominent shepherds in Israel's traditions, namely, Joseph and Moses. All three figures were younger brothers who went from tending flocks of sheep to

---

[57] 2 Sam 2:1–4a, 11. Note that McCarter views v. 11, however, as a deuteronomistic interpolation (see p. 28, above).

[58] Clements, *Abraham and David*, 51; also see, in particular, 56–57.

[59] On various possible kinds of connections between David, or the Davidic court, and the patriarchs (Abraham, Isaac, and Jacob), see, for example: ibid., 51, 56–57; Brueggemann, "David and His Theologian," 156–81; Rendsburg, "David and His Circle," 438–46; Rosenberg, *King and Kin*; Pleins, "Son-slayers," 29–38; Zakovitch, "Through the Looking Glass," 139–52; Sperling, *The Original Torah*, 82–90; Ho, "Stories of the Family Troubles," 514–31; Dietrich, "Die David-Abraham-Typologie," 41–55; Biddle, "Ancestral Motifs in 1 Samuel 25," 617–38; Rudman, "The Patriarchal Narratives," 239–49; Vaughn, "'And Lot Went with Him,'" 111–23; Watts, "Echoes from the Past," 481–508.

positions of leadership over God's people.[60] Joseph even has ties to Hebron, for it is from there that his father Jacob sent him to go and bring back word from his brothers on the well-being of the flocks.[61] The question might arise as to whether such parallels as these between David and other biblical figures are simply a natural "reader response" to the biblical editors' placing of HDR in the context of a much larger and grander narrative. The difficulty of substantiating such identifications and insights from "inner-biblical exegesis"[62] by appeal to "authorial intent" or some sort of inner-biblical dependence is widely recognized by critical scholars, particularly those inclined towards diachronic approaches.[63] But even if one concludes that these connections to which I have drawn attention were intended at some point, in their *sotto voce* form they are recognizable only by careful attention to the intertextual echoes of certain phrases and themes. Nothing, however, approaching the scale and tone of the comparisons between the reigning Hittite king and his "noble antecedents" is to be found

---

[60] Levenson draws attention to the analogies among these three figures in his essay on Joseph, "The Beloved Son," in *Death and Resurrection*, 144–45. Also see Levenson's 244 n. 2, where he points out the connection that *Exodus Rabbah* makes between God's dealings with David and Moses: ". . . before God confers greatness on a man He first tests him by a little thing and then promotes him to greatness. Here you have two great leaders whom God first proved by a little thing, found trustworthy, and then promoted to greatness. He tested David with sheep . . . God said to him: 'Thou hast been found trustworthy with the sheep; come, therefore, and tend My sheep' . . . Similarly in the case of Moses . . . God took him to tend Israel, as it is said: *Thou didst lead Thy people like a flock, by the hand of Moses and of Aaron* ([Ps.] LXXVII, 21)" (*Exod Rab.* 2:3, on Exod 3:1; quotation from Freedman and Simon, *Midrash Rabbah: Exodus*, 49–50).

[61] Gen 37:14. On the possible connections between David and Joseph, in addition to Levenson, *Death and Resurrection*, see Goetschel, "Le Messie fils de David," 265–75. And though he does not make an explicit connection between Joseph and David, Gary A. Anderson's essay on Joseph contains many helpful insights that are also relevant for understanding the significance of David's story in the books of Samuel; see Anderson, "Joseph," 198–215. On possible relationships between David and Moses, see, e.g., De Vries, "Moses and David," 619–39; Auld, *Kings without Privilege*; Knoppers, "David's Relation to Moses," 91–118.

[62] I use the term here to refer to both modern and traditional exegeses that attempt to discern connections or links in the biblical text, particularly across biblical books and/or corpora.

[63] On the general issues at stake in inner-biblical exegesis, and for specific examples, see, Sternberg, *The Poetics of Biblical Narrative*; Levinson, "The Right Chorale," 129–53; Eslinger, "Inner-Biblical Exegesis and Inner-Biblical Allusion," 47–58; Fewell, *Reading between Texts*; Vorster, "Readings, Readers, and the Succession Narrative," 395–407; Fishbane, "Inner-Biblical Exegesis," 33–48; Evans, Talmon, and Sanders, eds., *The Quest for Context and Meaning*; Tull, "Intertextuality and the Hebrew Scriptures," 59–90.

in HDR, the originally independent source as it has been reconstructed by modern scholars. This absence in HDR of even a single explicit connection between David and any one of his noble antecedents, especially given that such connections could have been readily established, must be recognized as rather bewildering for the theory that HDR functioned on David's personal behalf in largely, if not precisely, the same manner as the Apology of Ḫattušili functioned on behalf of the Hittite usurper. If anything, HDR enhances the image of David as an upstart. Not only does he lack meaningful ties to any noble antecedents, he is designated merely as "the son of Jesse" from the start, and on numerous occasions thereafter with derogative overtones.[64]

It would appear, therefore, that HDR is missing one of the most important personal apologetical motifs found in the Apology of Ḫattušili and the Proclamation of Telipinu: the indirect aggrandizement of the king through naming his predecessors who are highly honored in the people's collective memory, and also through his recounting some of their victories, judgments, and other deeds. This absence of any transparent ties to past figures, or noble antecedents, is difficult to explain if David's story in HDR was meant to function much like that of Ḫattušili. In HDR, however, YHWH's provision of and for David as Saul's replacement is depicted as sudden, unexpected, and even rather arbitrary. YHWH is not bound by any human claims or presumptions—He is free to choose and to "love"[65] whomsoever He wills.[66]

3) Historical Survey of the Unworthy Predecessor

The only formal element identified in the Hittite apologies that appears on the surface to be closely analogous to HDR is the "historical survey" of "the unworthy predecessor." Shawn Armington's assessment that this designation of Hoffner's "could serve as a good description of the whole sad story of

---

[64] Derogative overtones can be detected in 1 Sam 20:27, 30, 31; 22:7, 8, 9, 13; 25:10; outside HDR, see 2 Sam 20:1. On the use of "son of Jesse" as a derogative appellation for David, see nearly any of the major commentaries.

[65] On the covenantal nature of YHWH's "love" for His servants and people, see, among others, Moran, "The Ancient Near Eastern Background," 77–87; Kalluveettil, *Declaration and Covenant*.

[66] I shall elaborate on YHWH's unexpected favor for David in chs. 4 and 5, below. It should be noted here, however, that herein lies another highly significant parallel between David and the patriarchs. Again, on the surprising favor and choices of YHWH, see especially Levenson, *Death and Resurrection*; Anderson, "Joseph."

Saul"[67] might apply, perhaps, to some reconstructed version of the account in which Saul is presented as wicked and disobedient in contrast to a flat presentation of David as righteous and obedient. This, however, is certainly not what we find in the minimally reconstructed version of HDR or in any subsequent literary stage reviewed in chapter 1, not to mention the Masoretic form of the biblical account. Apart from superficial parallels, then, another highly significant but under-appreciated difference between the Apology of Ḫattušili and HDR can be seen in this formal element, that is, in portrayals of the unworthy predecessor(s), and in rehearsals of charges against them.

In numerous places, Ḫattušili speaks of his predecessors—his own countrymen whom he has replaced or deposed—with various terms of enmity. These include "enemy" (in singular and plural), "enviers," "opponent," and "opponent in court."[68] Furthermore, Ḫattušili himself enumerates the wicked deeds of those he deposed or otherwise bested. He tells how "Armatarḫunta, son of Zida, and other people as well began to cause me harm, they were evil to me." Even his brother Muwatalli believed them, for he "summoned [Ḫattušili] 'to the wheel'"[69] and gave Ḫattušili cause to speak of the lawsuit brought against him in Muwatalli's court as "an evil lawsuit," under the influence of "an evil deity," and possibly of Muwatalli himself as "enemy":

> Since the goddess, My Lady, held me by the hand, she never exposed me to an evil deity (nor) to an evil lawsuit [in a court governed by his own brother], never did she let an enemy weapon sway over me.[70]

Later, Ḫattušili declares that "when Armatarḫunta, son of Zida, saw the benevolence of Ištar, My Lady, and of my brother towards me, they (i.e., Armatarḫunta) with his wife (and) his son began to cast spells over me, because they were not successful in any (other) way. Even Šamuḫa, the city of the goddess, he filled with spells."[71] It appears to be a result of this witchcraft

---

[67] Armington, "Recurrent Narratives in 1 Samuel," 3 n. 9.

[68] Especially see van den Hout, "Apology of Ḫattušili III," 199–200 (§4).

[69] Ibid., 200 (§4). In a note at this point in his translation, van den Hout states: "Whereas the sumerogram for 'wheel' is written with the determinative for wooden objects in manuscript A (^{GIŠ}UMBIN), it is written with the divine determinative in B (^{d}UMBIN). Usually, this is taken to refer to some judicial procedure."

[70] Ibid.

[71] Ibid., 202 (§9).

that "the lawsuit was somehow reopened by the palace," but Muwatalli, his brother, "made [him] triumph over [Arma]tarḫunta." Armatarḫunta "with his wife (and) his sons" was in turn charged with witchcraft.[72] Ḫattušili also tells of the wickedness of Urḫitešub, whom Ḫattušili himself had made king and who, therefore, held legitimacy as suzerain at least in Ḫattušili's eyes. According to Ḫattušili, King Urḫitešub, too, "became envious of me, he [beg]an to harm me" after he "saw the benevolence [o]f the goddess towards me."[73] Urḫitešub "humiliated" him when "he took away from me all those in my service," as well as various other lands that Ḫattušili had resettled.[74] Ḫattušili submitted as long as he could—seven years—but finally "became hostile to him . . . in a manly way" because Urḫitešub "sought my destruction at divine and human behest."[75] He further explains his subjugation of Urḫitešub as the will of various gods:

> Because he [Urḫitešub] has now opposed me, the gods have made him succumb to me by (their) judgement.[76]

> When she [Ištar, My Lady] had left Urḫitešub no other way whatsoever, she locked him up in Šamuḫa like a pig in a sty.[77]

With all these epithets and asseverations of his predecessors' ill intent and wrongful actions against him, Ḫattušili presents himself as the innocent and righteous victim of power-mongers who are wholly unworthy to reign over Ḫatti. His deposing of them was inevitable and necessary.

We see little in HDR that resembles Ḫattušili's easy parsing of good and evil. HDR, by contrast, is remarkably nuanced in its portrayal of various pro-Davidic (including David himself) and anti-Davidic characters. As a result, the biblical account, in stark contrast to the Hittite text, risks communicating mixed messages regarding the worthiness of both Saul and David to be king.

---

[72] Ibid., 202 (§10a).

[73] Ibid., 202 (§10c).

[74] Ibid., 203 (§10c).

[75] Ibid. Instead of "in a manly way," Sturtevant and Bechtel have "as an (open) enemy"; *A Hittite Chrestomathy*, 77 (§11)."

[76] Van den Hout, "Apology of Ḫattušili III," 203 (§10c).

[77] Ibid., 203 (§11).

It is unquestionable, of course, that Saul is portrayed in a highly negative light in HDR. Among his heinous acts are his willingness to sacrifice the lives of his soldiers as he schemes to have David killed in battle;[78] his duplicitous dealings with his own children as he seeks to entrap David;[79] his numerous attempts on and unjust pursuits of David's life;[80] his massacre of a village of YHWH's priests and their families;[81] and his consultation of a forbidden medium.[82] In this enumeration of unworthy acts, we shall set aside his breaking of YHWH's commandment in 1 Samuel 13, where he offers the burnt offering instead of waiting on Samuel, and his "evil" act in 1 Samuel 15, where he spares some of the spoil and the life of King Agag, because these acts fall outside of the reconstructed History of David's Rise as reviewed in chapter 1.

In considering the significance of these acts, however, we might recognize a notable and even surprising contrast to the characterization of the consequences of the hostile and treacherous acts of Ḫattušili's enemies against him as reasons for their dethronement. In HDR, Saul's personal demise and the failure of any of his sons to assume his throne are not directly connected to, or, apparently, even hastened by, his treatment of David. After all, who is this "son of Jesse"? What is the offense if Saul removes the threat of one who has no natural claim to the throne? David is no Ḫattušili III, the "son" of a king and thus a direct descendant of the kings of old. Even if Saul's actions toward David and others function, in part, to demonstrate publicly his unworthiness as YHWH's anointed, neither that nor any worthiness on David's part is held up in HDR as a reason for YHWH's abandonment of Saul and David's replacement of him. That traces back, rather, to Saul's disobedience of YHWH's word before David is ever introduced. Here is another awkward gap—a gaping hole, really—that is left when HDR is read as a stand-alone account. Well before the introduction of HDR, in 1 Samuel 13 and 15, YHWH's rejection of Saul is decided and declared through the prophet Samuel. There is, of course, a brief allusion in 1 Sam 28:18 to the events of 1 Samuel 15: "Because you did not obey YHWH, and you did not execute His wrath upon Amalek, therefore YHWH has done this thing to you today." As I

---

[78] 1 Samuel 18[HDR] (see p. 16, above, on my use of this siglum).
[79] 1 Samuel 18–20[HDR].
[80] 1 Samuel 18–26[HDR].
[81] 1 Samuel 22.
[82] 1 Samuel 28[HDR].

have already noted in chapter 1, however, McCarter sees this reference to "the thoroughly prophetic account of the rejection of Saul" as "entirely superfluous and out of place here."[83] YHWH's rejection of Saul, then, is essentially left unexplained in the reconstructed History of David's Rise.

And yet, despite all this, as many scholars have persuasively argued, Saul comes across as a "tragic" and pitiful figure. This tragic aspect of Saul's life and kingship has drawn enough attention among biblical readers to fill a small library with their reflections on it.[84] The Hittite apology, in sharp contrast, portrays Hattušili's enemies in flatly negative terms. The assessment of Saul as such a tragic and pitiful figure stems in part from a reading of YHWH's rejection of Saul in 1 Samuel 13–15, but it certainly continues where McCarter's HDR begins in 1 Sam 16:14:

וְרוּחַ יְהוָה סָרָה מֵעִם שָׁאוּל וּבִעֲתַתּוּ רוּחַ־רָעָה מֵאֵת יְהוָה׃

Not only has "the spirit of YHWH deserted Saul,"[85] "an evil spirit from YHWH vexed him." Yet, even despite YHWH's abandonment of him, and even though he is heavily distracted by his increasing jealousy and fear of David, Saul continues doing that which a good king ought to do: He fights the enemies of his God and people.[86] In fact, Saul's desire to do precisely that (i.e., to defeat the Philistines marching against Israel), occasions the tragic story of Saul's visit to the medium at Endor and eventually leads to his ignoble death.

It is highly instructive to compare HDR's depiction of Saul in the account leading up to his death, particularly his inquiring of the medium, with Hattušili's indictments against Armatarhunta for practicing "witchcraft," for it is a prime example of the stark difference in the portrayals of the "unworthy

---

[83] See p. 33 n. 69, above.

[84] The following is a sampling of articles and monographs that address the topic directly: Brooks, *King Saul*; Humphreys, "The Tragedy of King Saul," 18–27; Gunn, *The Fate of King Saul*; Humphreys, "The Rise and Fall of King Saul," 74–90; Feldman, "Josephus' Portrait of Saul," 45–99; Humphreys, "From Tragic Hero to Villain," 95–117; Aschkenasy, "Biblical Substructures in the Tragic Form," 85–94; Exum and Whedbee, "Isaac, Samson, and Saul," 5–40; Zapf, "How Are the Mighty Fallen," 95–126; Humphreys, *The Tragic Vision*; Sanford, *King Saul, The Tragic Hero*; Exum, *Tragedy and Biblical Narrative*; Hawk, "Saul as Sacrifice," 20–25, 56; Cooper, "'Too Tall by Half,'" 5–22; Robert, "Saül, héros tragique dans un prophète incertain," 99–111; Couffignal, *Saül, héros tragique de la Bible*; Nicholson, *Three Faces of Saul*; Green, *How are the mighty fallen?*; Hentschel, *Saul*.

[85] Lit., "turned aside from being with Saul."

[86] E.g., 1 Sam 31:16; also see David's lament over Saul in 2 Samuel 1, esp. vv. 22–24. Also see 1 Sam 23:27–28, which is not included in McCarter's reconstructed HDR.

predecessors" in HDR and the Apology of Ḫattušili. Perhaps the best way to demonstrate this is to allow the texts to speak for themselves. First, consider Ḫattušili's indictments against Armatarḫunta:

> But when Armatarḫunta, son of Zida, saw the benevolence of Ištar, My Lady, and of my brother towards me, they (i.e., Armatarḫunta) with his wife (and) his son began to cast spells over me, because they were not successful in any (other) way. Even Šamuḫa, the city of the goddess, he filled with spells."[87]

Now, when it happened, that the lawsuit was somehow reopened by the palace, Ištar, My Lady, at that moment too showed (her) divine providence. The process resulted again in the verdict: They found witchcraft on Armatarḫunta, with his wife (and) his sons, and they charged him with it. He had filled Šamuḫa, the city of my goddess, with witch[craf]t, so the goddess, My Lady, made him succumb to me. And with his property, his wife (and) his son my brother turned him over to me and my brother said to me: "Šippaziti (is) not in(volved)." So, because my brother had made me triumph over [Arma]tarḫunta through the process, I did not fall back into further evil against him.[88]

Against this disdain and condemnation for his predecessor, compare HDR's depiction of Saul's sin of a related nature:

> [3] Now Samuel had died, and all Israel had mourned for him and buried him in Ramah, his own city. Saul had expelled the mediums and the wizards from the land. [4] The Philistines assembled, and came and encamped at Shunem. Saul gathered all Israel, and they encamped at Gilboa. [5] When Saul saw the army of the Philistines, he was afraid, and his heart trembled greatly. [6] When Saul inquired of the LORD, the LORD did not answer him, not by dreams, or by Urim, or by prophets. [7] Then Saul said to his servants, "Seek out for me a woman who is a medium, so that I may go to her and inquire of her." His servants said to him, "There is a medium at Endor." [8] So Saul disguised himself and put on other clothes and went there, he and two men with him. They came to the woman by night. And he said, "Consult a spirit for me, and bring up for me the one whom I name to you." [9] The woman said to him, "Surely you know what Saul has done, how he has cut off the mediums and the wizards from

---

[87] Van den Hout, "Apology of Ḫattušili III," 202 (§9).
[88] Ibid., 202 (§10a).

the land. Why then are you laying a snare for my life to bring about my death?" [10] But Saul swore to her by the LORD, "As the LORD lives, no punishment shall come upon you for this thing." [11] Then the woman said, "Whom shall I bring up for you?" He answered, "Bring up Samuel for me." [12] When the woman saw Samuel, she cried out with a loud voice; and the woman said to Saul, "Why have you deceived me? You are Saul!" [13] The king said to her, "Have no fear; what do you see?" The woman said to Saul, "I see a divine being coming up out of the ground." [14] He said to her, "What is his appearance?" She said, "An old man is coming up; he is wrapped in a robe." So Saul knew that it was Samuel, and he bowed with his face to the ground, and did obeisance. [15] Then Samuel said to Saul, "Why have you disturbed me by bringing me up?" Saul answered, "I am in great distress, for the Philistines are warring against me, and God has turned away from me and answers me no more, either by prophets or by dreams; so I have summoned you to tell me what I should do." [16] Samuel said, "Why then do you ask me, since the LORD has turned from you and become your enemy? [17] The LORD has done to you just as he spoke by me; for the LORD has torn the kingdom out of your hand, and given it to your neighbor, David. [18] Because you did not obey the voice of the LORD, and did not carry out his fierce wrath against Amalek, therefore the LORD has done this thing to you today. [19] Moreover the LORD will give Israel along with you into the hands of the Philistines; and tomorrow you and your sons shall be with me; the LORD will also give the army of Israel into the hands of the Philistines." [20] Immediately Saul fell full length on the ground, filled with fear because of the words of Samuel; and there was no strength in him, for he had eaten nothing all day and all night. [21] The woman came to Saul, and when she saw that he was terrified, she said to him, "Your servant has listened to you; I have taken my life in my hand, and have listened to what you have said to me. [22] Now therefore, you also listen to your servant; let me set a morsel of bread before you. Eat, that you may have strength when you go on your way." [23] He refused, and said, "I will not eat." But his servants, together with the woman, urged him; and he listened to their words. So he got up from the ground and sat on the bed. [24] Now the woman had a fatted calf in the house. She quickly slaughtered it, and she took flour, kneaded it, and baked unleavened cakes. [25] She put them before Saul and his servants, and they ate. Then they rose and went away that night.[89]

---

[89] 1 Sam 28:3–25 (NRSV). As I have noted in ch. 1 (esp. see 33 n. 69), McCarter thinks that the prophetic historian worked Samuel into this account. Whatever the case, the "tragic" depiction of Saul's helplessness in the face of YHWH's silence would remain in the view of most of the readers cited on p. 70 n. 84, above.

It is difficult to explain why a document aiming simply to legitimize David's usurpation, in part by delegitimizing Saul, would fail to capitalize on an opportunity such as this. Whereas the Apology of Ḫattušili emphatically denounces Ḫattušili's adversary for "filling" the city of the goddess with witchcraft, the biblical account begins by crediting Saul with having "expelled the mediums and the wizards from the land." Then, the text reports that Saul, in fact, "inquired of YHWH" when faced with the imminent threat of Philistine attack, but YHWH kept His silence. Only then, out of desperation, does Saul turn to seek out a medium. The text certainly does not justify Saul's act here, but what is more remarkable is that it does not explicitly condemn him for it. It misses the opportunity to portray Saul here as categorically "evil" or "wicked" (and thus to highlight further David's "righteousness," for he successfully inquires of YHWH on numerous occasions), but instead presents Saul as pitiful nearly as much as anything else. The private nature of the events depicted in this account does not allow one to explain away this soft portrayal of Saul on the basis that it must have been "too well known to be suppressed," as McCarter has argued, for example, with regard to David's life as an "outlaw" and "Philistine mercenary."[90]

Furthermore, some of the statements attributed to both Saul and David with regard to each other undermine or weaken the aims of delegitimizing Saul. For example, Saul is presented as remorseful and penitent, and that to a remarkable degree, for his actions against David:

> And Saul said, "I have sinned [חָטָאתִי]! Return, my son David, for I will not do evil to you again [כִּי לֹא־אָרַע לְךָ עוֹד]. For instead [of being harmed], my life was honored in your eyes today. But look [at me], I have acted foolishly, and I have erred most greatly [הִנֵּה הִסְכַּלְתִּי וָאֶשְׁגֶּה הַרְבֵּה מְאֹד]!"[91]

No enemy of Ḫattušili ever acknowledges his wayward ways. And not only does David refuse to speak against Saul, he laments his death and honors him through word and action in 2 Samuel 1:

---

[90] McCarter, "The Apology of David," 500. See "The Rhetorical Posture of HDR," 43–48, above.

[91] 1 Sam 26:21. Of course, we see a similar disposition in Saul in 1 Sam 24:17–23 as well. As I have noted on p. 30, above, some scholars also treat 1 Samuel 24 as part of the original HDR, though McCarter does not.

The ornament of Israel—
upon your heights, pierced!
How fell the mighty?!

Do not announce in Gath,
do not report in the streets of Ashkelon!
Otherwise the daughters of the Philistines will rejoice.
Otherwise the daughters of the uncircumcised will celebrate.

You mountains in Gilboa—
may there be neither dew nor rain upon you,
nor fields of offerings!
For there the shield of mighty ones [lay] defiled,
the shield of Saul unanointed with oil.

From the blood of the pierced,
from the fat of the mighty,
the bow of Jonathan did not recoil,
and the sword of Saul did not return empty.

Saul and Jonathan—
Beloved and dear in their lifetimes,
and in their deaths undivided.
They were swifter than eagles;
they were stronger than lions.

You Daughters of Israel, weep for Saul,
he who dressed you in ornamented crimson,
who outfitted your garments with gold ornaments.

How fell the mighty
in the midst of the battle!?

Jonathan—
upon your heights, pierced!
I am afflicted over you, my brother Jonathan!
You, to me, were most dear!

Your love to me was wondrous,
moreso than the love of women.

How fell the mighty?!
The instruments of battle have perished![92]

David speaks of Saul, together with his son Jonathan, as Israel's "ornament" (הַצְּבִי; v. 19); as "the mighty" or "mighty ones" (גִּבּוֹרִים; vv. 19, 21, 22, 25, 27); as "beloved and dear" (הַנֶּאֱהָבִים וְהַנְּעִימִם; v. 23); as "swifter than eagles" (מִנְּשָׁרִים קַלּוּ); v. 23); as "stronger than lions" (מֵאֲרָיוֹת גָּבֵרוּ; v. 23); and Saul as the one who dressed Israel's daughters "in ornamented crimson, [and] who outfitted [their] garments with gold ornaments" (v. 24).[93] By contrast, the Apology of Ḫattušili consistently describes and depicts his predecessors as "enemies" and "enviers," with no hint of any positive assessment by Ḫattušili or the people.[94]

There is another notable difference between the Apology of Ḫattušili and HDR. It is true that each text describes and/or depicts the ill will and hostile acts against the rising king, as well as his various responses to it, and thereby demonstrates the unworthiness of each one's predecessors. But whereas the Apology of Ḫattušili portrays Ḫattušili as wholly innocent and righteous and leaves nothing open to interpretation with regard to Ḫattušili's intentions and actions, the biblical account presents David's intentions and actions in far

---

[92] 2 Sam 1:19–27.

[93] VanderKam ("Davidic Complicity," 521–39) suggests that David's "every effort that is recorded in [2 Samuel 1] is calculated to divert from his person understandable suspicion. . . . All of the available evidence supports the conclusion that David had no part in Saul's death, but 2 Samuel 1 betrays David's fear that some might draw that inference" (529). In other words, he interprets David's treatment of the Amalekite gēr and his lament over Saul and Jonathan as a coverup. VanderKam presents his determination of what exactly the authors/editors were "calculating" to communicate in and through this narrative — i.e., David's innocence — as based on a "close reading" of the text. But this and other similar assessments of the narrative's rhetorical force, in fact, are heavily dependent upon a reconstructed historical context that he presumes must have evoked the text in the first place. His reading here and elsewhere is also prefaced by the removal of "editorial features" such as "the theme of the Lord's designation of David as king" and mention "at various junctures that the Lord was with David" (523–24). Having excised the "series of stories" from their literary and theological framework in the biblical narrative, the critic is able quite easily to attribute new motives and meanings as they seem to fit and make sense within the new framework, this time a reconstructed historical one. I shall return in ch. 3 to discuss in more detail the assumptions and conclusions that inform such a reading.

[94] Van den Hout, "Apology of Ḫattušili III," 200–4 (§§4, 9, 10c, 12b).

more ambivalent terms. This is certainly the case within the context of his full story in the biblical books of Samuel: In view of 2 Samuel, it might be argued that Saul's sins pale in comparison to David's. But even within the reconstructed HDR alone, David is not portrayed in flatly positive terms, as we shall see.[95]

Ḫattušili, on the one hand, asserts explicitly and unequivocally his innocence and faithfulness to his suzerain and goddess in numerous places. He acknowledges the "harm" caused him and the "evil" acted against him, but he explains that this was the work of envious men.[96] He declares his innocence and obedience and cites this as the cause of "My Lady" Ištar's favor:

> Whenever illness befell me, sick as I was, I looked on (it) as the goddess' providence. The goddess, My Lady, held me by the hand in every respect. But, since I was a man divinely provided for, since I walked before the gods in divine providence, I never did an evil thing against man.[97]

And later:

> Then the goddess, My Lady, appeared to me in a dream (saying): "Become my servant [with] (your) household!" so the goddess' [serv]ant with my household I became.[98]

Elsewhere Ḫattušili mentions his "service of the goddess . . . as a priest" by bringing offerings to her and worshiping her;[99] his setting up monuments and his weapon before her;[100] his taking a wife at "the behest of the goddess";[101]

---

[95] See, for example, the following works that identify a considerable degree of ambiguity in the characterization of David in the narrative accounts of David's rise: Miscall, *The Workings of Old Testament Narrative*; Noll, *The Faces of David*; and Biddle, "Ancestral Motifs in 1 Samuel 25."

[96] Van den Hout, "Apology of Ḫattušili III," 200, 202 (§§4, 9, 10c).

[97] Ibid., 200 (§4).

[98] Ibid., 202 (§9). For this last clause, Sturtevant and Bechtel have "And with my house I was true to the goddess" (*A Hittite Chrestomathy*, 75 [§9]).

[99] Van den Hout, "Apology of Ḫattušili III," 199, 202 (§§3, 9).

[100] Ibid., 201 (§§6, 7). A parenthetical question mark follows each occurrence of "monument" in van den Hout's translation, and also after Sturtevant and Bechtel's rendering of the term as "trophy" (*A Hittite Chrestomathy*, 71 [§§6:25; 7:44]). As van den Hout notes (201 n. 25), the context in each case suggests such a translation.

[101] Van den Hout, "Apology of Ḫattušili III," 202 (§9).

his dedication of his son to the goddess;[102] and his consecration and dedication to Ištar of various sites, including "the property of Armatarḫunta," the mausoleum that he built, and other property.[103]

In addition to his loyalty to the goddess, Ḫattušili asserts his fealty to Muwatalli, his brother and king:

> [When] my [bro]ther became [go]d[104]—because I [co]mmanded [Ḫatt]uša and (because) he had [...] me in lordship, I di[d] not [do] anything (evil) out of regard for [the love] for [m]y br[other. T]herefore, sin[ce] my brother did not have a [l]egitimate son, I took up Urḫitešub, son of a concubine. [I put] him into lordship over [Ḫa]tti Land and laid all of [Ḫattuša] in (his) hand, so that he was Great King over the Ḫatti Lands, while I was king of Ḫakpiš.[105]

As king, Urḫitešub "became envious" of Ḫattušili and "[beg]an to harm" him when he "saw the benevolence [o]f the goddess towards" him; he took away from Ḫattušili "all those in [his] service" and other depopulated lands that Ḫattušili "had resettled"; and he "humiliated" Ḫattušili. Yet, once again, Ḫattušili declares firmly: "Out of regard for the love for my brother I did not react at all."[106] And with regard to his eventual rebellion against Urḫitešub, Ḫattušili asserts that he was provoked, and that in making war against Urḫitešub, he "did not commit a moral offence."[107] He testifies to Urḫitešub's injustice and his own righteousness when he raises the question, "If he [Urḫitešub] had in no way opposed me, would they (i.e., the gods) really have made a Great King succumb to a petty king?" He then definitively answers his own question: "Because he has now opposed me, the gods have made him succumb to me by (their) judgement."[108] Again, after Ištar had given Ḫattušili victory over Urḫitešub and "locked him up in Šamuḫa like a pig in a sty," Ḫattušili declares his righteousness:

---

[102] Ibid., 204 (§12b).

[103] Ibid.

[104] I.e., when he died.

[105] Ibid., 202 (§10a).

[106] Ibid., 203 (§10c).

[107] Ibid. At 203 n. 50, regarding his rendering of "moral offence," van den Hout explains that "[t]he Hittite word used here refers to religious impurity which normally has to be removed by magic ritual."

[108] Ibid., 203 (§10c).

> Out of regard for the love of my brother I did not do anything
> (evil). I went back down to Urḫitešub and brought him down like a
> prisoner. I gave him fortified cities in the country of Nuḫašše and
> there he lived.[109]

And finally, once again, he declares his loyalty to his brother, the previous
king, because he placed Muwatalli's son upon his throne in Tarḫuntašša: "I
did not do anything (evil) out of regard for the love for my brother."[110] Now
let us turn to consider, in contrast, HDR's portrayal of David.

There is no question that David is portrayed throughout HDR largely
in harmony with the characterization of him in HDR's introduction—as a
man "who is skilled at playing, a man of valor, a man of battle, eloquent, a
comely man, and YHWH is with him." But the account also reveals enough
real and potential blemishes of character to question the validity of reading
and interpreting HDR as the same genre of royal apologetic literature as
that to which the Apology of Ḫattušili has reasonably been assigned. It is
not only that HDR fails to relate him explicitly to any noble antecedents, as
does the Hittite apology for Ḫattušili. The biblical source leaves more open
to interpretation than would seem reasonable for court propaganda, and thus,
in various instances, it risks casting—and sometimes does cast—David in a
poor or even negative light. Consider, for example, several characterizations
of David during his flight from Saul that seriously call into question David's
status as king-elect and future shepherd of YHWH's people. Ironically, at times
during David's flight from King Saul, he appears more like this king whom
YHWH has rejected than at any other point in his life.

First, David's flight from Saul, particularly at the beginning, is marked by
fear of man with little display of fear of God.[111] This is not to say that David
should have sat passively by without taking any action. Later, when David is in
Keilah and hears that Saul intends to besiege him there, his inquiring of YHWH
whether the people of Keilah will deliver him into Saul's hand enables him and
his men to go "wherever they could go" (וַיֵּצְאוּ מִקְּעִלָה וַיִּתְהַלְּכוּ בַּאֲשֶׁר יִתְהַלָּכוּ);
Saul gives up pursuit when he learns "that David escaped" (כִּי־נִמְלַט דָּוִד).[112]

---

[109] Ibid., 203 (§11).

[110] Ibid., 204 (§12b).

[111] For a fine discussion on the biblical notion of "fear of God," see Moberly, *The Bible,
Theology, and Faith.* Moberly describes Abraham (particularly as portrayed in Genesis 22)
as the paradigmatic God-fearer in the Hebrew Bible.

[112] 1 Sam 23:6–13.

But the characterization of David and his actions in 1 Sam 23:1–13 stand in marked contrast to that in 1 Samuel 21. Fear of Saul drives David to Nob and to lie to Ahimelech.[113] Out of fear of Saul he "flees" (וַיִּבְרַח) across the border to Gath,[114] even though, as it later becomes clear, God intended for him to remain for the time being in Judah.[115] When the Philistine courtiers attempt to provoke Achish to jealousy and alarm over how strong David had become, David becomes "very much afraid" (וַיִּרָא מְאֹד); fear of Achish and his servants, then, drives him to act like a madman and "escape" from Gath to Adullam.[116] Even if fear of all these men is understandable for anyone in David's circumstances, it is antithetical to "fear of God," which is marked by, among other things, a fundamental trust in God and His provision, and which must be demonstrated through careful obedience to the will of God. It should be noted, too, that this characterization of a "fearful David" is a significant departure from that which—toward the beginning of his introduction in the biblical drama—marks his splendid display of "fear of God" and disdain for his (or rather, YHWH's) human enemies when he single-handedly defeats the Philistine warrior in 1 Samuel 17.[117] Lack of "fear of God," then, implies a diminished trust in God's willingness to defend and care for his people. Should YHWH's anointed continue to live and act according to a fear of man instead of God, the consequences are serious. This is most poignantly demonstrated in the life of Saul. Fear of the Philistines was behind Saul's presumptuous and unlawful sacrifice in 1 Sam 13:5–9, and fear of the people led Saul to disobey YHWH's command to completely destroy the Amalekites. For these grave sins YHWH rejected Saul as king over Israel.[118]

Second, David is characterized as a lying, scheming, young rogue. His trickery, however innocent and driven by self-defense, begins in Gibeah

---

[113] 1 Sam 21:2–3, 9 (MT; vv. 1–2, 8 in most English versions).

[114] 1 Sam 21:11 (MT; v. 10 in most English versions).

[115] See 1 Sam 22:5.

[116] 1 Sam 21:13–22:1 (MT; vv. 12–22:1 in most English versions).

[117] In the context of 1 Samuel 17, also consider David's boldness before the seasoned Israelite soldiers, including his brothers, and King Saul, to whom he "boasts" of his fearless encounters with wild beasts while tending his father's sheep and declares that YHWH will deliver him from the Philistine just as He did from the lion and bear. Of course, as we have seen on p. 27, above, McCarter thinks that a less "idealized" battle account underlies the present one.

[118] 1 Sam 13:13–14; 15:1–35. Saul is further cast in a poor light when he is said to fear David in 1 Sam 18:12a, 29a; also cf. 1 Sam 17:11—probably not to be included in McCarter's reconstructed HDR—where Saul (together with "all Israel") is said to be "terrified and very much afraid" of Goliath.

with his scheme to expose, with Jonathan's aid, Saul's intent to kill him.[119] He resorts to more ruses in Nob to procure from Ahimelech both food and Goliath's sword,[120] and then again when he "changes his behavior" and feigns madness before Achish and his servants.[121] In this developing portrayal of David as one who meets his needs (even if they are the most basic needs of survival) through trickery, we again see some semblance of the characterization of Saul, who has also resorted to dishonesty and trickery to suit his own purposes. For example, Saul is dishonest to Samuel about having not kept YHWH's command to completely destroy the Amalekites,[122] and he schemes "to bring down David by the hand of the Philistines."[123] It is unsurprising that some biblical scholars have seen in 1 Sam 21:14 (v. 13 in most English versions) remnants of a tradition circulating among anti-David circles that wished to portray David as a madman possessed by an evil spirit.[124] Even if the tradition was transformed into a humorous story of David duping the foolish Philistine king and court, as some say, the image of God's chosen servant having resorted to clawing on doors and slobbering on himself like a rabid animal or demoniac is hardly edifying, if not simply embarrassing. Even here we are reminded of the rejected King Saul, who is frequently overcome by an "evil spirit from YHWH" (רוּחַ־רָעָה מֵאֵת יְהוָה) after YHWH's spirit deserts him,[125] and the tragicomical picture of Saul raving

---

[119] 1 Samuel 20[HDR]. In "Jonathan's Ruse," Ward notes that "David's skill at dissimulation is a common feature of numerous narratives in 1 Samuel 16:14–2 Samuel 5," and this can be seen in his trick to expose Saul's true heart toward him (1 Sam 20:1b–21:1). If Jonathan is unable to change his father's mind, David hopes to prove Saul's antipathy for him and thus "enlist Jonathan's sympathy and possibly his all-out support." Ward finds evidence of this second objective in David's conversation with Jonathan (and presumably, the successful results), but he has difficulty in determining David's sincerity (only for political gain? certainly this, but *only* this?) while Jonathan's loyalty is very clear. See Ward, "The Story of David's Rise," 40–41.

[120] 1 Sam 21:2–10. It is often difficult to discern with certainty when David is lying to Ahimelech. The king certainly did not order him on any business (1 Sam 21:3), and it seems highly improbable that David would have taken flight without a weapon of some kind (v. 9). But is David also lying or telling the truth about the whereabouts of his men (v. 3) and their ritual purity (v. 6)? This is all too unclear from Samuel's narrative.

[121] 1 Sam 21:13.

[122] 1 Sam 15:13.

[123] 1 Sam 18:17–27.

[124] See, e.g., Klein, *1 Samuel*, 216, and Klein's discussion of Crüsemann, "Zwei alttestamentliche Witze," 215–27.

[125] 1 Sam 16:14–16, 23; 19:9; also see 18:10, which is not included in McCarter's HDR.

mad and naked all day and night when he goes to find David but instead finds the Spirit of God.[126]

Third, David is portrayed as more reliant upon himself than upon YHWH. He does not express interest in knowing God's will until 1 Sam 22:3, after he has gathered a band of discontents and when he takes his parents to Moab. David's self-reliance is made all the more apparent by his failure to inquire of YHWH while visiting the sanctuary in Nob. His chief concern in the sanctuary and before the priest of YHWH has only to do with bread and weapons. Ironically, David, who once so boldly accused Goliath of relying upon his weapons and declared to him that "it is not with a sword nor by the spear that YHWH saves,"[127] now seeks the very sword Goliath used in battle against him. David prefers the sword of Goliath over the ephod behind which it lies; the Philistine's sword is given to David while the ephod sits there unused.[128] When reading this episode in the context of the entire Hebrew canon, the words of Deut 8:3—that "man does not live on bread alone, but . . . on all that comes from the mouth of YHWH"—quickly come to mind as an indictment against David here for seeking bread and a sword but not the word of YHWH.

How can I assert, based on the elliptical narrative and despite Doeg's testimony and Saul's charge against Ahimelech in 1 Samuel 22, that David does not seek an oracle from YHWH in Nob? 1) The actual narrative of David's trip to Nob, and the dialogue that transpired between him and Ahimelech, are conspicuously silent regarding any such inquiry. In the narrative David shows more interest in the weapon behind the ephod than in the ephod itself. I find no obvious reason for the narrator to mention (directly or through dialogue) Ahimelech's gift to David of food and sword and yet remain silent on the transaction that would prove most damning of Ahimelech in Saul's eyes. 2) The assertion that David inquired of YHWH occurs only in the reported speech of Doeg and Saul in 1 Samuel 22 (Ahimelech's self-defense before Saul in 1 Sam 22:14–15 is problematic; it is not clear whether he is admitting to have inquired of God for David on the particular occasion in question). Nowhere does the reliable narrator directly make such a claim. This can easily be understood as false testimony on the part of Doeg, and as a testimony that

---

[126] 1 Sam 19:22–24. Note, however, that McCarter considers this episode to be "a late accretion" (see p. 35, above).

[127] 1 Sam 17:45–47; as I have noted above, it is unclear, according to McCarter's view, precisely how much, if any, of 1 Samuel 17 in its present shape belonged to the original HDR.

[128] 1 Sam 21:8–10.

Saul is eager to accept as an excuse to execute the priests of Nob for treason. 3) Perhaps most telling, this would be the only time that David meets with failure immediately after inquiring of YHWH. If David sought YHWH's will while in Nob, how do we explain his decision to depart immediately for Gath? Did David receive no answer or a wrong answer from the ephod, or did he inquire of something unrelated to his most immediate need for guidance? It is unlikely that he inquired but received no answer. If so, that would hardly count as an inquiry worth reporting. Moreover, this would be the only time that YHWH remains silent in response to David. It is even more improbable that the ephod gave David a wrong answer. As we see, David goes immediately to Gath only to find threat of death and shameful scorn. There is a notable occasion of YHWH sending a "lying spirit" (רוּחַ שֶׁקֶר) to a king when Ahab is enticed to go up against and to fall at Ramoth-gilead in 1 Kings 22. The narrator there, however, elaborates considerably upon the circumstances and justification for why God would treat Ahab accordingly. Nowhere else is David (or any other Judahite king) given like treatment, and it is nearly inconceivable that God would intentionally deceive him at this crucial point in the early stage of his career. 4) The other possible explanation—that David asked for something other than direction for the next step in the midst of imminent danger—is also highly unlikely. Given David's "perfect record" whenever YHWH answers him through means such as the oracle, his dramatic unsuccess in King Achish's court indicates that it was not YHWH's will for David to go to and remain in Gath at this time.

David's trip to Gath nearly ends in disaster, whether it be death or the renouncing of his loyalty to YHWH and His anointed one. The seriousness of David's self-reliance becomes clear when we recall that YHWH's rejection of Saul stemmed, in part, from Saul's reliance upon his own wisdom in two critical incidents. In 1 Sam 13:11–13, Saul thinks it better to sacrifice unlawfully than to follow YHWH's directions; and in 1 Sam 15:7–15, he thinks it better to spare "all that was good" of the Amalekites, despite YHWH's command to destroy everything.

A fourth way in which David resembles Saul is that David shows himself quite unready to shepherd and protect YHWH's people. First, consider the hypothetical outcome if David's plan had worked and Achish had accepted the lone fugitive into his service at this point: The four hundred men (plus more later) who gathered around him would have likely remained without a commander;[129] his family and the sole surviving priest of Nob would have gone without protection;[130] the town of Keilah would likely have been destroyed by the Philistines;[131] and so on. But second, consider the actual outcome of David's concern only for himself in Nob: All but one of the priests of Nob, together with their families, are slaughtered. Saul, first and foremost, is the evil shepherd here. Because of his jealousy and fear of David, he has lost almost all capacity to act in the best interests of his people.[132] David, however, is also culpable. Although he knew that Doeg saw him in the house of the priests and "that he would definitely tell Saul,"[133] he did nothing to prevent it. David thus expresses his deep regret over not dealing appropriately with Doeg and essentially confesses to Abiathar that he is partly to blame for the mass sacerdoticide: "It was I who brought about [the death of] every life of your father's house."[134] He did not perceive the danger of his actions in Nob and the consequences for Ahimelech because his mind was clouded by fear, trickery, and thoughts of self-preservation; or worse, he was fully aware but unconcerned at the moment that he was putting Ahimelech in an awkward and dangerous situation. Whatever the case, he fails initially as a shepherd-in-training. In effect, although unwittingly, he partners with Doeg in sealing the doom of YHWH's priests, all except for Abiathar.[135] Doeg is the prosecutor and executioner, but David provides Saul with the opportune warrant (unfounded though it may be).

Fifth, we might also consider the later portrayal of David as perhaps more concerned for his own life—"And it was deeply distressful for David

---

[129] 1 Sam 22:2; 23:13; 30.

[130] 1 Sam 22:1, 3–4, 20–23.

[131] 1 Sam 23:1–6.

[132] In addition to his murder of the priests of Nob, he frequently uses resources to pursue David instead of real enemies. Earlier, he risks the lives of many men, no doubt, when he puts David in position to be killed by the Philistines (1 Sam 18:25). Ironically, David will take a similarly deplorable action with Uriah after he commits adultery (2 Samuel 11).

[133] 1 Sam 22:22.

[134] Ibid. אָנֹכִי סַבֹּתִי בְּכָל־נֶפֶשׁ בֵּית אָבִיךְ literally reads, "It was I who brought about every life of your father's house."

[135] Of course, it is also clear that this is the fulfillment of YHWH's word of judgment to Eli the priest in 1 Samuel 2. Nevertheless, as is so frequently the case in Scripture, David's role (direct or indirect) in the execution of God's will for the house of Eli does not exonerate him from culpability (consider, for example, the role of Joseph's brothers in God's rescuing the entire family from famine, or the Babylonians' role in executing judgment upon Judah).

[וַתֵּצֶר לְדָוִד מְאֹד], for the people talked of stoning him"[136]—than for the lives of his people who were captured when the Amalekites raided Ziklag. There is also the portrayal of his apparent inability to maintain firm command over his own men, or to execute justice against them and their "wickedness."[137]

In sum, the portrayals of Saul and David in HDR are a far cry from the flat portrayals of Ḫattušili's unworthy predecessors. In light of these considerations, then, the formal element that would appear to be most closely analogous demonstrates, rather, a notable difference between the Hittite and Israelite texts.

4) The Coup d'état

In the Apology of Ḫattušili, Ḫattušili acknowledges freely that he has seized the throne of Urḫitešub, and so his justification of that is a very important element in his account. According to the text, Ḫattušili himself "took up Urḫitešub, son of a concubine [of his brother, Muwatalli]" and made him king of Ḫatti.[138] Urḫitešub became hostile towards Ḫattušili, despite the latter's self-proclaimed innocence, and thus provoked Ḫattušili's uprising after seven years of pacifistic compliance.[139] As in HDR, the reigning king is depicted as envious and intent on destroying the one whom he perceives to be a threat toward his kingship. But in contrast to HDR, the Hittite account states that Ḫattušili "no longer complied and . . . became hostile to him,"[140] and that he acted, with Ištar's assistance, to dethrone and replace his predecessor.

It is highly significant that there is no analogy in any reconstructed form of HDR (and certainly not in the biblical narrative of 1 Samuel 16–2 Samuel 5) to the fourth element that Hoffner identifies as common to the Hittite royal apologies: the account of the coup d'état. To the contrary, HDR is notably concerned with declarations and demonstrations of David's remarkable refusal to kill Saul and execute a coup when, by all appearances, doing so might easily be justified precisely as the divine will. Instead, David refused to take matters into his own hands and left Saul's fate in the hands of YHWH. Whereas the Hittite apologies present Ḫattušili and Telipinu as essentially making themselves to be the determiners and executors of the will of the

---

[136] 1 Sam 30:6.

[137] Especially see 2 Sam 3:22–39.

[138] Van den Hout, "Apology of Ḫattušili III," 202 (§10b).

[139] The account of Ḫattušili's coup d'état can be found in ibid., 202–3 (§§10c–11).

[140] Ibid., 203 (§10c).

gods,[141] David is presented as doing no such thing. The Hittite analogies would lead us to expect the king's willingness to acknowledge that he carried out a coup based on this or that justification (and David had plenty to draw on, as we have seen), but this is not what we find in HDR.

It is notable and even somewhat ironic, then, that one of the primary reasons for classifying HDR as a personal royal apology of the same ilk as the Hittite text is a point where HDR exhibits such a critical dissimilarity to the Apology of Ḫattušili. Far from presenting any problem for comparativists who read HDR, along with the Apology of Ḫattušili, as primarily about an individual usurper's "political self-justification," this striking dissimilarity is grounds for deeming David's apologists all the more clever and effective. In Stephen McKenzie's view, for example, the authors of HDR took on "the role of 'spin doctors,' explaining that David's motives were virtuous and his actions justified."[142] In this view, David does not have to justify a coup d'état head-on for the simple reason that he is portrayed as playing no direct or knowing role in the demise of King Saul and his dynasty—and therein lies the brilliance of David's apology.

It is important to give further consideration, however, to the implications of this difference that I have highlighted between HDR and the Apology of Ḫattušili. First, even if David's legitimacy as king were in question, or his hold on his kingship tenuous and shaky, nothing in the Apology of Ḫattušili is parallel to, or prepares us for, the extremely high degree of subtlety that must be said to characterize HDR if it is to be understood as David's attempt at personal self-justification. This is particularly the case if one thinks, contrary to any existing or reconstructed account, that David did stage a coup.[143] Comparison with the Apology of Ḫattušili is once again instructive.

---

[141] Again, though Telipinu did not base his coup explicitly on divine will, he points to divine displeasure with his wicked predecessor and, thus, implies that he is acting justly as their agent. See Hoffner, "Propaganda and Political Justification," 53–54.

[142] McKenzie, *King David*, 35. See also, e.g., VanderKam, "Davidic Complicity."

[143] In his "biography" of David, McKenzie employs the "principle of analogy," which "asserts that David acted in accord with the customs and motives common among ancient Middle Eastern rulers and with general human tendencies in his acquisition and retention of power." He continues: "This principle calls into question any explanation of David's motives and deeds that appears to be apologetic. It assumes that 'where there's smoke, there's fire.' That is, the accusations against David that the History of David's Rise and Court History sought to explain away were probably historical. . . . One sign of apology in the narrative has been called the technique of 'overstress.' This is where the story repeatedly states David's innocence in regard to a particular accusation. The more the author protests, the more we

Hoffner points out that the oft-repeated phrase "out of regard for the love of my brother" indicates that "Muwatalli's line had many supporters still, and that Ḫattušili was resolved to win them over."[144] How did Ḫattušili attempt to win support? First of all, he did not deny that he seized the throne by force. Rather, he simply justified it. He exonerates his actions, in part, by appealing to his readers' sense of justice. Because Urḫitešub persecuted and provoked him without just cause, Ḫattušili's declaration of war against the king was not a moral offence. But at a more fundamental level, the legitimacy of his supplantation is justified well enough by Ḫattušili's successful outcome. And so he asks rhetorically, "[W]ould they (i.e., the gods) really have made a Great King succumb to a petty king?" Urḫitešub's defeat by Ḫattušili was taken as a clear sign of the former's wickedness and the latter's uprightness. If we learn anything from the examples of the Hittite royal apologies, perhaps it is how highly improbable would be David's or any other ancient Near Eastern king's need for so much subtlety in justifying his ascension to the throne. This is particularly so when we consider the relative ease with which David might have justified the killing of Saul and/or the aggressive seizure of his throne based on events such as Saul's earlier disobedience and rejection by YHWH;[145] the visible visitations upon Saul by the "evil spirit";[146] Saul's slaughter of the priests of Nob;[147] Saul's consulting a medium;[148] Saul's unjust pursuit of David motivated by envy and paranoia;[149] the arguably

---

suspect the charge was true" (*King David*, 45). In the next chapter, I shall take issue with the assumption, in the first place, that the chief aim of the account is to assert "David's innocence." My aim here, however, is to point out how McKenzie comes to the conclusion that David did, in fact, exercise force in taking Saul's throne, and that he was undoubtedly himself responsible for the deaths of his "opponents." Also see Brettler, *The Creation of History*, esp. ch. 6, "Ideology in the Book of Samuel," 91–111; Halpern, *David's Secret Demons*, xv–xvi, and esp. ch. 4, "King David, Serial Killer," 73–103.

[144] Hoffner, "Propaganda and Political Justification," 55.

[145] As I have acknowledged above(pp. 69–70), the narrative account of Saul's previous disobedience and rejection, of course, falls outside of HDR. Nevertheless, unless we dismiss as a harmonizing insertion 1 Sam 28:18 (as does McCarter; see p. 33 n. 69, above), where Samuel reminds Saul of the reason for YHWH's rejection of him, HDR manifests at least some assumption that Saul's fate was more or less sealed before David ever came into his court.

[146] 1 Sam 16:14–23; 19:9; also see 1 Sam 18:10 (McCarter considers this to be among the late accretions; see pp. 34–35, above).

[147] 1 Sam 22:18–19.

[148] 1 Sam 28:3–25[HDR].

[149] 1 Samuel 19–27[HDR].

providential frustration of Saul's attempts on David's life;[150] Saul's own life "falling" into David's hands;[151] the public acclaim that David enjoyed from the people and even from Saul's own children, Michal and Jonathan;[152] and perhaps most importantly, the simple fact that Saul dies in battle and David becomes king.[153] By ancient Near Eastern standards, the proposition that HDR resorted to the creation of highly nuanced fiction or "rhetorical posture" seems highly dubious, if not absurd. This leads to my second point.

Contra McCarter, we must conclude that HDR was not "an apology in the sense defined by Hoffner," that is, "a document composed for a king who had usurped the throne, composed in order to defend or justify his assumption of the kingship by force" (at least not precisely or fully in these terms).[154] For, whereas the Apology of Ḫattušili and the Proclamation of Telipinu transparently justify the forceful deposing of the previous king by the supplanter himself, HDR neither assumes nor justifies a coup d'état. If taken on its own terms, then, HDR is not a personal apology "for a king who had usurped the throne" or who had assumed "kingship by force."

Of course, many historians and biblical scholars assume that David did, in fact, exercise some force against Saul and/or his "house" and thus aggressively usurped his throne. And as I have noted above, some scholars, such as McKenzie and Halpern, even go so far as to argue that this narrative demonstration that David did not carry out a coup is in fact evidence that this is precisely what he must have done.[155] In their view it is likely that he played a decisive role in the deaths of Saul and all others who stood in his way to the throne. This raises an important distinction between two differing approaches to HDR that treat it as an apology of David himself. One approach takes it as a more or less true apology. Its testimony is considered

---

[150] 1 Sam 23:6–13; outside of McCarter's HDR, see 1 Sam 19:18–24; 23:24–28.

[151] 1 Samuel 26; outside of McCarter's HDR, see 1 Samuel 24.

[152] 1 Sam 18:6–8a, 16, 20, 28; 19:1–7, 11–17; 20:3; 22:14; outside of McCarter's HDR, see 1 Sam 18:1–5, 30; 20:41–42; 23:16–18.

[153] 1 Samuel 31; 2 Sam 2:1–7; 5:3.

[154] See n. 1, above. McCarter gives something of a mixed message on the nature of David's usurpation. Later, in a footnote, he states, "It seems unlikely that David set out from the beginning to seize Saul's kingship for himself. It is difficult to believe, however, that he did not at least close his eyes to the political assassinations that in the end placed him on the throne" ("The Apology of David," 502 n. 24).

[155] See pp. 85–86 n. 143, above.

to be true: David really did not kill Saul, nor did he kill Abner and others.[156] The other approach takes it as a remarkably subtle and deceptive apology. David is viewed as probably culpable in every death and action from which he somehow benefits.[157] In both cases, however, the positive narration is taken as having a largely negative significance inasmuch as it is understood as "really" amounting to a personal denial of wrongdoing, that is, an apology composed for the sake of a royal individual to refute claims or charges that he ascended his throne illegitimately.

Whichever approach one takes, it bears repeating that the detection of these charges is based not on a straightforward reading of either HDR or the final biblical account, but in large part, rather, on a "reading against the grain," "the principle of skepticism," and other such "hermeneutics of suspicion."[158] Whatever hermeneutical approach one might prefer, we must recognize the simple fact that, unlike in the Apology of Ḫattušili, in no place does HDR or the biblical text give any explicit indication that its purpose is to justify David's replacement (whether by usurpation or some other means) of Saul as Israel's king. This recognition (re)opens the possibility that intents and purposes other than personal self-justification or apology might drive the reconstructed biblical source and present text, whichever one considers. Perhaps it may be appreciated as a story with theological significance and aims that transcend the mundane, personal function(s) assumed in the two approaches described above. It will be my aim in chapters 4 and 5 to demonstrate that this is precisely the case.

5) The Merciful Victor

In the extended excerpt describing Ḫattušili's coup d'état, we see one example of Ḫattušili's "mercy" vis-à-vis his opponents. Because of "regard for the love" of his brother, Ḫattušili "did not do anything (evil)" but placed the subjugated Urḫitešub over "fortified cities in the country of Nuḫašše"; and when Urḫitešub began planning to take another land, Ḫattušili still did not

---

[156] This is the approach taken in, e.g., Gordon, *I & II Samuel*, 37–41, 207–23. For a concise statement of McCarter's position on the question of David's culpability for their deaths, see n. 154, above.

[157] This latter approach can be seen in, e.g., Brettler, *The Creation of History*; McKenzie, *King David*; Halpern, *David's Secret Demons*.

[158] Especially see McKenzie, *King David*, 44–46, where McKenzie describes how the principles of skepticism and analogy serve as guidelines for him in his reconstruction of David's history.

kill him but "seized him and sent him alongside the sea."[159] Later, in another act of "unselfishness" and "regard" for his brother, Ḫattušili states: "I took up my [nephew] Kurunta and installed him into kingship there on the spot which my brother Muwatalli had built into the city of Tarḫuntašša."[160]

It might appear that the Apology of Ḫattušili's "merciful victor" finds something of an analogous parallel in HDR. For example, David grieves publicly over the deaths of Saul and Jonathan, and he honors Saul by executing the Amalekite who claims to have assisted Saul's suicide;[161] he accepts the service of Abner, Saul's general who had formerly pursued David together with Saul, and grieves over him when he is murdered;[162] and he laments the assassination of Ishbosheth and punishes his assassins.[163] Of course, the most obvious parallel to Ḫattušili's treatment of his brother's sons is one that lies outside of the putative original HDR: David's demonstration of magnanimity towards Mephibosheth, son of Jonathan, son of Saul. After David is well established on the throne, he asks his servants: "Is there anyone still remaining in the house of Saul in order for me to deal loyally with him for the sake of Jonathan [וְאֶעֱשֶׂה עִמּוֹ חֶסֶד בַּעֲבוּר יְהוֹנָתָן]?"[164] Mephibosheth is then found and brought to David, and David declares to him: "Do not fear, for I will certainly deal loyally with you for the sake of Jonathan, your father. I will return to you all the fields of Saul, your [grand]father, and you shall always eat bread at my table."[165]

Many contemporary scholars, unsurprisingly, view these claims and displays of mercy with much skepticism. Regarding the Hittite kings' declarations of mercy and leniency, for example, Hoffner states:

> Only when there is something to be gained from magnanimity do [victors] make the effort [to be generous]. Both Telepinu and Ḫattušili make the effort, because the situation was still delicate and the stakes

---

[159] Van den Hout, "Apology of Ḫattušili III," 203 (§11). Urḫitešub, we will recall, was Muwatalli's "son of a concubine" (202; §10a).

[160] Ibid., 204 (§12b).

[161] 2 Samuel 1.

[162] 2 Samuel 3[HDR].

[163] 2 Samuel 4.

[164] 2 Sam 9:1.

[165] 2 Sam 9:7. There are also notable exceptions to David's "mercy," of course, such as David's treatment of the Jebusites in 2 Sam 5:6–10, and outside HDR, his execution of Saul's descendants in 2 Samuel 21.

for survival too high. Thus both documents are at pains to portray the new kings as men of mercy.[166]

Similarly, many have questioned David's real motives behind his mercy (or at least the reports of his mercy) and have judged his mercies to be self-serving at best, if not simply fictitious. For example, with regard to the self-serving mercy that David might have demonstrated through public expressions of grief and honoring his enemies with proper burials, scholars generally assume one of two possibilities. One view assumes that David probably played some role in the deaths of Saul, Saul's three sons who fell with him in battle, his commander Abner, and Saul's son Ishbosheth, and that he feigned grief and honor for selfish reasons. Another view is that David did not play any role in their deaths, but that he would have privately rejoiced over his good fortune, and so he must have feigned grief and honor for selfish reasons. Either way, the biblical narrative is undermined, and assumptions about "what really happened" play a determinative role in exegesis of the text.[167] There are few modern commentators, it appears, who allow their suppositions to be restrained by the biblical text or HDR and consider seriously the possibility that David played no part in their deaths and that his grief and honor were deeply heartfelt, as it is certainly portrayed in the biblical account.

Whatever the case, framing the discussion of HDR in terms of "David as merciful victor" and the like causes us to overlook an important and fundamental point: David is not a victor over Saul in any active way, for he did not personally achieve any "victory" over Saul or Saul's natural heirs to the throne as Ḥattušili did over his opponents. That accomplishment is directly attributed to the deeds of Israel's enemies, the Philistines;[168] of men in David's camp said to be "too savage" or "too severe" for David (קָשִׁים מִמֶּנִּי) and "the evildoer[s]" (עֹשֵׂה הָרָעָה);[169] and of "wicked men" (אֲנָשִׁים רְשָׁעִים)

---

[166] Hoffner, "Propaganda and Political Justification," 54.

[167] On this phenomenon in modern interpretation, see especially Frei, *The Eclipse of Biblical Narrative*.

[168] 1 Samuel 31.

[169] 2 Sam 3:39. See the characterization of David's men in 1 Sam 22:2, which probably applies also to the "sons of Zeruiah," as quite the motley group: "And every man in distress [כָּל־אִישׁ מָצוֹק], every man who had a debt-collector [after him] [וְכָל־אִישׁ אֲשֶׁר־לוֹ נֹשֶׁא], and every man whose life was bitter [וְכָל־אִישׁ מַר־נֶפֶשׁ] gathered to him. And he became commander over them, and with him there were around four hundred men."

in Saul's own camp.[170] Ultimately, however, that victory was reserved for
YHWH, as the biblical text implies in the account of David and Saul's last
meeting, when David says: "YHWH handed you over [נְתָנְךָ יְהוָה] today, but
I would not lay my hand on the anointed of YHWH. See how your life was
[judged] important in my eyes today. In the same manner now, may my life
be [judged] important in the eyes of YHWH, and may He rescue me from
every distress [וְיַצִּלֵנִי מִכָּל־צָרָה]."[171] In fact, David repudiated any attempts
at becoming the victor over Saul, and he showed numerous mercies to Saul
at the risk of his and his men's lives. In particular, he bravely fights Saul's
battles, although Saul's hope was to have David killed on the battlefield;[172]
he soothes Saul's spirit even after Saul had tried to kill him;[173] and he spares
Saul's life in the midst of grave danger.[174] Ḫattušili's "mercy" towards the
king he deposed, in contrast, consisted of subjecting him to public humiliation
and essentially exiling him instead of killing him.

6) The Edict

The "edict" in the Apology of Ḫattušili is quite brief, and it relates to the
required service of, and reverence towards, Ištar:

> Whoever will take away in future the offspring of Ḫattušili (and)
> Puduhepa from the service of Ištar (or) desires (so much as) a blade
> of straw from the storehouse (or) a chip of wood from the threshing
> floor of Ištar of Šamuha, let him be Ištar of Šamuha's court opponent!
> Let no one take them for levy (and) corvée![175]

> Whoever in future stands up against the son, grandson (or) offspring
> of Ḫattušili (and) Puduhepa, may he among the gods be fearful of
> Ištar of Šamuha![176]

---

[170] 2 Sam 4:11.

[171] 1 Sam 26:23–24. McCarter does not attribute to HDR several other passages in the
biblical text that are even more explicit that YHWH is the one who delivers David from his
enemies. See, e.g., 1 Sam 17:37, 45–47; 19:19–24; 20:15–16; 24:2–23; 25:28–31; 28:16–19;
2 Samuel 22.

[172] 1 Samuel 18[HDR].

[173] 1 Sam 19:7, 9–10.

[174] 1 Samuel 26 (as well as in 1 Samuel 24, which McCarter thinks was added later).

[175] Van den Hout, "Apology of Ḫattušili III," 204 (§13).

[176] Ibid. (§14).

The "legal section" of the Proclamation of Telipinu is considerably lengthier and introduces various legal reforms including those regarding royal succession and the king's execution of justice. According to Hoffner, although "superficially it might appear that the somewhat disorganized group of rulings at the end of Telipinu's text have no common theme, one can in fact relate all the rulings to the central concern of internecine strife and killings among the royal family!"[177]

If we limit our scope to McCarter's reconstructed HDR, there is no mention of an edict regarding legal reforms, cultic concerns, or other issues pertaining to royal justice. It is ironic, once again, that we do much better at finding at least something analogous in the Israelite setting (the detection of which is necessary for drawing meaningful comparisons and contrasts) by considering 1 Samuel 16–2 Samuel 5 within its larger biblical context. And yet, at the same instant that any analogies are drawn, the differences between them are thrown into clear relief. That is, consideration of how some semblance of this formal and thematic element of the Hittite apologies appears in the biblical text gives some insight into the particularities of each.

One might start with 2 Samuel 7 (especially YHWH's promises and instructions to David through the prophet Nathan), which many biblical scholars treat as a late addition and, thus, as falling outside the boundaries of HDR:

> And then say this to my servant David: "Thus says YHWH of Hosts: 'I took you from the pasture, from following after the sheep, to become sovereign over my people Israel. And I have been with you everywhere you have gone, and I have cut off all your enemies from before you. And [now] I will make for you a great name, like that of the great men of the earth. And I will establish a place for my people Israel and plant him[178] [there] that he may dwell in his place and tremble no more. And the sons of perversity shall not continue to afflict him, as at the first, from the day when I appointed judges over my people Israel. And now I will give rest to you from all

---

[177] Hoffner, "Propaganda and Political Justification," 56.

[178] Two points should be noted with regard to my usage of pronouns for Israel in this translation. First, my translation reflects biblical Hebrew's usage of grammatically masculine pronouns for "Israel," "my people Israel," etc., rather than the typical English practice of using grammatically feminine pronouns for nation-states. Second, though most English versions switch to the grammatical plural (e.g., "plant them . . . that they may dwell"), I have chosen to reflect biblical Hebrew's use of the singular form (e.g., "plant him . . . that he may dwell").

your enemies.' And to you declares YHWH, 'A house for you will YHWH make. When your days are full, you will lie down with your fathers, but I shall raise up your seed after you, going forth from your own issue, and I shall establish his kingdom. *He* shall build a house for my name. And I will establish the throne of his kingdom forever. *I* will be for him a father, and *he* shall be for me a son. When he does wrong, I will reproach him with the rod of men and with the blows of the sons of man. But my covenant-faithfulness will not leave him like I removed [it] from Saul, whom I removed from before you. Your house shall stand secure, and your kingdom forever before you. Your throne shall be established forever.'"[179]

YHWH declares that David's son is to build Him a "house" (בֵּית יְהֹוָה), and YHWH, in turn, will establish his house (בֵּית דָּוִד) "forever" (vv. 12–13, 16). He will discipline David's "son" "when he does wrong" (v. 14), but He will not withdraw His mercy from him as He did from Saul (v. 15). Jon D. Levenson remarks on the Davidic covenant presented here in 2 Samuel 7 and in Psalm 89:

> [I]t is important to remember that the Davidic covenant as presented in both 2 Sam 7:14 and Ps 89:31–38 would seem to presuppose obligation by the Sinaitic pact. If the king disobeys the *mitsvot*, he will be punished. No statement of the Davidic covenant identifies the state with the will of God or exempts the king from punishment.[180]

Indeed, within its larger context, the history of Saul's sins and the consequent miseries visited upon him, his house, and his people, as well as the history of David's sins and the resulting miseries visited upon him, his house, and his people, might be seen as a narrative demonstration and confirmation of the Mosaic "edict" or "law of the king" in Deut 17:14–20. As prophetic history (i.e., part of the *Nebiim*), 1 Samuel 16–2 Samuel 5, together with its larger context, functions, at least in part, to edict, that is, "to publish" or "to decree" faithfulness, repentance, and return to YHWH and the keeping of His *Torah*. In contrast to Ḫattušili, in the biblical account David himself does

---

[179] 2 Sam 7:8–16.

[180] Levenson, *Sinai and Zion*, 213. In connection with this, Levenson notes that de Vaux ("Le roi d'Israël," 119–33, at 125) and Weinfeld ("The Covenant of Grant," 184–203, at 189) have found a parallel to the Davidic covenant in the Hittite grant to Ulmi-Teshub of Dattasa.

not issue but receives from YHWH this "edict," which applies to him and his descendants, as well as the people that they represent before YHWH.

The last point above—together with others before it—raises questions once again about the validity of drawing too close an analogy between HDR and the Apology of Ḫattušili. It also raises an even more fundamental question about the adequacy of basing one's interpretation on an isolated collage of episodes selected according to certain preconceived notions regarding their significance or function. In the next chapter, I shall consider in more detail how characterizing the biblical account from the outset as the self-justification of an individual king results in reconstructions and weighted readings that naturally reflect the presumed character of the accounts. In the present case, we have seen how some scholars pare down the biblical account and reconstruct "the original History of David's Rise" based on their presuppositions regarding heavily propagandistic or ideological aims and then turn back and re-read 1 Samuel 16–2 Samuel 5 as a tale that is chiefly concerned with legitimating David vis-à-vis Saul in the same way that the Hittite texts legitimize the usurpers Ḫattušili and Telipinu. And so, for instance, McCarter goes on to demonstrate in his essay how his summation of HDR in terms of these themes, together with his "thematic analysis of the history of David's rise that is sensitive to the rhetorical posture of the author," "reveals the apologetic character of the composition."[181]

Independent First-Person Account vs. Embedded Third-Person Account

There are two other notable differences that we should touch upon. First, an obvious difference—and yet, I have seen no one discuss its rhetorical significance or impact—is that the Hittite apologies are in the first-person voice, whereas HDR occurs in a third-person narrative. Second, and perhaps even more importantly, whereas the Hittite apologies remain as independent histories, 1 Samuel 16–2 Samuel 5 is integrally embedded within the context of a much larger narrative. It is remarkable that recognition and appreciation of these fundamental differences are nearly lost in modern discussions about the texts. This is obscured, in large part, because scholars necessarily take on the third-person voice in presenting the accounts of Ḫattušili and others, and so, in their retelling, they begin to sound and feel more like the

---

[181] McCarter, "The Apology of David," 499.

biblical account and its putative source.[182] And yet, these differences are not insignificant. Indeed, they have major implications for how we should approach the respective texts. Because the differences (i.e., first-person vs. third-person, and independent vs. embedded) closely intersect, I shall take them up together.

Hittite scholars assume that the Apology of Ḫattušili and the Proclamation of Telipinu were composed during the lifetimes of the royal speakers in these texts and that they served primarily, if not solely, the immediate concern of legitimizing the individual kings themselves during their reigns (and all that it entails, such as delegitimizing their predecessors). This is indicated, in part, by the first-person voice and stand-alone form of these apologies, together with the lack of any evidence that they were recontextualized and used toward other ends, for example, as the fictional autobiography of a later ruler, or by historians in later eras to fill gaps in their epic histories. Their meaning, therefore, is largely determined, if not entirely exhausted, by the particular context and function for which they were originally composed.[183] This is not so for the biblical text or its putative source.

The biblical narrative of 1 Samuel 16–2 Samuel 5, in contrast, is an integral part of an over-arching history that functions to address concerns and issues that are not limited to the people of David's day. Of course, the biblical editors might have easily incorporated a first-person account from David's reign and used it to speak to later concerns. Indeed, biblical editors did not shy away from doing so with regard to the book of Nehemiah, for example.[184] But

---

[182] Partly for this reason, above I have quoted directly from the Apology of Ḫattušili and the biblical account more freely than most in similar comparisons. Reading portions from each one side-by-side is perhaps as helpful for understanding the rhetorical effect of each text as any scholarly exposition.

[183] While there is no indication that the Apology of Ḫattušili was ever used in any context other than Ḫattušili's own reign, one cannot assert with the same degree of certitude that the meaning of the Proclamation of Telipinu was "exhausted" within the context of Telipinu's reign. The Telipinu text may have been known by other Hittite rulers, including Ḫattušili, and recognized as somehow authoritative with regard to Telipinu's "rules" for royal succession. I owe credit to an anonymous reviewer of my manuscript for this important caveat. For recent discussions related to historians' interpretations and uses of Hittite sources, see, for example: Bryce, *The Kingdom of the Hittites*, especially Appendix 2, "Sources for Hittite History: An Overview"; and Klengel, "Problems in Hittite History," 101–9. For a helpful discussion of form-critical and historical issues related to genre identification and the reading of ancient Near Eastern "autobiographies" in general, and for specific examples from Akkadian texts in particular, see especially Longman, *Fictional Akkadian Autobiography*.

[184] See, e.g., Davies, *First Person*.

this is not what we have in 1 Samuel 16–2 Samuel 5. Here, rather, we have an "omniscient narrator"[185] whose account of Saul's rejection and David's election has implied relevance and meaning not simply for legitimizing the historical David vis-à-vis King Saul, but for the people of YHWH for whom this account is handed down and retold, if not composed in the first place. From a form-critical perspective, the "omniscient" third-person narrative form of this account and its integration into the grand "history" of God's people allow or even cause the biblical history to transcend the time of its *dramatis personae* and recorded events and to speak with meaningful relevance to reading/reciting communities long after David's day in ways that are impossible for the Hittite texts (or, to a lesser degree, a stand-alone HDR).

Conclusion

Without attempting to summarize my lengthy discussion above, let me conclude this chapter with several observations that follow from it.

There is no question that sometime in the thirteenth century B.C.E. a Hittite individual calling himself Ḫattušili forcefully seized the throne of his predecessor. The Hittite text generally designated as "the Apology of Ḫattušili," which is incontrovertibly dated to the lifetime of this particular Ḫattušili, freely acknowledges—one may say it even boasts—that he acquired his position through means of force against his predecessor. Likewise, there is no question that this independent, first-person account—some have even called it an "autobiography"[186]—was composed not merely in order to boast of his victories or offer praises to his goddess; it is also marked throughout by the explicit concerns of establishing this royal individual's innocence and the legality of his rise to the throne. In that sense, the apology is intensely personal. The matter is not nearly so straightforward for David and the account of his rise to kingship, although they have been likened to Ḫattušili and his apology more than to any other ancient Near Eastern usurper and his royal apology where it is extant.

First, there is considerable debate in some circles over the question of whether, in fact, sometime in the late eleventh and/or early tenth centuries B.C.E., a certain David became Israel's second king, following after a certain

---

[185] See Sternberg, *The Poetics of Biblical Narrative*; especially see ch. 3 "Ideology of Narration and Narration of Ideology."

[186] See, e.g., the brief discussion in Wolf, *"The Apology of Hattušiliš,"* 12–14.

Saul. And while most historians of ancient Israel believe he did, a minority among them argue that David and the events surrounding his rise and reign are the fictitious inventions of a much later age. I am convinced that those in the minority are wrong. Their ability to gain any foothold, however, bespeaks something about the nature of the biblical account that distinguishes it from the Apology of Ḫattušili: Whereas the latter only makes sense in light of the historical Ḫattušili's individual predicament, the biblical account (in any of the reconstructed stages we have seen, including McCarter's reconstructed HDR) can be read in light of multiple predicaments of multiple individuals and/or communities of people whom they might be understood as representing. The distinction here is subtle, perhaps, but it is there nonetheless.

Second, however commonplace it has become to speak of David as a "usurper," as having "forcefully seized Saul's throne," and the like, it should be recognized that this characterization runs counter to the biblical account (again, in any of its reconstructed or actual literary stages). Many may argue that the biblical account succeeds as a royal apology precisely because it demonstrates David's innocence so effectively. Whether or not that is the case, note carefully what follows from this observation. On the one hand, both "faithful readers" who take the Apology of Ḫattušili at face value (that is, those who allow their knowledge of Ḫattušili to be constrained by the text) and historians of Ḫattušili's life and times would reach the conclusion that Ḫattušili forcefully seized his predecessor's throne and, therefore, published the text as his personal exoneration. On the other hand, while historians of David's life and times may argue, as many do, that the historical David forcefully seized Saul's throne and, therefore, published the account as his personal exoneration, "faithful readers" who take any reconstructed stage of the biblical account at face value, would in sharp contrast to the readers of Ḫattušili's account, not easily arrive at either aspect of these historians' conclusion. Where skeptical historians now cannot help but find personal self-justification, such as in the extended narrative account of David's flight from Saul, "faithful readers" may reasonably find a reflection of David's people, that is, the people whom he embodies and represents.[187] I contend that the latter reading better accords with the logic of Hebrew Scripture.

---

[187] Note that McCarter interprets the account of David's battle with Goliath in 1 Sam 17:1–11, 32–40, 42–48a, 49, 51–54 (which he thinks was added to HDR by a Deuteronomistic historian) in this latter sense, that is, as a symbolic representation of Israel confronting its enemies; see my brief discussion of this in ch. 1, pp. 29–30, above.

Finally, it is highly questionable whether HDR can be extracted and read independently. Treatments of 1 Samuel 16–2 Samuel 5 as an individual royal apology generally obscure its embeddedness and dependence upon the surrounding biblical narrative, both within Samuel and beyond. This has become evident partly through my discussion of McCarter's source analysis in chapter 1, and partly in the review of HDR in light of Hoffner's analysis of the Hittite texts' apologetic form and themes, such as in places where possible analogues (although only partial and serving distinctive aims) between the Hittite and Israelite texts are apparent only when David's story is viewed within its larger biblical context. That it strains credulity to read 1 Samuel 16[HDR]–2 Samuel 5[HDR] as self-contained and independent of the surrounding narratives will become more evident in chapters 4 and 5.[188] Were we to accept one of the pared down versions of HDR that have been proposed, however, the "omniscient" third-person style or form (among other factors) that sharply distinguishes it from the Apology of Ḫattušili still lends to a reading of it within a number of historical contexts in service of aims other than personal exoneration and legitimization of David-the-usurper.[189] This, too, will become clearer in the following chapters.

---

[188] Consider this strong statement about David's "felt presence" in the biblical story before he emerges on the scene in "HDR": "David is not mentioned in the Bible until the Book of Samuel, but we can begin to hear the strains of the 'undersong' that Bible scholar Gerhard von Rad detected in the earliest passages of the Yahwist's primal history. In fact, the Five Books of Moses are seeded with clues that anticipate the coming of King David long before we actually encounter him. And these clues suggest that the Bible was first and always intended by its original authors to be a celebration of King David and the line of Davidic kings who sat on the throne of Israel and Judah for some five hundred years, the longest-reigning dynasty in the ancient Near East and one of the longest-reigning in world history" (Kirsch, *King David*, 11). Also see, e.g., Van Seters, *In Search of History*, esp. 264–71.

[189] As we have already seen in ch. 1, besides the Jerusalemite court in David's own day, scholars have variously proposed the days and courts of Solomon, Rehoboam and Jeroboam, Jehu, Hezekiah, Josiah, etc., for contexts in which the source or sources of 1 Samuel 16–2 Samuel 5 make sense, though it is still conceived chiefly in apologetic terms for an individual monarch in each case.

CHAPTER 3

A Reconsideration of the History of David's Rise as an Answer to Charges against David

In chapter 1, I introduced Kyle McCarter's argument that HDR has a certain rhetorical posture by analogy to the Hittite Apology of Ḫattušili:

> A careful reading leads to the conclusion that the author is speaking to one possible charge of wrongdoing after another in an attempt to demonstrate David's innocence in the series of events that led to his succession. This case for the defense is made by relating the events in question in a way intended to allay all suspicions, and though the author becomes quite explicit at times, as in his report of Abner's death (see below), he does not permit himself to step out from behind his narrative and comment directly on the issue at hand. Nevertheless, the charges against which he defends David are easily recognized.[1]

There I discussed briefly the following seven underlying allegations against David that McCarter detects based on this recognition of HDR's rhetorical posture, or apologetic character:

---

[1] McCarter, "The Apology of David," 499.

1) David sought to advance himself at court at Saul's expense.
2) David was a deserter.
3) David was an outlaw.
4) David was a Philistine mercenary.
5) David was implicated in Saul's death.
6) David was implicated in Abner's death.
7) David was implicated in Ishbaal's death.[2]

I concluded my discussion there by stating that these "charges" are not so obvious as McCarter indicates, but that they "must be inferred, in large part, from a prior determination about the genre of the text and apparent similarities between HDR and the Apology of Ḫattušili, from assumptions about the actual history behind the text, as well as from assumptions about human nature in general."[3] In chapter 2, I addressed the issue of HDR's genre by questioning the degree and nature of the similarities that McCarter has detected between the History of David's Rise and the Apology of Ḫattušili. There I introduced and discussed many dissimilarities that have gone almost entirely overlooked, and I concluded that the History of David's Rise is not so similar or parallel to the Apology of Ḫattušili as some have suggested. I shall turn in this chapter to consider questions of HDR's apologetic nature from a different angle.

In the following discussion, I shall revisit McCarter's reading of the History of David's Rise as a calculated response to each of the above charges; I shall discuss the logic behind McCarter's detection of HDR's particular apologetic or rhetorical posture; and I shall argue that while his claims about the meaning of the account make sense given his assumptions about the socio-historical events and context that he posits as the evocation of the text, they are not self-evident from a reading of his reconstructed source alone, and much less the present biblical account, as he appears to suggest when he states, for example, that "the charges against which [the author] defends David are *easily recognized*."[4] Willem S. Vorster's observations regarding interpretation of the "Succession Narrative" (2 Samuel 9–20; 1 Kings 1–2) might as well apply to interpretation of the biblical account of David's rise to kingship:

---

[2] Ibid., 499–502. See pp. 44–47, above.
[3] Above, p. 47.
[4] McCarter, "The Apology of David," 499 [emphasis added].

It is also clear that the pro- and anti-propaganda readings of the [biblical] text are perceptions of the text rationalized by assumptions about the dating and the purpose of the narrative and furthermore prompted by the composition and the assumed theme of the text. These readings offer interesting results because readers are constructively involved in attributing meaning to the text they are supposedly reading.[5]

I aim, in this chapter, to demonstrate how in McCarter's own work he bases his meaning-making with regard to HDR as much or more upon his historical reconstruction of the events behind HDR, and upon his resulting assumptions regarding its unstated aims and intended audience, as he bases it upon a careful reading of the account. This is a necessary step towards better understanding why McCarter and others have detected the rhetorical posture discussed above not only in the reconstructed HDR but also in the full edition to which we have access.[6]

Speech-Act Theory

Before I continue with my discussion of McCarter's reading of the History of David's Rise as a response to various accusations against the historical David, it is necessary to introduce some of the terminology of speech-act theory, which distinguishes between the various acts, or usages, of language. The three basic acts of language that are relevant for the present discussion are:

1) the locutionary act (or, simply, the locution)—the basic act of utterance

2) the illocutionary act (or, simply, the illocution)—the particular force or use of a locution

3) the perlocutionary act (or, simply, the perlocution)—the consequence or accomplishment achieved by the locution

The classic text on speech-act theory is J. L. Austin's *How to Do Things with Words*. Here is his concise explanation of the three terms and concepts:

> We . . . distinguished a group of things we do in saying something, which together we summed up by saying we perform a *locutionary*

---

[5] Vorster, "Readings, Readers, and the Succession Narrative," 403.
[6] See, for example, p. 18 n. 21, above.

act, which is roughly equivalent to uttering a certain sentence with a certain sense and reference, which again is roughly equivalent to 'meaning' in the traditional sense. Second, we said that we also perform *illocutionary acts* such as informing, ordering, warning, undertaking, &c., i.e. utterances which have a certain (conventional) force. Thirdly, we may also perform *perlocutionary acts*: what we bring about or achieve *by* saying something, such as convincing, persuading, deterring, and even, say, surprising or misleading. Here we have three, if not more, different senses or dimensions of the 'use of a sentence' or of 'the use of language' (and, of course, there are others also). All these three kinds of 'actions' are, simply of course as actions, subject to the usual troubles and reservations about attempt as distinct from achievement, being intentional as distinct from being unintentional, and the like.[7]

Perhaps it will be helpful to consider each term and concept in light of a simple illustration taken from the book of 1 Samuel.

Consider, for instance, the following locutionary act, which is attributed to YHWH addressing Samuel at the opening of 1 Samuel 16:

Locution: "How long will you mourn for Saul?"

The meaning of this utterance, or locution, might initially appear to be simple and straightforward. Understanding its meaning becomes more complicated, however, when we recognize the range of possible illocutionary forces that may have been intended by the speaker and/or narrator. The illocutionary act intended by the locution "How long will you mourn for Saul?" might be any of the following (and this list is a mere sampling of possible illocutions):

Illocution 1: to request information

Illocution 2: to show displeasure over the mourner's excessive mourning

Illocution 3: to command the mourner to stop mourning

Note that a speaker may intend to convey only one or multiple illocutions with one locution. In spoken language, the speaker uses tone of voice and body language (such as facial expressions), in particular, to help the addressee, and any others listening in, to correctly interpret the intended illocutionary

---

[7] Austin, *How to Do Things*, 108–9 [emphasis in original]; see, in particular, "Lectures" VIII–XII.

force. Knowledge about the speaker(s), recipient(s), and the wider context of their conversation are also important indicators of meaning. Finally, to continue with the above example, the intended and desired perlocutionary act might be any of the following (again, one could conceive of a much more extensive list of possible perlocutions):

Perlocution 1: to evoke an answer to the request for information

Perlocution 2: to make the mourner think or feel a certain way about Saul or himself

Perlocution 3: to cause the mourner to stop mourning

Again, note that a speaker and/or narrator may attempt to perform only one or multiple perlocutions through one locution.

Each of these acts of language usage—that is the locutionary, illocutionary, and perlocutionary acts—requires much nuance, both in its own right and in relation to others. This brief introduction to speech-act theory, however, should sufficiently meet our present need to establish some basic theoretical terms for the following discussion of the message and function of the History of David's Rise.[8]

McCarter's Identification of Charges Against David—A Reconsideration of the Illocutionary Force of the Biblical Account of David's Rise to the Throne

I would now like to consider at some length the grounds for McCarter's assertions in his thematic analysis, which I introduced in chapter 1. His exposition of the narrative's rhetorical posture as a response to numerous underlying charges against David raises many questions. For example: Is the illocutionary force or meaning of HDR really self-evident from a close reading of the biblical account of David's rise to the throne, as McCarter has indicated? Can we conclude with certainty that the locutions that McCarter has attributed to HDR were evoked for and employed with the same sort of

---

[8] More generally speaking, some reference by biblical scholars to speech-act theory would be helpful for thinking about the many and various ways in which authors, editors, and tradents, among others, attempt and in fact do different things with the same locutions. For more recent discussions on these and other aspects of speech-act theory in the context of biblical interpretation, see Wolterstorff, *Divine Discourse*; Briggs, *Words in Action*.

illocutionary force and perlocutionary aims as the Apology of Ḫattušili? What assumptions inform these conclusions? And furthermore, what themes are missing from McCarter's analysis that might suggest other possibilities with regard to HDR's illocutionary force and perlocutionary aims?

I shall treat, in turn, each of the underlying charges that McCarter has detected and posited as the principle impetus for HDR's composition. My chief aim is to show that McCarter is often guided by premises—for example, the premise that HDR is essentially defensive in its composition—based primarily on extratextual information and not just on a careful reading of the biblical account. As we shall see, all but one of the charges that McCarter detects are not givens; rather, they can be recognized only after, or simultaneous with, the determination to view HDR through the primary lens of royal apology for an individual king. McCarter's assumptions about the original goal of the History of David's Rise—that is, his assumptions about the illocutionary force and perlocutionary aims of personal self-justification by, or on the behalf of, King David—are determinative in his exposition of the real meaning of the text. To restate McCarter's view in terms of speech-act theory, HDR's locutions carried the illocutionary force of declaring that David had risen to Saul's throne not by unlawful usurpation, but legitimately. By this, it aimed to perform the perlocutions of persuading any doubters that the outstanding charges against David were false, convincing people that David's rise to kingship was lawful and legitimate (indeed, the will of YHWH), silencing any remaining detractors of David, and the like. Based on his understanding that HDR's illocutionary force and perlocutionary aims are fundamentally akin to those evident in anyone's reading of the Hittite Apology of Ḫattušili, then, McCarter makes logical inferences about the historical or real meaning of HDR's positive locutions regarding David's rise to the throne, that is, that they are postures composed for the purpose of refuting unstated accusations. Let us turn, now, to see how this is worked out in each case.

1) David Sought to Advance Himself at Court at Saul's Expense

In McCarter's view, the real meaning, or illocutionary force, of 1 Samuel 16–19[HDR 9] (i.e., of its locutions) is the denial of rumors of David's self-

---

[9] See p. 16, above, on my terminology and sigla for the biblical text and its sources. According to McCarter, 1 Samuel 16–19[HDR] consists of: 1 Sam 16:14–23; an earlier battle account in which David wins much acclaim by virtue of his success against Israel-Judah's enemies in place of chs. 17; 18:6–8a, 9, 12a, 13–16,

aggrandizement in Saul's court and army by demonstrating that David passively entered Saul's service, where he served his king loyally and bravely, and that he was the passive recipient of the king's daughter as his wife. The perlocutionary aim of this account is to convince the audience that the historical David did not aggressively seek Saul's throne but advanced "step by step toward the kingship almost in spite of himself."[10] To what degree is McCarter's determination based simply upon a careful reading of HDR? Let us consider the logic behind McCarter's easy recognition of the charge that "David sought to advance himself at court at Saul's expense," and his exposition of the text's rhetorical posture.

First, McCarter obviously accepts as historically true the "claims" of the biblical text that a) the historical David achieved extraordinary attainments in Saul's court through his many battle victories; b) he established ties to the royal family through his marriage to Michal and his friendship with Jonathan;[11] and yet, despite his many contributions to Saul's cause, c) he did not rise but fell from favor with Saul. Second, however, McCarter does not accept as historically true the reasons given in HDR for David's falling out with Saul (e.g., Saul's intense jealousy and paranoia that were brought on, in part, from his affliction by an "evil spirit from YHWH"). He infers from the facts of a, b, and c, rather, that David probably "acted out of a strong and perhaps unscrupulous self-interest while in Saul's service."[12] There is also the unstated inference that the portrayal of such an aggressive David at this stage in his life would have been damning of him in the eyes of the people of Israel, as if passivity with regard to his position and rank in Saul's service were a virtue in David's day. Third, therefore, McCarter thinks that this particular account in which David happens to become Saul's servant—and even his son-in-law—and, thereafter, serves Saul nobly and loyally, both in and out of the king's presence, means that David must have stood accused of self-aggrandizement, and that this accusation needed to be refuted. The

---

20–21a, 22–29a; and 19:1–17. Again, see my presentation of McCarter's source analysis in ch. 1.

[10] McCarter, "The Apology of David," 503.

[11] See p. 113 n. 38, below, for the passages related to David's relationships with Michal and Jonathan, and for which of these McCarter attributes to the original HDR.

[12] McCarter, "The Apology of David," 499. VanderKam ("Davidic Complicity," 524) states, for example, "A close reading of 1 Samuel 16–2 Samuel 1 discloses that good sense, not madness, led Saul to suspect David as a dangerous rival to his throne from a very early stage (cf. 1 Sam 18:8–9; 20:30–31; 22:6–8; 24:20)."

true or historical meaning of the locutions, then, has more to do with David's shrewd and self-interested acts and political maneuvers than with Saul's actual treatment of David.[13]

McCarter's assessment of HDR's meaning here is not so self-evident as he indicates immediately prior to his analysis. He appears to concede the inconclusiveness of his determination when he states that "[t]he extraordinary attainments of the young Judahite at the Benjaminite court, especially in light of his subsequent fall from favor, *might suggest* that he acted out of a strong and perhaps unscrupulous self-interest while in Saul's service."[14] Indeed, his assessment that these accounts were composed to discount the stated charges hinges, rather, on his suspicion that David was unscrupulously self-promoting. As we have seen already in chapter 2, Steven McKenzie also articulates several principles underlying this and other assumptions. First, according to the "principle of skepticism," asserts McKenzie, the characterizations of Saul and David "should make us skeptical about whether Saul was really as inept and unstable as 1–2 Samuel portray him."[15] Second, based on the "principle of analogy," he asserts, our knowledge of "the customs and motives common among ancient Middle Eastern rulers" and of the "general human tendencies" of people in positions of power are better guides in determining David's "real motives" than is the biblical account's depiction.[16] McKenzie goes on to speak, then, of the "technique of 'overstress'":

> [Overstress] is where the story repeatedly states David's innocence in regard to a particular accusation. The more the author protests, the more we suspect the charge was true.[17]

But where can it be said that "the story repeatedly states David's innocence in regard to a particular accusation," or that the author is explicitly protesting some charge?

There are instances in the narrative, of course, where David's innocence is an issue. Consider the following: 1) David's innocence vis-à-vis Saul, and his unjust treatment by Saul, are explicitly addressed by David and Jonathan

---

[13] On this, see, in particular, McKenzie, *King David*, 77–88; Halpern, *David's Secret Demons*, 280–84.

[14] McCarter, "The Apology of David," 499–500 [emphasis mine].

[15] McKenzie, *King David*, 44.

[16] Ibid., 44–45.

[17] Ibid., 45.

at two different points.[18] 2) Ahimelech the priest declares David's faithfulness to Saul.[19] 3) Abigail causes David to realize the importance of allowing YHWH to avenge his enemies.[20] 4) David refuses to kill Saul when given the opportunity, and he contrasts his mercy towards Saul with Saul's unjust treatment of him.[21] And finally, 5) David's uninvolvement in Joab's murder of Abner is an important point in that account.[22] It would be a true statement, then, for readers to observe David's innocence in these several instances, and to make this assertion: "David is depicted as innocent in the biblical account." But the assertion that this depiction of David's innocence can only be read sensibly in terms of its functioning in service of the historically particular aims of denying underlying charges by insurrectionists and discontents that David is to blame—partly or wholly—in the deaths of Saul, the priests of Nob, Nabal, and Abner, among others, does not necessarily follow.

The interpretation that the account is refuting real-world accusations against David is derivative of, and driven by, the assumption that the meaning of the text is exhausted by what it might tell us about historically located struggles in and around the Davidic court for power. It fails, therefore, to recognize other potential illocutionary forces and perlocutionary aims of these accounts, such as their functioning to demonstrate dramatically the innocent suffering of God's people in the face of injustice, God's providential and mysterious preservation of His suffering servants, and so on. Instead, the interpretive key for McCarter (along with others I have cited) comes from critical assumptions about the historical reconstruction of the events behind HDR (itself reconstructed in light of these assumptions). That is, he bases his conclusion regarding the illocutionary force of the text primarily on his assumptions about the original function of HDR, which he grounds in his view of what might have really happened: David probably was more aggressive and self-aggrandizing than the narrative suggests, and so his court produced a document akin to the royal propaganda of the Hittites and other neighbors to legitimize his actions.

---

[18] 1 Sam 19:1–7, and 1 Samuel 20[HDR].

[19] 1 Sam 22:14.

[20] 1 Sam 25:23–27, 32–35, 39; McCarter does not attribute vv. 28–31 to the original HDR.

[21] 1 Samuel 26; also see 1 Samuel 24, which McCarter attributes to the Deuteronomist.

[22] 2 Samuel 3[HDR]. See my discussion of McCarter's fifth, sixth, and seventh charges further below.

In light of McCarter's assumptions and conclusion, it is unsurprising — and yet easily overlooked — that McCarter's summation of HDR has its own rhetorical effect. Having raised his suspicions concerning what went on behind the scenes, McCarter selectively highlights and frames certain events in HDR as the obvious answer to the presumed allegations:

> The narrator, however, shows that David came to court at Saul's behest (1 Sam 16:19–22) and that as long as he was there he was completely loyal and indeed did much to help Saul's own cause (cf. 1 Sam 19:4–5). He did not seek out his marriage to the princess Michal, the most conspicuous sign of his elevated position, but instead protested his unworthiness of the match (1 Sam 18:23), which was in fact Saul's idea (vv 20–21a), until persuaded by the insistence of Saul's courtiers.[23]

McCarter hereby inscribes and reflects his assumptions regarding the illocutionary force of the text — that is, to prove David innocent of the charge that he "sought to advance himself at court at Saul's expense" — in this highly condensed paraphrase of a few locutions in 1 Samuel 16–19[HDR].

The illocutionary force of the narrative even in McCarter's reconstructed History of David's Rise, however, is not so clear-cut. David is indeed invited to Saul's court. But what is the illocutionary force here? Based on HDR's locutions alone, a simple assertion of innocence, in this case that "David did not manipulate people and events so as to enter Saul's court," is certainly not the only possible illocution. Other illocutionary aims of the unexpected invitation are easily conceivable. For example, it might function to make a positive and dramatic statement about YHWH's provision for David[24] and David's emerging identity as YHWH's elect, for it is here that he is first distinguished and set apart in the eyes of Saul and his court. Likewise, that David "did not seek out his marriage to the princess Michal" is an accurate statement about the narrative of HDR. But the text itself does not speak in these terms. That is, it is not self-evident that the chief illocutionary force of this account is the declaration that David is innocent of charges that he cleverly orchestrated events in order to become the king's son-in-law. Again, alternative explanations for the narrator's telling of these events are not only possible, but they are at least as credible. The illocutionary force of David's

---

[23] McCarter, "The Apology of David," 499–500.

[24] I shall discuss this theme of YHWH's provision in ch. 4.

protestations to the proposal of Saul's servants might be, for example, to communicate something about the poor and lowly estate of his father's house (whatever one might presume to have actually been the case). Indeed, David refers explicitly to this when Saul's servants, at Saul's prodding, suggested that he "become now the king's son-in-law": "Is it a small thing in your eyes to become the king's son-in-law? *I* am a poor man and of small repute [וְאָנֹכִי אִישׁ־רָשׁ וְנִקְלֶה]!"[25] Michal's unbesought "love,"[26] coupled with Saul's offer of her hand to David (albeit to evil ends), might as well have been recounted to demonstrate David's increasingly elevated and beloved position in the eyes of the people and Saul's court, even if against Saul's will.[27]

Furthermore, depending on the assumptions that we bring to the text, we can easily reach varying conclusions regarding the illocutionary force of the many episodes and details that are missing from McCarter's concise summary above. What of the illocutionary force of HDR's reference to the various movements of YHWH's spirit in 1 Samuel 16[HDR] and 18[HDR], for example? It is hardly surprising that modern scholars typically view this as a theological leitmotif that is conveniently employed—much like Ḫattušili's invocation of Ištar's name—as the ultimate demonstration and proof of David's innocence and legitimacy.[28] In this view, once again, the only conceivable perlocutionary aim is that of retaining and/or accruing power. Is it not possible, however, that the intended and interpreted illocutionary force of the references to YHWH's spirit was something other than a theological leitmotif in service of personal self-justification by (or for) an individual king? Within the context of ancient Israel, it is conceivable, for instance, that one of the perlocutionary aims here was that YHWH should receive credit and honor for the mysterious way in which He confirmed His rejection of Saul and election of David as king of his people. I shall elaborate further on these and other possibilities in the following chapters.

To take a different approach, we might apply McCarter's logic regarding the text's rhetorical posturing to various narrative details to see where it takes us. According to his logic, many statements in the account can be

---

[25] 1 Sam 18:23. David also speaks in a self-effacing manner in 1 Sam 18:18, after Saul offers to David his elder daughter Merab for a wife: "Who am I, and what is my life, [or] my father's family in Israel, that I should become the king's son-in-law?" McCarter, however, attributes 1 Sam 18:17–19 to proto-MT editors (see pp. 34–35, above).

[26] "And Michal, Saul's daughter, loved [וַתֶּאֱהַב] David" (1 Sam 18:20).

[27] I shall return to this theme in ch. 5.

[28] E.g., McCarter, "The Apology of David," 502–4.

taken in defensive or negative terms and turned on their heads as rhetorical posturing. But unless the defensive aims are explicitly stated in the locutions themselves, such readings rest largely on assumptions and conclusions about illocutionary and perlocutionary aims that are unstated and, thus, must be detected on the basis of something outside of the mere locutions. Consider, for example, the locution regarding David's physical appearance[29] in 1 Sam 16:12:

> He was ruddy [אַדְמוֹנִי], with beautiful eyes [עִם־יְפֵה עֵינַיִם], and good-looking [וְטוֹב רֹאִי].

Then again, in 1 Sam 17:42:

> And the Philistine looked and saw David, and he despised him because he was a boy, and [because he was] ruddy [וְאַדְמֹנִי] with a pleasing appearance [עִם־יְפֵה מַרְאֶה].

In another passage, YHWH chastises Samuel in 1 Sam 16:7 for assuming that Jesse's eldest son is "YHWH's anointed" (v. 6) based on his impressive height and pleasing appearance, as the text implies:

> But YHWH said to Samuel, "Do not look to his appearance or to the height of his standing [אַל־תַּבֵּט אֶל־מַרְאֵהוּ וְאֶל־גְּבֹהַּ קוֹמָתוֹ], because I have rejected him. For it is not that which man sees, because man sees the appearance [lit., "the eyes"; כִּי הָאָדָם יִרְאֶה לַעֵינַיִם]. YHWH, however, sees the heart.

---

[29] For a modern parallel, one might find it instructive to read accounts of Abraham Lincoln's physical appearance by his supporters; to contrast these with descriptions of him by his opponents; to compare both of these with portraits of Lincoln; and to consider how verbal and visual portraits function to exalt or demean the man and all that he represents. Consider, for instance, one biographer's reports about Lincoln as he traveled from Springfield to Washington for his inauguration in February of 1861. After Lincoln passed secretly through Baltimore because of an uncovered assassination plot, opponents "taunted Lincoln [in local newspapers] as a hick with a high-pitched voice and a Kentucky twang, an ugly 'gorilla' and 'baboon.'" Others who saw the president-elect along the route, though, saw him in a starkly different light. According to one man: "He is a clever man, *and not so bad looking as they say*, while he is no great beauty. He is tall . . . has a commanding figure, bows pretty well, is not stiff, has a pleasant face, is amiable and *determined*" (Freedman, *Lincoln: A Photobiography*, 70 [emphasis in original]). On the early study of Lincoln portraiture, see Peterson, *Lincoln in American Memory*, 146.

Shall we conclude, as some have with regard to other texts, that the author(s) "doth protest too much"? According to the skeptical logic of "overstress" or "rhetorical posturing," it is conceivable that we might take all this as evidence that, in fact, David was rather physically unappealing and, therefore, characterized by all that physical blemishes and ugliness might imply in an ancient Israelite context—evil, uncleanness, and general unsuitability as a servant of YHWH.[30] Saul M. Olyan, for instance, argues that in Deut 15:21 and 17:1, "evil" (raʿ) "has a physical sense and is perhaps best translated 'disfiguring' or 'ugly.'" In contrast, he states, "[i]ts antonym 'good' (ṭōb) also has a physical sense and is best translated 'beautiful' in contexts in which the physical sense is intended."[31] Olyan proceeds, then, to draw numerous connections in the Hebrew Bible between physical ugliness, or blemishes, and one's unsuitability to come before YHWH in worship for reasons such as ritual uncleanness.[32] In view of Olyan's observations, it would be rather easy to conceive of numerous contexts that could have evoked the above descriptions of David. But this is the critical point to note: Conclusions regarding these sorts of illocutionary force and perlocutionary aims depend heavily on extratextual assumptions or predeterminations about the historical event or situation that evoked the account. Apart from the sort of historically conditioned external information that McCarter and others have proposed, therefore, the possibility that the text is "addressing itself to issues exposed to actual or possible public censure"[33] is not "easily recognized," as more than two millennia of readings without these assumptions abundantly indicate.

2) David Was a Deserter

McCarter draws special attention to how 1 Samuel 19–21[HDR][34] casts David as faithful to Saul to the point of risking his life on numerous occasions—he leaves Saul's court only when it is certain that to stay would mean sure death—particularly in order to show as false the outstanding accusations in Israel that David was unfaithful to Saul, and that he was essentially a deserter. As in the case of the first charge discussed above, McCarter begins his brief

---

[30] See Olyan, *Rites and Rank,* 103–14.

[31] Ibid., 103–4, 170 n. 8; see 1 Sam 16:12.

[32] Ibid., 104–14.

[33] McCarter, "The Apology of David," 499.

[34] According to McCarter, 1 Samuel 19–21[HDR] consists of: 1 Sam 19:1–17; 20:1–10, 18–22, 24–39; and all of ch. 21.

discussion of HDR's depiction of David's flight from Saul with a qualified assertion: "The circumstances of David's departure from court *might lead* to the suspicion that he shirked his responsibilities to Saul and deserted."[35] It is apparent from his summary, though, that McCarter has no doubt that the account of David's flight from Saul was composed for the illocutionary purpose of declaring David's undying loyalty to Saul:

> The narrator of the history of David's rise, however, takes special pains to show that David was forced to leave in order to save his life (1 Sam 19:9–17) and that he did so reluctantly, having first explored every possibility of remaining. In short, he was driven away from the place of his true loyalties by Saul's hostility (cf. 1 Sam 26:19). Moreover Saul's own daughter and his son, the crown prince, saw the rightness of David's side and aided his escape (1 Sam 19:11–17; 20:1–21:1).[36]

My above discussion of the rhetorical effect of McCarter's own summary of HDR applies here as well: He focuses attention on selected details, and he presents them in a way that exudes certainty about their illocutionary force and perlocutionary aim, that is, that the author took special pains to compose these passages to prove David's innocence of any wrongdoing, to convince all of Israel to accept David as the rightful king, and to silence his critics.

Once again, it is easy to overlook how certain assumptions about what actually happened, or presuppositions external to the text, inform decisions about the illocutionary force and perlocutionary aims of the text. McCarter does not specify precisely how "[t]he circumstances of David's departure from court," or which circumstances, might have made people suspicious that David acted unfaithfully in Saul's court and eventually deserted him. On this point, McKenzie once again invokes the technique of "overstress":

> The stories in 1 Samuel 18–20 urge strongly that David was innocent of any intention to overthrow Saul. The modern reader "against the grain" is compelled by their "overstress" on this point to suppose precisely the opposite. I would speculate that the ultimate reason for Saul's pursuit of David was a failed coup attempt. All the ingredients were present. David had the power and the ambition to try to overthrow Saul. The biblical story admits that he was suspected of plotting to do just that. The apology protests so much

---

[35] McCarter, "The Apology of David," 500 [emphasis in original].
[36] Ibid.

against this accusation that one can hardly avoid the suspicion that there is something to it. Saul drove David out and sought to kill him because David had tried to overthrow Saul.[37]

It is clear from the biblical account, indeed, that there are several obvious points of contention for Saul: the love of Saul's children, Jonathan and Michal, for David;[38] the people's (particularly the singing women's) high praise and growing love for David;[39] David's apparent military strength as evidenced by his great success on the battlefield;[40] David's running to Samuel for refuge;[41] and David's absence from Saul's feast.[42] But McCarter and McKenzie cannot be referring solely to the circumstances that the narrative of HDR depicts.

Even McKenzie's statement above that "[t]he biblical story admits that he was suspected of plotting to [overthrow Saul]" is based not on any explicit "admission of suspicion," but rather on descriptions of Saul's "fear" and "awe" of David,[43] and on Saul's statement to Jonathan that "all the days that the son of Jesse lives on the earth, you and your kingdom will not be established."[44] Despite McKenzie's trust in the rationality of Saul's emotions and statements, the text admits of no such plot against Saul—to the contrary, the narrative demonstrates David's respect for YHWH's anointed on more than one occasion, as I point out below—and there is no clear indication in the text that Saul's fear and ill will against David were motivated by anything other than irrational jealousy and paranoia. McKenzie, in fact, appears to acknowledge this in a statement following directly upon the above quotation:

---

[37] McKenzie, *King David*, 87.

[38] 1 Sam 18:20, 27–29; 19:1–7, 11–17; 20; 22:8. Also see 1 Sam 18:1–4; 20:11–17, 23, 40–42; and 23:16–18, though McCarter excludes these from the original HDR.

[39] 1 Sam 18:6–8a, 16. As 1 Sam 21:11 indicates, David's acclaim had even spread among Israel's enemies.

[40] As we have seen in ch. 1, McCarter thinks that some battle account in which David is victorious underlies the story of David's defeat of the Philistine champion in 1 Samuel 17, but he does not attempt to reconstruct it. First Samuel 18:6 apparently picks up where the original account left off, in McCarter's view. See, therefore, 1 Sam 18:6–8a, 9, 12, 13–16, 27–29.

[41] 1 Sam 19:18–24. Though McCarter attributes all of David's interaction with Samuel to the prophetic historian, as we have seen, he does not do so with David's interaction with the prophet Gad in 1 Sam 22:5.

[42] 1 Samuel 20[HDR].

[43] 1 Sam 18:12a, 15, 29a.

[44] 1 Sam 20:31.

This is a radical suggestion, and impossible to prove. But it would account for the events the Bible describes as well as the vehemence of its apologetic denial of such a charge.[45]

Not only is McKenzie's claim that David attempted a coup "a radical suggestion" and "impossible to prove," so is his claim that the biblical account is "vehemently" responding with an "apologetic denial of such a charge."

It is one thing to observe, for example, that Jonathan's attempts to turn Saul's heart back toward David show that David would have preferred to remain in Saul's service. But it is quite another thing to determine, in light of what one thinks is more likely to have really happened, that the narrator's primary message and aim, that is, the illocutionary force and perlocutionary aim of the narrative, are chiefly to declare and prove that David was not a willful deserter or an insurgent. Or, to give another example, it is important to observe that throughout the course of the narrative David exhibits his high esteem and respect for "YHWH's anointed": David does not take up arms against Saul when Saul first tries to kill him in 1 Samuel 18–20[HDR], when Saul murders in cold blood those who have assisted David in 1 Samuel 22, when Saul pursues him in 1 Samuel 23–26[HDR] (especially here, where David spares Saul's life though he has the opportunity and is urged by his men to kill him),[46] and when the Philistines march against king Saul's army in 1 Samuel 29, 31. Also, in 2 Samuel 1, David responds to the news of Saul's death with a public lament, and he executes the man who claims to have killed Saul. But far more information than the narrative itself provides is needed to interpret the illocutionary force of these accounts as a vehement denial of an unstated charge of sedition. The latter determination requires going beyond (or behind, as it were) the narrative of HDR to the historical events themselves. Only in the face of certitude about the hypothetical historical situation that McCarter, McKenzie, and others have posited can the positive portrayal of David vis-à-vis YHWH's anointed in the biblical account be characterized as a vehement apologetic denial.

---

[45] McKenzie, *King David*, 87–88.

[46] Characteristically confident in his assessment of the real David, regarding the portrayal of David's reverence for the anointed of YHWH, McKenzie later states: "It goes without saying, in light of their apologetic nature, that the value of these two chapters [1 Samuel 24 and 26] for historical reconstruction is virtually nil. It is extremely unlikely that David ever found himself with any such advantage over Saul. Indeed, the historical David would doubtless have taken advantage of the opportunity to kill Saul had it been presented to him" (ibid., 96).

Apart from the unearthing of new textual evidence from David's or Saul's courts, we will never be able to state with absolute certainty the originally intended illocutionary force and perlocutionary aims of HDR, if then. My aim here is to show that, without assumptions or theories about "what actually happened," the actual locutions contained in McCarter's reconstructed HDR (not to mention the biblical text) do not require that we read it as a rhetorically charged apology that is closely parallel to the Apology of Ḥattušili and the like. If we suspend the presupposition that what the historical David would have needed from a history of his ascension to an unrelated neighbor's throne is a positively spun defense, then we can begin to recognize other possible illocutionary meanings and perlocutionary aims for the biblical text, which has been identified as essentially the equivalent of HDR. It is plausible, then, as we will see in the following chapters, that herein might be seen a dramatic statement to the people of YHWH about the belovedness of His elect.

3) David Was an Outlaw

McCarter essentially argues that the illocutionary force of 1 Samuel 20–30[HDR 47] is to portray David as remaining loyal to his king and countrymen even when he served as a fugitive commander over hundreds of men, many of whom were transparently "wicked and worthless men" (אִישׁ־רָע וּבְלִיַּעַל)[48] and, thus, true outlaws. He maintains that because the narrator could not erase the memory of David as an outlaw leading outlaws, the narrator spun it in the best light he could. In McCarter's view, then, there is only one conceivable explanation for the inclusion of the extended narrative in 1 Samuel 20–30[HDR]. David's life as an outlaw had disturbed some, perhaps many:

> The fact that David was known to have spent part of his life as leader of a band of outlaws—a fact that, we must assume, was too well known to be suppressed—would surely have inspired public disapprobation. The narrator is careful to show, however, that David at that time was a fugitive from Saul's unjust pursuit and that he earnestly

---

[47] McCarter's 1 Samuel 20–30[HDR] includes: 1 Sam 20:1–10, 18–22, 24–39; all of chs. 21–22; 23:1–13; 25:1b–27, 32–44; all of chs. 26–27; 28:1–10, 12b–13, 21–25 (an anonymous apparition appeared in the place of Samuel in the original version); all of chs. 29–30.

[48] 1 Sam 30:22; also see 1 Sam 22:2.

sought reconciliation (cf. 1 Sam 26:18–20). Saul even recognized this state of affairs himself in his rare lucid moments (v 21).[49]

It is quite evident that McCarter determines the illocutionary force of the account based on his assumptions regarding the historical fact of David's life as an outlaw among outlaws. In the locutions that describe David's heroic attempts to rescue, aid, and prosper his fellow Judahites and be reconciled to Saul at the same time, McCarter discerns a perlocutionary aim that is fundamentally apologetic: to repair David's all-too-well-known reputation as a renegade among renegades. He states that this "fact" of David's past "would surely have inspired public disapprobation," which is what forced the hand of the narrator to come to David's defense. Underlying this certainty that the public must have disapproved of David's outlaw days is the assumption that the historical public had no cause to believe that the historical David might have any good or legitimate reason for living the life of an outlaw.[50] This is also the obvious implication behind McCarter's and many other critics' assumption that the narrator would have "suppressed" mention of this part of David's life if it were not so widely known already.

In keeping with this logic, one might assert, in a similar fashion, that Joseph's experiences in "the pit" and in an Egyptian prison[51] were "too well known to be suppressed" and "would surely have inspired public disapprobation"; the "vehemence of its apologetic denial" that Joseph committed any crime worthy of such treatment suggests that he was guilty, but the narrator has recast suspicion, instead, on his brothers and Potiphar by characterizing them as unjust. Most biblical scholars would recognize that this misses the point of the narrative of Joseph's suffering.[52] There is a strong interest throughout biblical literature in the fate of figures and groups who flee from someone or something (e.g., famine) and/or who are exiled or displaced, sometimes

---

[49] McCarter, "The Apology of David," 500.

[50] McKenzie's view of the true nature of David's days on the run from Saul is clear in the title of the chapter in which he discusses it: "Holy Terrorist: David and His Outlaw Band," in *King David*, 89–110. Earlier in his book, McKenzie compares David to Saddam Hussein: "Both were clever politicians and military commanders. Both led outlaw bands that rivaled the ruling family. Both eventually replaced their rivals, leaving a trail of dead bodies behind. Both gained and retained power through military force" (ibid., 22). Also see VanderKam, "Davidic Complicity," 524; Halpern, *David's Secret Demons*, 284–87.

[51] Gen 37:24–28; 39:20–41:14.

[52] On this, see "The Beloved Son as Ruler and Servant," in Levenson, *Death and Resurrection*, 143–69; Anderson, "Joseph."

temporarily and sometimes permanently, and who often increase in wealth and strength during their time abroad. Some of the variations of this theme or "type scene"[53] include Adam and Eve's expulsion from Eden; Cain's life as "a fugitive and a wanderer on the earth"; Abram's flight from Canaan into Egypt, and later into Gerar; Lot's escape from Sodom; Isaac's sojourn in Gerar; Jacob's flight from Esau and, later, his leaving Laban; Jacob and his family's flight from famine into Egypt; Moses' flight from Pharaoh into the land of Midian; Samson's sojourn among the Philistines; David's flight from Absalom; Absalom's flight from David to the king of Geshur; Shimei's servants' flight to King Achish; Jeroboam's flight from Solomon to King Shishak; Elijah's flight from Ahab; and Jonah's flight from God.

Because scholars have more solid bases for approaching David's story in light of historical questions and assumptions than, for example, those of the patriarchs, "history" plays a far greater role in informing their assessment of the text's meaning (that is, its illocutionary forces and perlocutionary aims). In the present case of David, however, it is not self-evident from the text itself that David's flight from Saul and his life in exile, even in service of a foreign king, were utterly shameful and best forgotten, or that this account was originally evoked by his need for personal justification and redemption of his character because it could not be forgotten. To the contrary, the author allots an inordinately large amount of space to this period in David's life, and later editors, by McCarter's count, add even more. Indeed, it is quite remarkable that, whereas McCarter and many other scholars assume that David's life as a fugitive outlaw must have been an acute embarrassment that, in the end, the Davidic court's spinners could not fix completely, this account of David's suffering as a fugitive from Saul's unjust pursuit preoccupied the author of HDR, and particularly the editors of the books of Samuel and Psalms, more, perhaps, than any other story.

---

[53] Drawing from the concept of "type-scenes" in Homer scholarship, Alter (*The Art of Biblical Narrative*, 51) describes Biblical type-scenes as "a series of recurrent narrative episodes attached to the careers of biblical heroes that are analogous to Homeric type-scenes in that they are dependent on the manipulation of a fixed constellation of predetermined motifs. Since biblical narrative characteristically catches its protagonists only at the critical and revealing points in their lives, the biblical type-scene occurs not in the rituals of daily existence but at the crucial junctures in the lives of the heroes, from conception and birth to betrothal to deathbed."

4) David Was a Philistine Mercenary

In depicting David's Philistine sojourn, according to McCarter, the primary illocutionary force of 1 Samuel 27–30[HDR 54] is to characterize David as ever loyal to Saul and Israel-Judah—and all the while undermining Philistine interests—during his exile in the land of the Philistines and his "service" under Achish. Again, this was done specifically to recast David's prior loyalties and deeds in a manner as unobjectionable—even favorable—as possible. The problem here is similar to the one discussed immediately above. Here, McCarter assumes that the narrator's hand has been forced by widespread knowledge of, and objections to, David's service to the Philistine King Achish:

> The public knowledge that David had served in the army of a king of the Philistines, Israel's most hated foe, would certainly have provoked objections. Again this must have been too widely known to be denied. The narrative, however, makes it clear that David was forced into Philistine service as a desperate last resort. . . . It is scrupulously shown, moreover, that while he was in the Philistine army, he never led his troops against any Israelite or Judahite city, though he deceived Achish of Gath, his lord, into thinking so (1 Sam 27:8–12). Indeed he took advantage of the power of his position to attack Israel's enemies and thereby to enrich Judah (1 Samuel 30).[55]

Again, presumed historical realities external to the text inform McCarter's determination of its illocutionary force. McCarter assumes that David's court would have altogether denied his past fraternizing with the Philistines if it could have done so credibly. McKenzie, likewise, states that David's Philistine service "was a great embarrassment to the writer of David's apology."[56] But because David's court could not deny this, it made the best it could of potentially damning circumstances and, for example, showed how David made fools of the Philistines. As in the case with the third charge, above, this assessment implies that David did, in fact, do something wrong by the people's standard (at least in the estimation of those among whom it

---

[54] See p. 115 n. 47, above.

[55] McCarter, "The Apology of David," 500.

[56] McKenzie, *King David*, 107. It would have been a "great embarrassment" in McKenzie's view because he concludes that "it is historically doubtful that David maintained his loyalty to Saul" (ibid., 114).

"would certainly have provoked objections"[57]) and that 1 Samuel 27–30[HDR] was composed only out of necessity to interpret in David's favor, as much as possible, the suspect nature of his prior loyalties and deeds. The illocutionary force, or the message, of the account of David's sojourn in Philistia, then, functions primarily, if not solely, as a declaration that he was not disloyal despite all appearances.

It is not my aim to argue that this rather ingenious interpretation of what the text is really about is implausible as an explanatory theory. My argument, rather, is that the text, or locutions, of HDR itself does not require this interpretation; this explanation makes sense only after the introduction of the historical assumptions that I have pointed out. In fact, in light of the prevalence of the biblical theme of personal flight from danger, exile, and even service under foreign authority-figures, some of whom were also Philistines, such as we have seen above, it is strange that McCarter and others so easily assume the worst about David's true motivations and reasons for serving under Achish—none of which they think could have been legitimate in the eyes of the people—and then give those assumptions primacy in formulating the real meaning and purpose, the illocutionary force and perlocutionary aim, of the account of David's Philistine sojourn and service. It is highly conceivable, however, as I have already argued, that the author(s)/editor(s) of these accounts, at any stage in their literary history, might have enthusiastically included this account of David's exile from the land of Judah/Israel and to a foreign king.

5–7) David Was Implicated in Saul's, Abner's, and Ishbaal's Deaths

McCarter's final three assessments of HDR's illocutionary force, which relate to the untimely deaths of Saul and his three sons on Mount Gilboa, Abner, and Ishbaal, can be grouped and discussed together. First, with regard to Saul's death, in McCarter's view 1 Samuel 29 recounts the story of Achish leaving David behind as an alibi for the purpose of proving that David had nothing to do with the deaths of Saul and his sons, as many people must have suspected. David's show of respect for the anointed of YHWH in 1 Samuel 26 and 2 Samuel 1 underscore this, according to him. Second, 2 Samuel

---

[57] McCarter, "The Apology of David," 493. Also see, e.g., Halpern, *David's Secret Demons*, 287–94, where he concludes that David colluded with the Philistines.

2–3[HDR] [58] tell why and how Joab eventually killed Abner, though the latter had entered into David's service, so as to exonerate David from the abounding accusations against him. Third, 2 Samuel 4 gives account of the treacherous assassination of Ishbaal by his own men as yet another alibi for David, who stood to gain the most from his death and, thus, must have been accused by many as having played an indirect or direct role in it.

McCarter draws his assumption that David needed "an apology in the sense defined by Hoffner"—that is, "a document composed for a king who had usurped the throne, composed in order to defend or justify his assumption of the kingship by force"[59]—from the "principle of *cui bono*." The "principle of *cui bono*" refers to the observation that David personally benefited and was propelled in his rise to the throne by the deaths of certain human obstacles. Regarding Saul's death, McCarter asserts:

> *Some must have suspected*, if only on the ground of *cui bono*, that David was involved in the demise of his predecessor.[60]

Likewise regarding Abner's death:

> *Suspicion must have fallen* on David in regard to the death of Abner, inasmuch as it was he who set Ishbaal on his father's throne (2

---

[58] According to McCarter, 2 Samuel 2–3[HDR] includes: 2 Sam 2:1–9, 12–32; 3:1–8, 11–18a, 19–39.

[59] See p. 39 n. 92, above.

[60] McCarter, "The Apology of David," 500 [emphasis in original]. The full quotation from McCarter (ibid., 500–1) reads:

> Some must have suspected, if only on the ground of *cui bono*, that David was involved in the demise of his predecessor, especially since Saul died fighting against the Philistines at a time when David was in the Philistine army. Indeed the forces of Achish were known, it seems, to have participated in the battle of Mount Gilboa (cf. 1 Sam 29:1–2)! Nevertheless, David was not, we are told, with Achish at Gilboa (1 Sam 29:11), and it is subtly but clearly implied that if he had been, he would have fought *with* [emphasis in original] Saul rather than against him. In 1 Sam 29:8, having been told by Achish that he must quit the march north, David expresses a wish to "go out and fight against the enemies of my lord, the king." Though Achish assumes the reference is to him, the irony is not lost on the audience. Elsewhere in the story, moreover, David is shown to have been fastidious about the sanctity of the person of Saul, the anointed of Yahweh, refusing an opportunity to slay him when it is offered (1 Samuel 26) and strictly punishing the violator of his person (2 Sam 1:14–16).

Sam 2:8–9) and *seemed, therefore, to have been the major obstacle to David's kingship over the northern tribes.*[61]

And, finally, also concerning Ishbaal's death:

> As in the cases of the deaths of Saul and Abner, David *must have been suspected* of treachery in the murder of Ishbaal.[62]

With Abner gone, Ishbaal was the last significant human obstacle to David's reign over a united Israel-Judah, and his murder came at an opportune moment for David. McCarter presumes, therefore, that many among David's

---

[61] Ibid., 501 [emphasis added]. McCarter's full passage (ibid., 501) on David's suspected complicity in Abner's murder reads:

> Suspicion must have fallen on David in regard to the death of Abner, inasmuch as it was he who set Ishbaal on his father's throne (2 Sam 2:8–9) and seemed, therefore, to have been the major obstacle to David's kingship over the northern tribes. The narrative shows, however, that David and Abner had reached an accord before the latter's death, inasmuch as Abner, having quarreled with Ishbaal (2 Sam 3:7–11), had actually begun to champion David's cause in the north (vv 17–18) and had offered him the kingship of Israel (v 21a). In particular we are informed three times (!) that after their last interview Abner left David "in peace" (vv 21b, 22, 23). In other words, the narrator means to show us that here as in the previous cases suspicion of David is groundless. Instead Abner died in consequence of a private quarrel with Joab, David's commander-in-chief (2 Sam 2:12–32; 3:22–30), and David knew nothing, as we are explicitly advised in 2 Sam 3:26b, of the deception that finally cost Abner his life. When he learned of Abner's death, we are told, David declared, "I and my kingship are innocent before Yahweh forever of the blood of Abner, son of Ner!" (2 Sam 3:28). Furthermore, he pronounced a curse upon Joab's house (v 29) and led the mourning for Abner himself (vv 31–35), much to the approval of the people (v 36). "All the people and all Israel knew at that time," says our narrator (v 37), "that it had not been the king's will (*kî lōʾ hāyĕtâ mēhammelek*) to kill Abner, the son of Ner."

[62] Ibid. [emphasis added]. And finally, regarding the seventh charge that McCarter detects (ibid., 501–2):

> As in the cases of the deaths of Saul and Abner, David must have been suspected of treachery in the murder of Ishbaal. The narrative shows, however, that Ishbaal was slain without David's knowledge by a pair of Benjaminites (2 Sam 4:2–3), opportunists who hoped to gain David's favor by taking the life of their master (vv 5–8). But David was not pleased by the news and indignantly condemned the assassins to death (vv 9–12a). It was David, moreover, who arranged for the honorable burial of Ishbaal's remains.

contemporaries would have naturally suspected him of having some hand in the deaths of Saul (and presumably his sons, including Jonathan), Abner, and Ishbaal, if only because of the personal convenience and benefit that David derived from the removal of these "obstacles" to his kingship over a united kingdom. McKenzie and Halpern go beyond McCarter, who is definitive only with regard to the presence of suspicion of David, and argue that the historical meaning of this apologetic text is that David was an "assassin," or a "serial killer."[63]

If these conclusions were based solely on a reading of the text, it would be a curious thing to speak of these various figures as obstacles to David, at least in the sense that McCarter implies. That is, at work in his reading is the fundamental assumption that David aspired to be king and was determined to do what was necessary to attain the throne. Within the realm of the narrative, it is not problematic, of course, to ascribe some royal aspirations to David, or even to recognize his willingness to act in ways that are beneficial to him and his family, followers, and countrymen. The thrust of HDR's account, and of the present biblical account even more so, however, is that it is first and foremost YHWH who aspires, and acts providentially, to seat David on the throne.

It is simplistic, therefore, to assert the principle of *cui bono* as the chief impetus or evocation of these accounts. Many benefited in various ways from the deaths recounted in the narrative. V. Philips Long succinctly states this problem with the above interpretation:

> Quite apart from the serious question whether such a principle [of *cui bono*] assumes a far too mechanistic view of historical occurrence, it is doubtful in any case how often the application of the rule of *cui bono* would isolate David as the prime suspect. After all, the Philistines benefited from Saul's death on Mount Gilboa, Ishbaal's assassins hoped to benefit from his death, Joab benefited (emotionally and politically) from Amnon's death. This review leaves only the cases of Nabal and Uriah. The biblical narrators make no attempt to hide David's culpability for the death of Uriah, and why they would go out of their way to provide David with an alibi in the death of the brutish Nabal is difficult to see, when they apparently

---

[63] So McKenzie (*King David*, 111–27) aptly titles his chapter on David's career in 2 Samuel 2–5 "Assassin." Halpern (*David's Secret Demons*, 73–103), likewise, calls one of his chapters "King David, Serial Killer." See also, e.g., VanderKam, "Davidic Complicity," and p. 75 n. 93, above.

felt no compunction about recording David's violent excursions into the countryside—"leaving neither man nor woman alive" (1 Sam. 29:9ff.)—while sojourning in Ziklag. One could still claim that the common benefactor in all the deaths was David, but even this claim would be open to challenge with respect to Abner, Amasa, Amnon, and perhaps others. *The point is that nothing is innately implausible in the biblical ascription of motive and means with respect to each death.*[64]

Some readers will undoubtedly take this discussion as an attempt to whitewash David and retort that it is further proof of the Davidic apology's effectiveness at convincing readers—modern as well as ancient ones—of David's innocence. But that would miss the point of my discussion here. My central focus is not the question of whether the historical David was, to put it simply, good or bad. My purpose, rather, is to show how the privileging of certain historical concerns and assumptions has resulted in claims for meanings and aims—both illocutions and perlocutions—that are not only not self-evident, but that also downplay or miss altogether other probable meanings and aims of the account and even run counter to the narrative's emphasis that YHWH and His people ultimately benefited from the recounting of these events.[65] This requires further discussion of the question of whether the narrative's primary, or even only, purpose is to refute implied charges and allay suspicion of David's complicity.

The discussion becomes more complicated when we turn to consider the question of whether, on textual grounds, we can assert that the sole or chief illocutionary force of HDR each time a significant figure dies is to declare David's innocence, not simply within the narrative world but to the implied readers of the account. It will be helpful to focus on the account surrounding the death of Abner because, of the three accounts mentioned above, it appears to pose the greatest challenge to my argument: It is the only one of the three that is explicitly concerned with establishing David's innocence within the narrative world. The narrator reports twice, and the servants of

---

[64] Provan, Long, and Longman, *A Biblical History of Israel*, 220–21 [emphasis added].

[65] The question of precisely how they benefited goes beyond the removal of "obstacles" to David. For example, it might be argued that YHWH's word of judgment against Saul proved true in his fate, and that the people of Israel benefited by "witnessing" that. Or, for example, it might be argued that the people benefited in various ways by "witnessing" the treachery and immediate or eventual judgment against Abner's and Ishbaal's murderers.

David once, that Abner "went in peace" (וַיֵּלֶךְ בְּשָׁלוֹם).[66] Joab hears of this and—unbeknownst to David—has Abner brought back to Hebron, where Joab murders Abner to avenge the death of his brother, Asahel. When David discovers this, he swears on behalf of his own innocence and against Joab and his father's house:

> Later, when David heard about it, he said, "Forever innocent before YHWH am I and my kingdom from the blood of Abner son of Ner. May [this guilt] fall on Joab's head, and on his father's entire house. May there never cease to be, from Joab's house, one with a discharge, one with a skin disease, one who holds the spindle, one who falls by the sword, and one who lacks bread."[67]

David then leads the people in lamenting for Abner, and he swears that he will fast until sundown. According to the narrator, David's lamenting and fasting had a powerful effect on "all the people":

> All the people acknowledged [David's words and/or actions], and it was pleasing in their eyes, just as all that the king did was good in the eyes of all the people. Then all the people, and all Israel, knew on that day that [the order] to kill Abner son of Ner was not from the king.[68]

David further praises and laments over Abner—"And the king said to his servants, 'Do you not know that a commander, and a great one, has fallen today in Israel?'"—and once again decries "the evil" of "the sons of Zeruiah."[69]

Leaving the illocutionary force of this account aside for the moment, at the locutionary level—that is, in the actual words and sentences of the account—both David and the narrator explicitly assert that David played no role in the murder of Abner.[70] Among other things, this account portrays a David who is genuinely fearful within the narrative world that this turn of events might be held against him, and who wishes to exonerate himself from having had any part in such a treacherous and grievous act. In other words, within the

---

[66] 2 Sam 3:21–23.
[67] 2 Sam 3:28–29.
[68] 2 Sam 3:36–37.
[69] 2 Sam 3:38–39.
[70] By David in 2 Sam 3:28, and by the narrator in 3:37.

narrative world, the depiction and establishment of David's innocence vis-à-vis a treacherous and grievous deed in Israel is an explicitly critical element in the larger story of David's becoming king over Israel as well as Judah. Here we have, then, a transparent apology made both by David and on David's behalf. But here, too, arises an interesting problem. The narrative—in the reported speech of David and in the words of the narrator—defends David's innocence too transparently, in fact, to be characterized as the same sort of rhetorical posturing that McCarter perceives in the responses to the other putative charges. That is, this is the only obvious instance in the seven charges that McCarter has enumerated where an explicit apology of sorts is made by and/or for David within the narrative world. In all the other cases, the apology is not found explicitly functioning at the locutionary level inside the narrative world. According to McCarter and many others, rather, the account itself functioned as an apology outside the narrative world.[71]

This brings me back to the question of whether the illocutionary force of this account of Abner's death boils down to the denial of implied charges against the historical David (or possibly one of his descendants) by demonstrating his innocence. Stated differently, is its perlocutionary aim to allay suspicion towards David in the real world as part of the effort to win more supporters for David and silence all his detractors?

After enumerating the seven "charges" that he has detected, McCarter states that "[s]ome or all of these charges must actually have been made during David's lifetime. The issues they raise concern his personal behavior and would have been liveliest during his own reign."[72] This claim, together with his preceding discussion, demonstrates something of the extent to which his conclusions about the text are undergirded by historical considerations, that is, in terms of how the narrative relates to what actually happened. Essentially, he is asserting that this account only makes sense when taken as addressing the historical David's own "personal behavior."[73] McCarter's

---

[71] McCarter ("The Apology of David," 499) acknowledges the distinctively explicit nature of the report of Abner's death.

[72] Ibid., 502.

[73] Similarly, McKenzie sides with those scholars who "suggest that these source documents were written during or shortly after David's reign. They point out that accusations listed earlier were against David personally, not his dynasty. These would have been controversial only during David's lifetime or shortly afterward, and an apologetic response would have been unnecessary after he had been dead for several generations and his dynasty firmly established" (*King David*, 35).

theory for HDR's historical setting and function is attractive, among other reasons, because it offers a plausible rationale for how the text makes sense in a particular, historical context.

With regard to these final three charges, however, there are unresolved questions if we interpret the narrative as answering to charges of murder, including regicide, that "would have been liveliest during his own reign." First, if these accounts were composed to counter charges against David for complicity in, or direct responsibility for, the deaths of Saul, Abner, and Ishbaal, it is extremely odd that the only explicit assertion of David's innocence—and one quite strenuous at that—is given in the face of Abner's murder, and not after the deaths of YHWH's anointed or his rightful heirs (including Saul's sons killed at Gilboa and Ishbaal). Second, it begs the question of how the account continued to make sense as it was transmitted from generation to generation, when the issues of the historical David's life were no longer "lively." In fact, plausible illocutionary meanings in various contexts, including an original one in David's own lifetime, can also be formulated. For example, the accounts of the deaths of Abner and Ishbaal dramatically demonstrate the ongoing threat against God's elect from the treachery and lies of enemies, whether from within or without. When we bracket McCarter's assumptions about the historical David and how he actually rose to sit on Saul's throne, therefore, the illocutionary and perlocutionary possibilities that might be discerned behind the story of David's election and confirmation far exceed the need simply to prove David's innocence vis-à-vis certain charges.

Conclusion

One of the chief questions that so many interpreters (perhaps most interpreters, apart from newer literary critics) seem to be interested in asking and in attempting to answer is historical in nature: What really happened? That is, is "the History of David's Rise" a truthful account of how David came to power? Or, as VanderKam, McKenzie, and Halpern essentially characterize it, is it mostly a cover-up of a calculating, Saddam Hussein-like ancient Near Eastern tyrant who left in his rise to the throne a trail of corpses? These are deeply important questions, for it does matter whether or not there was a historical David and what really happened in his life and times. As should be fully clear by now, however, the present study is not yet another attempt to get at the events behind the text and reconstruct the "real" history of David's rise.

I have attempted to demonstrate, rather, how some scholars' determination of HDR's meaning is heavily informed by something in addition to a close reading of the text. And here we see the inevitably circular nature of the reasoning behind their conclusions. External assumptions and conclusions regarding HDR's original historical shape, context, and function, as well as assumptions about what really happened, lead McCarter, McKenzie, and others to read the locutions in HDR as ultimately defensive and amounting to apologetic posturing for the sake of an individual king. They generally assume that David usurped Saul's throne (that is, that he took it by force) and therefore needed to give some reasonable explanation for why the people should accept him as their legitimate king.[74] Their reading of the History of David's Rise as an exemplar of the genre of ancient Near Eastern royal apology composed to exonerate an individual king, therefore, becomes the interpretive key necessary for understanding and appreciating the original illocutionary force and perlocutionary aims that pertain to HDR's locutions. Furthermore, this determination that the illocutionary force of HDR's narratives is rhetorical posturing (in other words, that it is the *sotto voce* declaration that David is innocent of all detected charges) becomes an important part of the circumstantial evidence supporting the characterization or interpretation of HDR as an independent apology for an individual monarch. In short, among those who hold to this view, assumptions regarding HDR's function as a personal apology are critical for detecting and exposing with any certainty the sort of defensive or rhetorical posturing in the text that has been detected. Read in that light, the rhetorical posture of the text is "easily recognized" and appears so obvious that it seems to stand on its own. This obvious rhetorical character or posture, then, is taken to shore up prior observations and conclusions regarding the genre and historical function of HDR.

When we restrict our attention to the locutions of HDR and bracket these assumptions about the historical David, however, McCarter's assessment of HDR's illocutionary force and perlocutionary aims becomes far less compelling. His approach of determining the meaning and purpose of HDR largely on the basis of his many assumptions about the historical David and what really happened in his ascent to the throne still has some plausibility,

---

[74] Again, note that McCarter's position on the nature of David's usurpation is slightly nuanced compared to that of McKenzie and others (for example, see p. 122, above).

and it will undoubtedly remain attractive to interpreters whose primary interests lie in using the text as a window to what they would describe as the historical reality, persons, and events behind the text. We are now better positioned to recognize, however, that the highly favorable and positive portrayal of David that McCarter sees in HDR is not inexplicable apart from his suspicious reading, which rests on the exposé of underlying charges that might have evoked such a portrayal or characterization. There are, in fact, other equally plausible and sensible explanations of how this particular story of David's election and confirmation, in the midst of danger from all sides, might have been recounted and transmitted towards other ends.

CHAPTER 4

YHWH's Initial and Immediate Act of Finding, Choosing, and Providing Himself a King in the Person of David

In the preceding chapters, we have seen how, in searching for and determining the real purpose of the biblical narrative of David's rise to kingship, Kyle McCarter, Steven McKenzie, and others have detected, embedded within the Masoretic account, an originally independent "History of David's Rise" that they date to David's own lifetime. They conclude that someone close to David composed it as an apologetic account primarily, if not solely, to justify and legitimize David's usurpation of Saul's throne. In McCarter's estimation, the author refuted various charges against David of personal wrong-doing, including lese-majesty, while simultaneously demonstrating David's ability to act as king, his loyalty to Saul, his blamelessness before Saul, and his favor with YHWH. In short, the purpose of the account, according to this view, was to silence any accusers and to convince the rest of the people that David was the right individual to assume Saul's throne and reign as their king. Inasmuch as this reading is planted firmly in the *res*, or "stuff," of an easily imaginable and reconstructable history, it offers a reasonable account for various features of an original History of David's Rise.

It is important to recognize, however, that scholars have based their assumptions and conclusions about the text's true meaning—that the narrative is posturing (deceitfully or not) to defend the historical David from implied allegations and, simultaneously, to prove his fitness to be king—upon more than merely a close reading of the text. As we have seen above, especially in chapters 2 and 3, certain predetermined assumptions about what really happened, human nature, and so on, contribute significantly to this particular construal of the account's meaning and purpose, however reasonable it may be. This is true even if one concludes, with McCarter, that the narrative makes it "clear that David's rise to power was made possible, indeed inevitable, by the special favor of the god of Israel, 'Yahweh is with him' being . . . the leitmotif of the entire composition."[1] For if one assumes that the account's original readers approached it in search of justification that David was, contrary to some contemporary claim, fit to be king, then YHWH's election of and presence with David constitute one of no less than five legitimizing themes identified by McCarter. These are:

1) David's capability to lead and wage war
2) David's service to Saul's house, and the royal house's display of loyalty to David
3) David's absolute loyalty to Saul and passivity concerning the accrual of power
4) David's blamelessness and moral rectitude before Saul
5) David's receiving the divine mandate and assistance[2]

According to this reading, which looks to the Apology of Ḫattušili for corroboration, all of these narrative themes become essential elements in the refutation of presumed accusations against David, and, at the same time, evidence of David's fitness to be king. I do not mean to suggest that McCarter and others dismiss or even downplay data that attribute the king's success to divine favor. Indeed, they treat appeals and other references to divine favor and causation as extremely important for what they reveal about how ancient Near Eastern kings such as David and Ḫattušili justified their usurpations. It is important to note, too, that whereas some reduce the claims of divine election and favor to the level of base fabrication or religious charlatanry,[3] others such as McCarter refrain from passing such judgments. Whatever the case, the purpose of the account's depiction of YHWH's election of and presence

---

[1] McCarter, "The Apology of David," 499.

[2] My summary of McCarter's enumeration of HDR's five major themes; see p. 42, above, for more detail.

[3] We have seen several examples of this already in the preceding chapters, in the numerous quotations from McKenzie, *King David*; Halpern, *David's Secret Demons*; Brettler, *The Creation of History*; and VanderKam, "Davidic Complicity."

with David, in this reading, are identified, first and foremost, in terms of their rhetorical function, together with other legitimizing acts of rhetoric, to protect and bolster the power base of King David. That is, in this approach, the depictions of YHWH's dealings with David in the biblical account find their meaning largely exhausted in their capacity to contribute to the personal self-justification of David.

It has been important for the sake of my argument until now to limit my reconsideration of the significance of the story of David's rise almost entirely to a reconstructed, independent version in which it is thought by some to have originally existed. By doing so, I have been able to uncover many problematic assumptions and conclusions of this approach, and to demonstrate that the approach fails in numerous respects to make sense of the biblical account even in the original and independent literary stage that McCarter has reconstructed and dated to David's own lifetime. There is no longer a compelling reason to interpret the account of David's rise in terms of the ostensible meaning of a putatively original source presumed to have been composed independently of the surrounding narrative. The validity of the assumptions and propositions supporting its detection and subsequent interpretation is dubious at best, as I have argued extensively in the preceding chapters. It is time, therefore, to shift our attention from the hypothetically reconstructed text of HDR to the story of David's rise to kingship in its present biblical shape.[4] Inasmuch as I shall center my discussion in this chapter around YHWH's initial election of David, and in the following chapter around YHWH's confirmation of David as His elect, I shall focus chiefly upon the narrative in 1 Samuel 13–31. As my exposition from this point forward will demonstrate, and as I have indicated at several points already, the extended account of Saul and David as transmitted in the books of Samuel—including 1 Samuel 13–31 but also extending beyond—exhibits enough of a literary coherence to warrant its analysis as an integrated and coherent account.

We should begin by recognizing the special importance of the narrative prior to David's enlisting in Saul's service—that is, the accounts of Saul's election, reign, and rejection, and, in particular, of Samuel's visit to Bethlehem to find and anoint a new king for YHWH—for properly appreciating the significance of the larger account. As we shall see in considerable detail, the narratives leading up to David's anointing establish YHWH's election of and presence with David as the primary basis of, and essential means by which,

---

[4] See my discussion of my approach to the Hebrew text on pp. 6–11, above.

David rises to his royal office, and not simply as one of several legitimizing motifs, even if deemed to be the most important of those. Nearly everything that happens to David in the biblical narrative is conceived as being the consequence of YHWH's prior determination and act. First, therefore, I shall discuss the nature and significance of YHWH's initial election of David in terms of His "finding," "choosing," and "providing" Himself a new king in the person of David. YHWH's initial act of election, then, initiates the finding, choosing, and providing of and for David by YHWH's people. Then, in the following chapter, while concentrating primarily on the biblical account leading up to the deaths of Saul and his sons in 1 Samuel 31, I shall argue that YHWH's election of David is confirmed or embodied in and through the gradual emergence of David as the beloved son of Jesse, the beloved son of Saul, and finally, the beloved son of YHWH and the people of Israel.[5]

YHWH's Immediate and Mediate Election of David

In order better to understand the nature of YHWH's election of David and the function of the various episodes recounted in the story of David's rise to kingship after his anointing, it is helpful to distinguish between YHWH's immediate election and mediate election of David in the biblical narrative. By "YHWH's immediate election" of David, I refer to that act of election that is attributed directly to YHWH by His own word, whether spoken via His prophet or by Himself.[6] The majority of studies that are concerned primarily with YHWH's election of David and the Davidic line in the books of Samuel are centered upon 2 Samuel 7.[7] The centrality of this passage for election theology in the Bible is widely recognized, and it is certainly an important example of YHWH's immediate election, for in this text the narrator, the prophet, and YHWH Himself all speak of YHWH's election and confirmation of David and his sons to reign forever. I am mostly interested, however, in a deeper understanding of

---

[5] I shall, of course, develop this theme more fully below. For now, I might simply note that my understanding of the "beloved son" motif in the Hebrew Bible is deeply informed by the following two works in particular: Levenson, *Death and Resurrection*; Anderson, "Joseph."

[6] Via the prophet in 1 Sam 13:14; 15:28; 28:17; and by YHWH Himself in 16:1, 12. See, too, the following, in which others essentially announce or declare YHWH's election of David: 1 Sam 25:28, 30; 2 Sam 3:9–10, 18; 5:2, 12.

[7] See discussion and bibliography, for example, in Gakuru, *An Inner-Biblical Exegetical Study*.

YHWH's initial act of election which thrusts David onto the scene and propels him on the road to kingship. In this chapter, therefore, I shall concentrate on the multivalent significance within the biblical narrative's larger context of YHWH's announcement to Samuel in 1 Sam 16:1 that "רָאִיתִי בְּבָנָיו לִי מֶלֶךְ" (literally, "I have seen among his sons a king for me"). The term most under question here is רָאִיתִי (literally, "I saw" or "I have seen"), which is translated variously as "I have found," "I have chosen," and "I have provided." I shall discuss, therefore, the merits of conceiving of YHWH's initial and immediate election of David in these various senses.

Next, I shall proceed with a discussion of YHWH's mediate election of David. I shall contend that the events surrounding David's anointing, his subsequent successes, and the responses by various and diverse figures confirmed, or mediated, YHWH's pre-determined election of David. While arguing that YHWH's immediate election of David is the basis of His mediate election of him, I recognize the possibility, of course, that ancient readers, not to mention the figures depicted in the narrative, would not have seen any significant distinction between the immediacy and mediacy of divine election, as I have characterized it. Be that as it may, I hope to demonstrate in the present study that the distinction is discernible and heuristically helpful for understanding the nature of David's election in the books of Samuel. Before I begin my inquiry into the nature of YHWH's immediate election of David, allow me to address in more detail the question of the timing of his election.

The Timing of YHWH's Election of David

Biblical commentators frequently depict Samuel's anointing of David in 1 Sam 16:1–13 as the moment of YHWH's election of David.[8] Inasmuch as the important event of 1 Sam 16:13—Samuel's anointing of David and the rushing

---

[8] See, e.g., McCarter, *I Samuel*, 277–78; Brueggemann, *First and Second Samuel*. On YHWH's declaration over David in 1 Sam 16:12, for instance, Brueggemann says, "Yahweh does a quick heart examination and renders the verdict, 'This is he'" (123). McCarter, as we have seen in the preceding chapters, attributes 1 Sam 16:1–13 to the prophetic historian and, therefore, assumes that it was unknown in the original HDR. In his view, it seems, this addition does not essentially change the interpretation of HDR but simply explains or makes more explicit from the beginning the leitmotif that "YHWH was with David." I shall demonstrate, however, that this account, together with the preceding accounts of Saul's rejection, has a far greater importance in the framing and reading of David's rise to kingship.

of YHWH's Spirit upon him—represents the first public confirmation of YHWH's election, it is certainly natural to conceive of the figures within the narrative world of the biblical account as identifying this as the moment of YHWH's election of David, whether they realize it at the time or only in retrospect.[9] One might argue, then, that readers should not make the sort of distinction that I have suggested above. Nevertheless, in the view of the readers of the biblical account, there is a moment of divine election that originated in the hidden but decisive will of YHWH that precedes Samuel's anointing of David. For that reason, I treat David's anointing as a confirmation, or manifestation, of YHWH's prior election.

King Saul's disobedience of YHWH's commandment and his rejection of YHWH's word in 1 Samuel 13 and 15 expose his unsuitability to reign over the people of Israel as YHWH's vicegerent.[10] YHWH "rejects" (מאס) Saul as king.[11] At the same time, upon declaring His rejection of Saul, YHWH also declares through His prophet that He "has appointed" (וַיְצַוֵּהוּ) "a man according to His heart,"[12] and, later, that He "has given" (וּנְתָנָהּ) the kingdom of Israel to a "neighbor" of Saul's better than he.[13] And finally, for the third time in the biblical narrative, but this time speaking directly in the first person, YHWH declares, "I have seen [רָאִיתִי] myself a king" among the sons of a certain Bethlehemite.[14] This last case occurs in the context of YHWH's reason for sending Samuel to Jesse the Bethlehemite. And although the phrase "רָאִיתִי בְּבָנָיו לִי מֶלֶךְ" has been rendered variously, all would appear to agree that YHWH's instructions to Samuel in 1 Sam 16:1 are based on something—whether a decision or certain act(s)—that has already occurred in the mind of YHWH. YHWH has, in some important sense, already elected David. It might be that the Hebrew phrasing allows for both past and future

---

[9] I shall return in ch. 5 to consider this and other questions related to the degree to which the events (and their significance) in 1 Sam 16:6–13 are publicized.

[10] On this topic, particularly on the issue of reading these chapters synchronically as part of a coherent narrative, see Long, *Reign and Rejection of King Saul.*

[11] On the language of YHWH's rejection of Saul, see 1 Sam 13:13–14; 15:22–29, 35; 16:1.

[12] 1 Sam 13:14. See p. 137 n. 24, below.

[13] 1 Sam 15:28.

[14] 1 Sam 16:1. I shall return to discuss the translation of רָאִיתִי in considerable depth below. Robert Alter explains the first-person form here, which stands in contrast to the earlier passages where YHWH's will is reported by Samuel, as achieving the effect that "God's judgments are rendered with perfect, authoritative transparency. Evidently the writer (or redactor) felt that the initial election of David had to be entirely unambiguous" (*The David Story*, 95).

dimensions in the statement, as the NJPS, for example, makes explicit with its translation, "I have [at some point in the past] decided on one of his sons to be king [at some point in the future]." But the Hebrew phrasing also allows for the possibility that the one that YHWH has "seen" is in some sense already king in YHWH's view, even if not yet in view of the people. This way of thinking about the chosen one becomes all the more conceivable when, a few verses later, Samuel says over Eliab: "Surely before YHWH is His anointed!" (אַךְ נֶגֶד יְהוָה מְשִׁיחוֹ).[15] It is possible, of course, that מְשִׁיחוֹ here simply means "the one who is to be anointed." But it seems more likely that in this context, the event that makes מְשִׁיחוֹ a true descriptor (or would have if Samuel had not misidentified מְשִׁיחוֹ) is the prior decision or act(s) of YHWH as much or more so than the ceremony that is to follow. Whatever the case, by the time YHWH sends Samuel the prophet to Bethlehem to anoint for Him the one whom He will declare to Samuel,[16] His decision is firmly made, even if suspense continues building over the identity of YHWH's king-elect.

Let us turn, now, to consider the nature of YHWH's initial and immediate election of David prior to His confirmation of that decision to others (though, from the first indication of His new election in 1 Samuel 13, He increasingly makes His will known to the prophet Samuel).

"I Have Seen Myself a King"

After reaffirming His rejection of Saul from reigning as king over Israel, YHWH issues this command to Samuel in 1 Sam 16:1: "Fill your horn with oil and go—I am sending you to Jesse the Bethlehemite." As I noted above, translations diverge significantly in their rendering of the last part of verse 1—כִּי־רָאִיתִי בְּבָנָיו לִי מֶלֶךְ—which is given as part of YHWH's motive for sending Samuel.[17] For example:

KJV: ". . . for I have provided me a king among his sons."

NRSV and ESV: ". . . for I have provided for myself a king among his sons."

NJPS: ". . . for I have decided on one of his sons to be king."

---

[15] 1 Sam 16:6.

[16] 1 Sam 16:1, 3.

[17] The other part of YHWH's reason is indicated at the beginning of v. 1: "I have rejected [Saul] from being king over Israel."

NIV: "I have chosen one of his sons to be king."

McCarter: ". . . for I have found me a king among Jesse's sons."[18]

YHWH's act of "seeing" (ראה) is translated and conceived variously in terms of "finding" (McCarter), "choosing" (NIV, NJPS), and "providing" (KJV, NRSV, ESV). Below, I shall argue that each of these translations captures and reflects certain aspects of YHWH's election of David as it is depicted in Samuel. The point of the discussion is not to determine the best English translation; rather, I offer this as a helpful way to approach three related yet different conceptual frameworks within which to think about the nature of YHWH's immediate election of David.[19]

"I Have Found Myself a King"

One construal of YHWH's words to Samuel in 1 Sam 16:1 is McCarter's translation of ראה in the sense of "to find": ". . . for I have found me a king among Jesse's sons."[20] Eugene Peterson also follows this sense and nicely communicates in English the visual way in which YHWH finds His king: "I've spotted the very king I want among his sons."[21] The term is used in this sense just a few verses later. When Saul's servants suggest in 1 Sam 16:16 that he command his servants to "seek [וְבַקְשׁוּ] a man who is skilled at playing the lyre," Saul responds in verse 17: רְאוּ־נָא לִי אִישׁ מֵיטִיב לְנַגֵּן וַהֲבִיאוֹתֶם אֵלָי. The NJPS and McCarter render רְאוּ־נָא לִי here as "Find me," and the NIV simply as "Find."[22] But does "find" or "find me" make sense in the context of 1 Sam 16:1? There are, in fact, warrants in the immediate and larger biblical contexts for conceiving of YHWH's election of David in terms of divine discovery, and thus we should recognize the possibility that YHWH's statement in 1 Sam 16:1 conveys the sense that He has "spotted" Saul's replacement among the sons of Jesse, presumably after conducting a search of sorts.

---

[18] McCarter, *I Samuel*, 273.

[19] This study will be a good example of how "information" from both the immediate and larger contexts informs differing interpretations that lead to various translations. Those interpretive and translation decisions, in turn, inform subsequent readings in other contexts, and so the hermeneutical circle continues.

[20] McCarter, *I Samuel*, 273.

[21] Peterson, *The Message*, at 1 Sam 16:1.

[22] 1 Sam 16:18 shows the difficulty of always using the same English term for the Hebrew. The servant who tells Saul about David replies: הִנֵּה רָאִיתִי בֵּן לְיִשַׁי בֵּית הַלַּחְמִי. In this case, רָאִיתִי should be rendered "I have seen."

Some of the warrants to which I am referring are to be found in other biblical depictions of YHWH's searching for and finding people. Later, 2 Chr 16:9 portrays YHWH as conducting an extensive search (כִּי יְהוָה עֵינָיו מְשֹׁטְטוֹת בְּכָל־הָאָרֶץ; "For YHWH's eyes range through the whole earth"), though for more general purposes, that is, in order "to strengthen those with their heart wholly toward him" (לְהִתְחַזֵּק עִם־לְבָבָם שָׁלֵם אֵלָיו). And specifically with regard to David, a psalmist has YHWH declaring outright: "I have found David, my servant" (מָצָאתִי דָּוִד עַבְדִּי).[23] Furthermore, the book of 1 Samuel portrays YHWH as one who searches and finds. When Samuel confronts Saul at Gilgal for breaking YHWH's commandment, he declares to him that YHWH will no longer establish his kingdom. Instead, he says in 1 Sam 13:14, "YHWH has sought [בִּקֵּשׁ] for Himself a man according to His heart."[24] It is implied here that YHWH found the sort of man for whom He had searched, for the second half of the verse states that "YHWH has appointed him [וַיְצַוֵּהוּ] ruler over His people." Also, note the structural parallel between Samuel's statement in 1 Sam 13:14 and YHWH's in 16:1 (find translations of both passages above):

Samuel (13:14):	בִּקֵּשׁ יְהוָה לוֹ אִישׁ כִּלְבָבוֹ
YHWH (16:1):	רָאִיתִי . . . לִי מֶלֶךְ

In each case, YHWH is the subject of a perfective verb that ascribes an action to and for Himself, as indicated by the prepositional constructions לְ/לִי/לוֹ, with the one who is to replace Saul as the object of the verb. This parallel structure suggests that Samuel and YHWH might be speaking about the same act—that is, YHWH's searching and finding for Himself someone to replace Saul as king.[25]

---

[23] Ps 89:21.

[24] See McCarter's alternative translation, "a man of his own choosing" (*I Samuel*, 225). McCarter argues that "the expression *klbb*, 'according to (one's) heart,' has to do with an individual's will or purpose. . . . The present passage, therefore, asserts the freedom of the divine will in choosing a new king in the spirit of the prophetic theology of leadership" (229).

[25] Verbal and thematic links such as this that span the sources thought to underlie the books of Samuel frustrate source-critical attempts to demarcate the sources definitively. Of course, because McCarter attributes both of these verses to the hand of his eighth-century prophetic historian, this particular case would not pose the problem for him that it might for others who attribute 1 Sam 16:1–13 to the HDR that they think was originally independent from the rest of Samuel. On this and other source-critical issues, see ch. 1, above.

YHWH's special interest in the heart is also seen in 1 Samuel 16, and this concern with the heart might support the portrayal of YHWH there as announcing that He has "found" Himself a king, as Samuel essentially announces in 1 Samuel 13. Having heard YHWH say "רָאִיתִי" a king among Jesse's sons, Samuel goes to Bethlehem to look for and find him. When he saw (וַיַּרְא) Eliab, he thought "surely" that he had found YHWH's anointed.[26] But immediately YHWH tells him:

> Do not look [אַל־תַּבֵּט] to his appearance [מַרְאֵהוּ] or to the height of his standing, because I have rejected him. For it is not that which man sees [יִרְאֶה] [that YHWH sees], because man sees the outward appearance [lit., "sees the eyes"; יִרְאֶה לַעֵינַיִם]. YHWH, however, sees the heart [יִרְאֶה לַלֵּבָב].[27]

Neither the narrator nor YHWH explicitly state in 1 Samuel 16 what it is about the heart that YHWH sees or looks for when deciding whom to reject and whom to choose. But when YHWH says to Samuel regarding David, when he has just been brought before Samuel, "Rise and anoint him, for this is he,"[28] the implication is that YHWH has seen—in the sense of "found"—what He was searching for in David's heart, but not in his brothers' hearts. It is easy to see, then, how this might (re)inform our reading of YHWH's announcement to Samuel at the beginning of chapter 16:

מַלֵּא קַרְנְךָ שֶׁמֶן וְלֵךְ אֶשְׁלָחֲךָ אֶל־יִשַׁי בֵּית־הַלַּחְמִי
כִּי־רָאִיתִי בְּבָנָיו לִי מֶלֶךְ:

YHWH sent Samuel to anoint David because there was something in or about the heart of this one among the many sons of Jesse, indeed, among all the sons of Israel, that YHWH saw or found to meet His good pleasure. If YHWH's announcement to Samuel in 1 Sam 16:1 can be understood in this way, it is more than a restatement of His findings initially reported in 1 Sam 13:14. There, Samuel (and Saul) learned only that YHWH had sought out and found someone else, namely, "a man according to His heart" (אִישׁ כִּלְבָבוֹ). In 1 Sam

---

[26] 1 Sam 16:6.
[27] 1 Sam 16:7.
[28] 1 Sam 16:12.

16:1, YHWH prepares to reveal the identity of the one He has seen or found: He is in Bethlehem, of the house of Jesse, "among his sons."[29]

In the end, "I have found" is not to be preferred as the English rendering of רָאִיתִי in 1 Sam 16:1 because, as we will see below, the term ראה in this context allows for and, indeed, suggests a multivalence that is closed off by the English verb "to find." Nevertheless, inasmuch as my aim is not primarily to determine the best translation but to understand better the varied ways in which the biblical text depicts YHWH's election of David, consideration of this particular translation is helpful, if merely on a provisional basis, for recognizing a significant aspect—YHWH's finding of David—in the language of election in 1 Samuel.

"I Have Chosen Myself a King"

The NJPS (with "I have decided on") and the NIV (with "I have chosen") render רָאִיתִי in the sense of "to choose" or "to select." What might account for this rather idiomatic and unusual translation of the verb ראה, which in its most basic sense means "to see"? First of all, at the sentence level in verse 1 there is an implicit contrastive sense drawn between David—whom we later discover to be the one that YHWH has "seen"—and the other sons of Jesse: רָאִיתִי בְּבָנָיו ("I have seen *among his sons*"). In some sense, YHWH has seen one among many sons. And whether or not this act of divine seeing is best rendered here as "I have decided on" or "I have chosen," YHWH's interaction with Samuel in Bethlehem, and Samuel's with Jesse, over Jesse's sons as they are paraded before the prophet one by one demonstrate that there is a particularistic sense to רָאִיתִי בְּבָנָיו. First, YHWH declares that He has "rejected" the firstborn (מְאַסְתִּיהוּ). Next, with regard to each of the second- and third-born sons, YHWH declares to Samuel, or Samuel declares to Jesse, "YHWH has not chosen this one either" (גַּם־בָּזֶה לֹא־בָחַר יְהוָה).[30] Then, after seeing each of Jesse's first seven sons, Samuel declares to him, "YHWH has not chosen these" (לֹא־בָחַר יְהוָה בָּאֵלֶּה).[31] Finally, then, when David appears before Samuel, YHWH tells Samuel, "Rise and anoint him, for this is he

---

[29] Between the pronouncement to Saul in 1 Sam 13:14 and YHWH's command to Samuel in 16:1, there is just one other reference to the one who will replace Saul—to a "neighbor" of Saul's in 1 Sam 15:28.

[30] 1 Sam 16:7, 8, 9. I shall return to address the question of the speaker's identity (or speakers' identities) in these verses in the next chapter.

[31] 1 Sam 16:10.

[כִּי־זֶה הוּא]."[32] YHWH has rejected the rest because He has chosen this one, as is implied by the negative declarations over David's brothers. From this distinction alone, drawn as it is between David and the rest of Jesse's sons, it is easy to see why the NJPS and the NIV translators emphasize the aspect of decision or choice in their interpretation of the nature of YHWH's act of seeing in 1 Sam 16:1.

David's brothers, however, are not the only ones whom YHWH rejects. YHWH's choice of David was precipitated, in the first place, by His rejection of Saul. YHWH's command in 1 Sam 16:1 for Samuel to fill his horn with oil and go to Jesse the Bethlehemite is enveloped between a negative and a positive reason for going. We have examined the positive reason: "because I have seen myself a king among his sons" (כִּי־רָאִיתִי בְּבָנָיו לִי מֶלֶךְ). But this is preceded by the negative reason that YHWH has "rejected [Saul] from being king over Israel" (וַאֲנִי מְאַסְתִּיו מִמְּלֹךְ עַל־יִשְׂרָאֵל).[33] Again, however we decide to render רָאִיתִי, we must recognize the implicit contrastive sense drawn here not only between David and his brothers, but also between David and Saul.

"I Have Provided Myself a King"

The majority of English Bible versions, including the KJV, the NRSV, and the ESV, agree in their translation of רָאִיתִי in 1 Sam 16:1 as "I have provided." There is significant textual justification beyond the verse in question for conceiving of YHWH's election of David in terms of His provision, and in more than one of the English term's related senses. The term "provide" might connote 1) the act or exercise of foresight, quite literally reflecting the Latin *providere*, from *pro*, "before in time," and *videre*, "to see" (largely obsolete today, though it was common at the time of the KJV translation); 2) the act of preparation, that is, "to prepare, get ready, or arrange (something) beforehand," or "to supply or furnish for use"; and 3) the act of equipping, that is, "to equip or fit out (a person, etc.) with what is necessary for a certain purpose."[34] Let us consider how YHWH's act of seeing (ראה) might

---

[32] 1 Sam 16:12.

[33] Also see 1 Sam 15:35, where it states that YHWH "regretted that He had made Saul king over Israel."

[34] See "provide, *v.*" in *OED Online* <http://dictionary.oed.com/cgi/entry/50191067>. Consider "providence," from the same root. In early usage, "providence" was used more generally than today for "[t]he action of providing; provision, preparation, arrangement"; and "[F]oresight, prevision; *esp.* [emphasis in original] anticipation of and preparation for the future; 'timely

be depicted and conceptualized in Samuel as His act of provision in these intersecting senses.

Perhaps the best example of how רָאָה is used to signify God's provision elsewhere in Scripture is seen in Gen 22:8, when Abraham tells Isaac, אֱלֹהִים יִרְאֶה־לּוֹ הַשֶּׂה. This is translated as "God will provide for himself the lamb" (ESV), "God himself will provide the lamb" (NRSV), "God will see to the sheep" (NJPS), and the like.[35] Putting aside the question of Abraham's own assumptions or expectations about how God might provide or see to the lamb,[36] the statement proves to be true: God provides or sees to the sacrificial offering presumably by 1) leading a ram to the appropriate spot;[37] 2) allowing Abraham to "see" it (וַיִּשָּׂא אַבְרָהָם אֶת־עֵינָיו וַיַּרְא) there at the appropriate moment; and 3) accepting the ram in place of Abraham's son, Isaac.[38] The animal is God's provision in a double sense. In the first sense, God has made the appropriate preparation beforehand so that, at the opportune moment, He might supply Abraham with the object that he needs (a ram) to carry out his assigned task. And in the second sense, the object of YHWH's provision is also the subject (that is, the means) of His provision to Abraham by virtue of its becoming the substitution for Isaac, his beloved son.

Apart from basic differences of tense and speaker, and the addition of a couple of elements in Gen 22:8, Abraham's reason to Isaac why there is no lamb and YHWH's reason to Samuel for going to Jesse the Bethlehemite are structured very similarly:

| Gen 22:8 | אֱלֹהִים יִרְאֶה־ לּוֹ הַשֶּׂה |
| 1 Sam 16:1 | וַיֹּאמֶר יְהוָה . . . רָאִיתִי בְּבָנָיו לִי מֶלֶךְ |

Based on these linguistic similarities, together with the larger context in 1 Samuel, it is reasonable to understand YHWH's announcement in 1 Sam 16:1—רָאִיתִי . . . לִי מֶלֶךְ—as meaning that here, too, in His foresight,

---

care' . . . hence, prudent or wise arrangement, management, government, or guidance." Today, of course, the term is most commonly employed to denote "[t]he foreknowing and beneficent care and government of God (or of nature, etc); divine direction, control, or guidance." See "providence, *n.*" in *OED* <http://dictionary.oed.com/cgi/entry/50191069>.

[35] As the NJPS shows, this is an instance where the more literal translation of "see" or "see to" works nicely.

[36] On this, see Levenson, *Death and Resurrection,* esp. 134–37.

[37] Precisely how this happens—whether through the agency of visible or invisible "angels," such as in the episode involving Balaam and his donkey (Numbers 22), or through some mysterious exercise of God's will over the animal—is left to the imagination.

[38] Gen 22:13.

He has already prepared and supplied (that is, provided) Himself with the object that He needs (a king) for His purposes. In this case, too, the object of YHWH's provision (a king for Himself, at this point) will also, in time, become the subject, means, or agent of His provision for His people. As such, the provision of this king also necessitates his becoming equipped to fulfill YHWH's purposes. Remarkably, at the point of David's introduction into the narrative, there is an unmistakable sign of YHWH's provision. He has already begun grooming and preparing David to shepherd His people:

> And Samuel said to Jesse, "Are all of the young men here?" And he said, "There still remains the least, but look, he is tending the sheep [וְהִנֵּה רֹעֶה בַּצֹּאן]."[39]

YHWH's seeing to a king for Himself constitutes not merely His finding and choosing the right man, but also His providing and equipping a good shepherd for His people.[40]

There is further indication in 1 Samuel that YHWH is providing for Himself a king to tend to His people through the early training and equipping of David. Of course, it is one thing to determine that David is prepared, to some extent, to become the next king even before he is anointed. It is yet another thing to give YHWH the credit for whatever preparedness David has obtained even before Samuel calls him. The most obvious basis in the biblical narrative for doing both is David's shepherding experience. Beyond its highly symbolic significance, at a critical point in the life of the nation David testifies that YHWH has used this experience to prepare him to fight His battles. When David offers to fight the Philistine who is taunting the Israelite army, Saul declares that he is no match for the Philistine, who "has been a man of battle from his youth," for David is still "a boy."[41] The evidence that David offers King Saul to convince him that he is able and ready to face "this Philistine" is a story from his past:

---

[39] 1 Sam 16:11a.

[40] See, for example, 2 Sam 5:2: "Even in times past, when Saul was king over us, *you* were the one leading out and bringing in Israel [to and from battle]. And YHWH said to you, '*You* shall tend my people Israel [אַתָּה תִרְעֶה אֶת־עַמִּי אֶת־יִשְׂרָאֵל], and *you* shall be ruler over Israel.'" Also, see Gen 37:2; Ex 3:1; 2 Sam 7:7–8; and Ps 78:71. These are just a few of the passages that depict (future) leaders of God's people as shepherds. Also see pp. 64–65, above.

[41] 1 Sam 17:33.

And David said to Saul, "While your servant was tending his
father's sheep [רֹעֶה הָיָה עַבְדְּךָ לְאָבִיו בַּצֹּאן],[42] there would come
the lion or the bear and take a lamb from the flock. And I would
go out after it, and I would strike it and deliver [the lamb] from
its mouth [וְהִכִּתִיו וְהִצַּלְתִּי מִפִּיו]. And it would rise up against me,
but I would take it by its beard, strike it, and kill it. Your servant
has defeated both the lion and the bear. Now, this uncircumcised
Philistine will be like one of them, because he has defied the battle
lines of the living God."[43]

It is not primarily his experience or personal qualifications, however, to
which David appeals. He professes that it was YHWH who accomplished
this through him:

And David said, "YHWH who delivered me [יְהוָה אֲשֶׁר הִצִּלַנִי] from
the paw of the lion and from the paw of the bear, He will deliver
me [הוּא יַצִּילֵנִי] from the paw[44] of this Philistine!"[45]

David persuades Saul that he is as capable as any of Saul's men (at the very
least, he is more confident and willing), and so Saul sends David with his
benediction: "Go, and may YHWH be with you!" (לֵךְ וַיהוָה יִהְיֶה עִמָּךְ).[46]
David's words—but more importantly, YHWH's provision[47]—are proved true
when he slays the Philistine.

---

[42] Again, see Gen 37:2: הָיָה רֹעֶה אֶת־אֶחָיו בַּצֹּאן . . . יוֹסֵף ("Joseph . . . was tending
the sheep with his brothers"); Ex 3:1: וּמֹשֶׁה הָיָה רֹעֶה אֶת־צֹאן ("Now Moses was tending
the sheep"); 1 Sam 16:11: עוֹד שָׁאַר הַקָּטָן וְהִנֵּה רֹעֶה בַּצֹּאן ("There still remains the least,
but look, he is tending the sheep"). As I acknowledge in ch. 2, I credit Jon D. Levenson's
work for drawing my attention to many of the verbal and thematic parallels here and also
with regard to Genesis 22, which I note at numerous points both above and below.

[43] 1 Sam 17:34–36.

[44] Or, "from the hand." "From the paw" better reflects the comparison between the
Philistine and wild beasts of prey; the MT has מִיַּד for all three.

[45] 1 Sam 17:37a.

[46] 1 Sam 17:37b.

[47] It should be noted that even in presuming an entirely synchronous reading of the
biblical text, the narrative does not allow certainty about the timing of this "preparation" or
"provision." There are narrative gaps in 1 Samuel 16–17 that allow for different possibilities
with regard to when David battled with the wild animals while keeping his father's sheep.
Most interpreters assume, it appears, that David is referring to recurring episodes over a
long period of time, extending back to well before his anointing by Samuel. But it is also
possible within the framework of the narrative that these battles with "the lion" and "the
bear" occurred during the period of time when "David went back and forth from Saul in

If David's battles with animals in the wilderness were part of YHWH's provision of and for him, all the more so is his battle with Goliath (among other battles to come). Unlike the case with the sacrificial animal that YHWH "provides" in Genesis 22, the provision of a king is not a one-time event but an ongoing process. And in David's public battles against and his defeat of the enemies of God's people, we see a demonstration of God's provision that is even more complicated than the double sense of which I spoke with regard to His "seeing to the sheep" in Genesis 22. In the case of David's battle against Goliath, for example, David is the object of YHWH's provision (that is, YHWH provides David as Israel's representative against the Philistine champion); he is the subject of YHWH's provision (that is, in YHWH's name, David prevailed over the Philistine and set the enemies of God's people to flight); and in and through this experience, David himself is the recipient of YHWH's provision (that is, just as with his earlier shepherding experience, this new training is part of his equipping as Israel's future shepherd and king).

Conclusion

YHWH's election of David as His new king is established beyond question before David even appears or is named in the biblical narrative. When YHWH "sought for Himself a man according to His heart," He found David. When YHWH "rejected Saul from being king over Israel," He chose David. When YHWH determined Saul to be inadequate and unfaithful as the shepherd of His people, He provided David. Because David is an upstart and "the son of a nobody," as I shall discuss in more detail in the next chapter, YHWH's election of him is surprising and inexplicable, but David's legitimacy is not a problem for the readers. In the present biblical account, because YHWH's rejection of Saul and His election of David are determined and disclosed to the readers by the first half of 1 Samuel 16, the implied or ideal reading community is not looking for exoneration of David from this point forward. Rather, the readers stand poised to witness the surprising and wondrous manifestation—the confirmation and embodiment—of YHWH's immediate and decisive election of David. Let us consider, then, how YHWH's mediate, or mediated, election of David unfolds in the biblical story of David's rise to the throne of all Israel.

---

order to tend his father's sheep in Bethlehem" (1 Sam 17:15), that is, after his anointing by Samuel and the vision of YHWH's spirit upon him (1 Sam 16:13).

CHAPTER 5

The Surprising Election and Confirmation of David as YHWH's Beloved Son

YHWH's Confirmation of David as His Beloved Son

The commissioning of Samuel by YHWH to go and anoint a king for Him among Jesse's sons, together with all the drama surrounding this event (which is at least semi-public), begins the second stage of YHWH's election of David. This second stage is what I have termed YHWH's mediate election of David. It is the manifestation and confirmation of YHWH's prior and immediate election of David embodied in the narrative, both in the finding, choosing, and providing of and for David by numerous individuals and groups, and in the public demonstration of YHWH's ongoing provision of and for David, particularly in the midst of his many battles and other trials. YHWH's heretofore hidden election is subsequently made public, starting with his anointing, as he is gradually revealed to everyone—from his own family to the king—as YHWH's anointed king who will replace Saul. That is, beginning in 1 Samuel 16, YHWH begins allowing others to see (that is, find, choose, and provide) for themselves the next king—even if only gradually—that He has already seen (that is, found, chosen, and provided) for Himself in the person of David. In 1 Samuel 16 is the first public and official manifestation before the watching eyes of the people of what has been true for some time: "This is he," זֶה הוּא, that is, "YHWH's anointed," מְשִׁיחַ יְהוָה, the one that YHWH has already seen. This gradual confirmation of David's divine election occurs with great surprise and wonder as he is preferred time and again by various ones—who thereby function in part as mediators of YHWH's election of David—above the sons of Jesse, above the sons of Saul, and above Saul himself.

David, Beloved Son of Jesse

The Seer Looks for the Son of Jesse Whom YHWH Has Seen

Samuel arrives in Bethlehem knowing that his task is to anoint one of Jesse's sons, but he does not know which one. YHWH gives no name or other identifier by which Samuel might also "see" or find him, but He simply instructs him as follows:

> And YHWH said, "You shall take a heifer [עֶגְלַת בָּקָר תִּקַּח בְּיָדֶךָ]¹ and say, 'I have come to sacrifice to YHWH.' And you shall call Jesse to the sacrifice. Now *I* will show you [וְאָנֹכִי אוֹדִיעֲךָ] what you shall do, and you shall anoint for me the one whom I shall tell you [אֵת אֲשֶׁר־אֹמַר אֵלֶיךָ]."²

YHWH emphasizes here that He will tell Samuel what to do, that is, whom to anoint. Samuel is presumptuous, however, and he allows his own sight to guide him in identifying the one whom YHWH has seen. When Samuel sees Eliab (וַיַּרְא אֶת־אֱלִיאָב), Samuel—and not YHWH—says confidently (וַיֹּאמֶר אַךְ) that YHWH's anointed is there before Him.³ What follows is a pedagogical moment for Samuel and the others present,⁴ and, of course, for the readers. YHWH instructs Samuel that he is using the wrong criteria—all based on sight according to human perspective—for truly seeing His newly chosen king. Samuel cannot identify (אַל־תַּבֵּט) YHWH's anointed based

---

¹ Lit., "you shall take in your hand."

² 1 Sam 16:2b–3; italics added to the translation to show the emphasis in the Hebrew text. The language and instructions here are reminiscent of Gen 22:2:

> And [God] said, "Take [קַח־נָא] your son, your only son, whom you love—Isaac—and go [וְלֶךְ־לְךָ; compare with 1 Sam 16:1, וְלֵךְ] to the land of Moriah. Then offer him there as a burnt offering on one of the mountains that I shall tell you [אֲשֶׁר אֹמַר אֵלֶיךָ]."

³ 1 Sam 16:6. Does Samuel state this audibly for others to hear? Or does he think it, as the translators of the NRSV, NIV, NJPS, and ESV, among others, conclude? Again, I shall return to discuss this in more detail further below.

⁴ See the note above. Further below, I shall also consider the question of who is present for Samuel's anointing of David, and the degree to which various ones are privy to the exchanges between YHWH and Samuel.

on "his appearance" (מַרְאֵהוּ), "the height of his standing" (גְּבֹהַּ קוֹמָתוֹ), or "the outward appearance" (lit., "the eyes," לַעֵינַיִם) for it was not these that caught YHWH's attention but, rather, "the heart" (וַיהוָה יִרְאֶה לַלֵּבָב).[5] The chief criterion for YHWH's choice (or His seeing) of His king, then, is neither pedigree nor physical appearance nor anything else visible to the human eye. Ironically, the seer's vision is impaired by his own expectations for Israel's next king[6]—apart from YHWH's word, he sees as any other man—as well as his failure to wait for YHWH first to declare to him whom he is to anoint, as he was instructed before going to Bethlehem.[7]

Perhaps it is because of Samuel's mistaken certainty about Jesse's firstborn as the most natural and obvious choice for king, and/or perhaps it is because of an implicit contrast between Eliab and Saul,[8] but YHWH's reaction against Eliab is stated more strongly than with the others to follow. Of Eliab, YHWH declares, in first-person form, "I have rejected him" (מְאַסְתִּיהוּ).[9] By contrast, either YHWH or Samuel—the text is ambiguous at this point—says of the next two eldest sons in third-person form, "YHWH has not chosen this one either" (גַּם־בָּזֶה לֹא־בָחַר יְהוָה).[10] And finally, of the first seven as a group, it is identifiably Samuel who declares, "YHWH has not chosen these" (לֹא־בָחַר יְהוָה בָּאֵלֶּה)[11] Whether or not we should read into this a more strenuous rejection of Eliab than of the others is not fully clear. Whatever the case, with each passing son of Jesse in this drama of YHWH's rejection, the education of the seer (and witnesses) with regard to how YHWH sees things

[5] 1 Sam 16:7.

[6] One might also say that Samuel's vision is impaired partly by David's absence. Despite YHWH's warning in v. 7, it is clear from v. 12—וְהוּא אַדְמוֹנִי עִם־יְפֵה עֵינַיִם וְטוֹב רֹאִי—that physical appearance is not altogether insignificant. It is not the basis for seeing or choosing God's king, but it still may be one of many factors or indicators that confirms for human eyes his chosenness. Samuel's ability to see and discern YHWH's choice, therefore, is not impugned as much as it would have been had David also been present when Samuel says that Eliab must surely be YHWH's anointed.

[7] 1 Sam 16:3.

[8] See 1 Sam 9:2 on Saul's appearance (also see p. 164 n. 69, below). McCarter, for example, appears to agree with Mettinger and others who see in YHWH's words to Samuel in 1 Sam 16:7 an implicit criticism of Saul, whom the biblical narrative describes in similar terms (see 1 Sam 9:2; 10:23). McCarter (*1 Samuel*, 277) quotes Mettinger (*King and Messiah*, 175): "Eliab is something of a 'new Saul,' so that in his rejection Saul is denounced in effigy."

[9] 1 Sam 16:7.

[10] 1 Sam 16:8–9. I shall discuss this ambiguity further below.

[11] 1 Sam 16:10.

continues: Neither physical stature nor social prominence (in this case, as determined by birth order) are determinants.

Just as importantly, however, suspense mounts with each named introduction and rejection of Jesse's first three sons, and then with the telescoped introduction and rejection of the next four, until a perplexed Samuel finds that he still does not see among Jesse's sons the one whom YHWH has seen. Only upon questioning Jesse does Samuel discover that one more son of Jesse remains, but he is not even present—he has not been called to the sacrifice, as Samuel had instructed. Instead, Jesse answers, "There still remains the least, but look, he is tending the sheep."[12]

YHWH's Surprising Choice of "the Least" of Jesse's Sons

By way of Jesse's reply to Samuel in 1 Sam 16:11, the biblical narrator explicitly designates David (who still remains unnamed at this point) as הַקָּטָן among Jesse's sons. All of the major English versions render הַקָּטָן in this verse as "the youngest."[13] This is an understandable choice of terms because הַקָּטָן (or the variant הַקָּטֹן) functions here and in other places to differentiate younger/youngest siblings from the elder/eldest.[14] Yet, it is also clear that in certain contexts קָטָן carries other connotations. For example, the term might simply be rendered as "small" or "little";[15] as "least," or "small(est)" "with added idea of weakness";[16] or "small" with the sense of "insignificant" or "unimportant."[17] Herein lies, of course, one of the difficulties with any translation, for whereas the Hebrew often allows for two or more nuances or meanings of a particular term in certain contexts, its rendering by one English term usually closes off all but one of those potential nuances or meanings. I suggest that this has been the case with English renderings of הַקָּטָן as "the youngest" in the context of 1 Sam 16:1–13. Here, as we will

---

[12] 1 Sam 16:11. In ch. 4, I have already discussed the great significance of the fact that David is "tending the sheep" (וְהִנֵּה רֹעֶה בַּצֹּאן) when Samuel discovers him, that is, when he is first introduced into the narrative (though still not by name).

[13] Including the KJV, NRSV, NJPS, NIV, and ESV.

[14] See, for example, Gen 9:24; 42:13.

[15] E.g., 2 Sam 12:3: כִּבְשָׂה אַחַת קְטַנָּה "one little ewe lamb."

[16] Francis Brown et al., *The Brown-Driver-Briggs Hebrew and English Lexicon*, 882, at קָטָן 2.a. In 2 Kgs 18:24//Isa 36:9, for instance עַבְדֵי אֲדֹנִי הַקְּטַנִּים is translated as "the least of my master's servants" in the NRSV, NJPS, and ESV.

[17] E.g., 1 Sam 15:17: הֲלוֹא אִם־קָטֹן אַתָּה בְּעֵינֶיךָ רֹאשׁ שִׁבְטֵי יִשְׂרָאֵל אָתָּה, "Even if you are small in your own eyes, are you not the head of the tribes of Israel?"

see, הַקָּטָן functions together with the dramatic narrative to present David not simply as the "youngest" of his brothers, but also to characterize him as the "smallest" (or, at least smaller than the eldest) and, as "man sees" him relative to his brothers, the "least significant." Perhaps, then, rendering הַקָּטָן as "the least" is the best that one can do to capture in English these various nuances in the context of 1 Sam 16:1–13. Unlike "the youngest" or "the smallest," "the least" can be taken as referring to his relative age (i.e., the least in years), his relative physical stature (the least in size), and/or, as an extension of the first two, the relative degree of weight or significance that he commands in the eyes of his family (as the youngest and smallest, quite naturally he is honored the least).[18] Let us see how these various nuances are developed in the narrative.

In the first place, Jesse is certainly using the term comparatively to denote David's birth order in relationship to his other sons: David is the youngest among eight sons.[19] Besides this explicit statement, David's low position in relation to his brothers is punctuated in dramatic fashion by the recounting of Samuel's examination, in order of birth, of Jesse's firstborn (vv. 6–7), second-born (v. 8), third-born (v. 9), and fourth-, fifth-, sixth-, and seventh-born sons (v. 10). If only by virtue of his birth order, David is the most unlikely and improbable one among Jesse's sons to come to the prophet's attention or receive special treatment.[20] In approaching David last, then, Samuel treats David as "the least," fully in accordance with all expectations.

Jesse's designation of David as הַקָּטָן might refer comparatively, in the second place, to David's physical stature by indicating that David is "the smallest." This is the case, at least, in comparison to Jesse's eldest son, Eliab.

---

[18] Peterson's *The Message* is one translation—although, on the whole, it is more of a highly colloquial paraphrase—that diverges on this point. Its colloquial expression, "Well, yes, there's the runt," quite nicely captures something of the nuanced sense of הַקָּטָן that I detect.

[19] The issue of the much-discussed discrepancy between this text and 1 Chr 2:15, which names David as the seventh son of Jesse, is unimportant for the present study. Interested readers might consult the brief discussions in, e.g., McCarter, *I Samuel*, 276; and Gordon, *I & II Samuel*, 151.

[20] On the rights and privileges of eldest sons in biblical literature, see, in particular, "First-Born and Late-Born, Fathers and Mothers" (ch. 7), in Levenson, *Death and Resurrection*, 55–60. Also see, e.g., de Vaux, *Ancient Israel*, 41–42, 59–60. On the other hand, for a treatment of the recurring biblical motif of younger brothers receiving preferential treatment, and a challenge to the view that kingship in ancient Israel passed through primogeniture, see Greenspahn, *When Brothers Dwell Together*.

The sight of Eliab (together, presumably, with the assumption or full awareness that this is Jesse's firstborn son)[21] leads Samuel to remark, "Surely before YHWH is His anointed!" (אַךְ נֶגֶד יְהוָה מְשִׁיחוֹ).[22] YHWH's response effectively describes what it is about Eliab's appearance that has evoked Samuel's high esteem for him, but at the same time, implies that the one Samuel is to anoint is not as physically impressive:

> But YHWH said to Samuel, "Do not look to his appearance or to the height of his standing, because I have rejected him. For it is not that which man sees, because man sees the outward appearance. YHWH, however, sees the heart."[23]

This does not mean that David's physical appearance is irrelevant. As I have already noted above, while it does not provide any basis for finding or choosing YHWH's king, as Samuel's reaction to Eliab would have suggested, it is one of several confirmations of David's elect status that is visible to human eyes. Even then, however, it is notable that the narrative's later description of David—"he was ruddy, with beautiful eyes, and good-looking" (וְהוּא אַדְמוֹנִי עִם־יְפֵה עֵינַיִם וְטוֹב רֹאִי)[24]—makes no reference to "the height of his standing," such as in the case of Eliab and, earlier, Saul. The implication is that David does not measure up to his eldest brother, at least in this one regard.[25]

Besides the clear contrasts between David and his brothers in terms of birth order and physical stature, David is portrayed as הַקָּטָן in a third sense in 1 Sam 16:1–13. Because Samuel does not find the one whom YHWH has seen among Jesse's sons who are present, he asks Jesse if he has any more children (הֲתַמּוּ הַנְּעָרִים). Jesse does not offer to send for his remaining son, "the least"—he does not even refer to him by name—but he simply answers Samuel: "There still remains the least, but look, he is tending the sheep" (עוֹד שָׁאַר הַקָּטָן וְהִנֵּה רֹעֶה בַּצֹּאן).[26] Jesse's locution is brief—only six words

---

[21] Another factor that must be considered in Samuel's positive assessment is that the only other man he has anointed as king also stood head and shoulders above the rest (1 Sam 9:2; see p. 147 n. 8, above, and p. 164 n. 69, below).

[22] 1 Sam 16:6.

[23] 1 Sam 16:7.

[24] 1 Sam 16:12.

[25] On the importance of David's physical appearance, despite YHWH's command to Samuel in 1 Sam 16:7, see Hamilton, *The Body Royal*, 129–30.

[26] 1 Sam 16:11.

in the Hebrew—but the illocutionary force of his reply goes far beyond a simple "yes," which would have sufficed.[27] If nothing else, he is offering here his excuses for why he did not call all of his sons before Samuel, as Samuel presumably intended.[28] If this is the extent of the meaning of Jesse's reply, the *waw*-conjunction might be taken as a loose conjunction setting up a simple additive structure that draws Samuel's attention to what "the least" (David's only designation up to this point) is doing at the present moment: "There still remains the least. See [over there], he is tending the sheep."[29] But it is also possible to translate the *waw* here in a contrastive sense: "There still remains the least, but look, he is [busy now] tending the sheep."[30] The context seems to support the latter translation, that is, the contrastive sense, for it appears that Jesse is also indicating by his actions and response to Samuel why it is unnecessary even now for his eighth son to appear before the prophet. In contrast to Jesse's unprompted calling and parading his other sons before Samuel one by one whenever Samuel had finished with each previous one, Jesse does not treat David in the same way. Not only must Samuel ask Jesse if these are all of his sons, when Jesse replies to Samuel that "[t]here still remains the least" (עוֹד שָׁאַר הַקָּטָן) and shows no inclination towards calling David, Samuel must tell Jesse, with some urgency: "Send and get him, for we will not sit down [around the table] until his arrival here."[31] The denouement of the revelation—both to Samuel and to the readers—that David was not among those called,[32] and the likely possibility that Jesse still thinks David's

---

[27] There is yet more significance in Jesse's terse reply that goes beyond what Jesse could have intended, namely, his statement that David is out tending the sheep. See my discussion above (as well as that of numerous other commentators) on the significance of David's transition from shepherding his father's sheep to shepherding, as king, God's people.

[28] See 1 Sam 16:5.

[29] So, e.g., the KJV: "There remaineth yet the youngest, and, behold, he keepeth the sheep"; and the NJPS: "There is still the youngest; he is tending the flock."

[30] So, e.g., the NRSV: "There remains yet the youngest, but he is keeping the sheep"; the NIV: "'There is still the youngest,' Jesse answered, 'but he is tending the sheep'"; and the ESV: "There remains yet the youngest, but behold, he is keeping the sheep."

[31] 1 Sam 16:11. On the bracketed insertion of "around the table," see my discussion below at p. 181.

[32] My wording here is intentionally ambiguous in order to reflect the ambiguity of the text regarding the prophet's invitation to Jesse and his sons to the sacrifice in 1 Sam 16:5. It may be, on the one hand, that we are to conceive of David as never receiving or even hearing the invitation (certainly not from the prophet, but neither from his father or brothers). It is

place is with the sheep, not with the prophet, dramatically demonstrates how Jesse, and probably his first seven sons, see David.

One might assume that the father, Jesse, is ultimately responsible for David's absence. In Jonathan and David's ruse at Saul's feast in 1 Samuel 20, however, it is David's brother who is reported to have commanded David to attend the family sacrifice:

> And Jonathan answered Saul, "David strongly requested leave of me to go to Bethlehem. He said, 'Please give me leave, because we have a family sacrifice in the city, and my brother has commanded me [to attend] כִּי זֶבַח מִשְׁפָּחָה לָנוּ בָּעִיר וְהוּא צִוָּה־לִי אָחִי]. Now, if I have found favor in your eyes, grant me escape so that I may see my brothers.' Therefore he has not come to the king's table."[33]

Though Jonathan's claim is a lie designed to test Saul's true intent towards David, this would indicate that elder or eldest sons were at least sometimes responsible for overseeing family sacrifices and calling their younger brothers to attend. Perhaps there is also a hint of irony here, even if only apparent to the readers. In 1 Samuel 20, Jonathan portrays David's presence at the family sacrifice as being in such demand that his brother would call him back from a considerable distance, even away from the king's feast, to attend. In 1 Samuel 16, however, neither his brother nor anyone else calls him away from tending the nearby sheep to a sacrifice administered by the prophet himself. Though Samuel has invited Jesse and "his sons" to the sacrifice, they have apparently determined that it is unnecessary for הַקָּטָן, the least, to attend. And when the prophet shows a special interest in examining each of Jesse's sons, apparently it does not occur to them that Samuel's interest might extend to הַקָּטָן, who is certainly the youngest, possibly the smallest, and consequently the least of Jesse's sons. Inadvertently, then, Samuel, too, treats David as the least in approaching him last.

All this—the unfolding drama of rejection, the revelation that "the least" has not been called and is not present, and the concealment of his identity while Samuel and Jesse discuss his absence and send for someone to bring him— functions to demonstrate (and ultimately to effect in the reader) the surprise and wonder that YHWH has seen (that is, found, chosen, and provided) the least

---

also conceivable, on the other hand, that David at least knew of the prophet's invitation, but was unable to attend the sacrifice.

[33] 1 Sam 20:28–29.

instead of any of the rest. Samuel is eager to see him, for he states, "Send and get him, for we will not sit down [around the table] until his arrival here."[34] The sight of David is impressive enough to merit description. This time, however, it is not his size or stature that catches the eye, and it is YHWH, not Samuel, who speaks and says "this is he" (כִּי־זֶה הוּא), the one whom Samuel is to anoint.[35] Only after receiving YHWH's confirming word can Samuel be certain that he has seen the one whom YHWH has first seen "among [Jesse's] sons," and he proceeds to anoint him there "in the midst of his brothers" (בְּקֶרֶב אֶחָיו). The Spirit of YHWH "rushed upon David[36] from that day on," and Samuel, his business now complete, departs to Ramah.[37]

In sum, 1 Sam 16:1–13 depicts, among other things, the initial and surprising emergence of the least of Jesse's sons to some position of prominence among his brothers as they begin receding into the background. It is significant that the eldest three, in particular, are introduced by name in order of their birth, but by the end of the account, they are identified not by name but in terms of their relation to David (אֶחָיו). In contrast, David is first introduced in terms of his relation to his brothers (הַקָּטָן), but at the end of the account, he is the only one among them who is named. There is a progression in the public (or semi-public) confirmation of David as YHWH's newly elected king. At the beginning of the account, only YHWH sees David in an exalted position vis-à-vis the other sons of Jesse. Though relatively slow in getting there, and surprisingly dull for a seer, Samuel is the next to perceive David's identity as YHWH's king. Perhaps Samuel assumes that David must be the one at the moment that Jesse points to the remaining son tending the sheep and/or when he sees his beautiful eyes, but David is confirmed for Samuel as the one whom YHWH has first seen among Jesse's sons only by the word of YHWH: "Rise and anoint him, for this is he." Unless YHWH's word, "this is he," comes via some oracular device in response to an audible inquiry by Samuel, David is first set apart in view of all the other worshipers—certainly his father and

[34] 1 Sam 16:11.

[35] 1 Sam 16:12. Again, see 1 Sam 16:3, where YHWH tells Samuel that He would say which one Samuel is to anoint: וְאָנֹכִי אוֹדִיעֲךָ אֵת אֲשֶׁר־תַּעֲשֶׂה וּמָשַׁחְתָּ לִי אֵת אֲשֶׁר־אֹמַר אֵלֶיךָ; "Now *I* will show you what you shall do, and you shall anoint for me the one whom I shall tell you."

[36] David is named here for the first time in the books of Samuel.

[37] 1 Sam 16:13.

brothers, but perhaps the elders and their families as well[38]—when Samuel takes the horn of oil and anoints "him in the midst of his brothers," and perhaps subsequently through some visible manifestation of YHWH's Spirit rushing upon him. It is only at this point that David is finally named for the readers. The ideal or inscribed reading community knows David's identity all along, but by withholding David's name in this way, the narrative effectively reproduces some sense of the inexplicable discovery experienced by the various characters in the unfolding drama.

From "One Among Jesse's Sons" to "the Son of Jesse"

David continues on this trajectory vis-à-vis his brothers. In the account immediately following David's anointing, Saul's servants suggest that he command his servants to "seek a man [וִיבַקְשׁוּ אִישׁ] who is skilled at playing the lyre." To this, Saul responds: "Find me a man [רְאוּ־נָא לִי אִישׁ] who can play well and bring him to me."[39] Immediately upon hearing Saul's command,[40] one of his servants tells Saul about David: "See here, I have seen a son of Jesse the Bethlehemite."[41] Only the readers (as opposed to any of the characters in the story) are positioned to detect the similarity between YHWH's announcement to Samuel in 16:1 and the servant's announcement here to Saul:

וַיֹּאמֶר יְהוָה . . . רָאִיתִי בְּבָנָיו [יִשַׁי בֵּית־הַלַּחְמִי] לִי מֶלֶךְ   16:1

. . . וַיֹּאמֶר   הִנֵּה רָאִיתִי בֵּן לְיִשַׁי בֵּית הַלַּחְמִי . . .   16:18

---

[38] On questions concerning the public nature of David's anointing, see pp. 180–86, below.

[39] 1 Sam 16:16, 17.

[40] The possibility that the narrative assumes but simply omits mention of a search between vv. 17 and 18 is precluded by 1) the lack of any narrative report of a search; 2) the fact that the servant appears to be replying directly to Saul's command (וַיַּעַן . . . וַיֹּאמֶר); and, perhaps, 3) the servant's designation as אֶחָד מֵהַנְּעָרִים ("one of the servants") to distinguish him from the first group of servants (v. 15: עַבְדֵי־שָׁאוּל) who give Saul the idea, in the first place, to commission the search (that is, it does not appear that one of the servants who recommended the idea to Saul subsequently went out to find someone and is reporting back).

[41] 1 Sam 16:18. Among those versions with "I have seen" for רָאִיתִי are the KJV, NRSV, NIV, and ESV. NJPS diverges slightly with "I have observed," and McCarter has here "I have noticed."

Here is a remarkable verbal link between the divine act of seeing David among Jesse's sons, reported earlier, and a human act of seeing "a son of Jesse." It is as if the servant is seeing with YHWH's eyes, that is, as "YHWH sees," and not as "man sees."[42] Whereas even the seer was initially misled by his eyes, as we saw above, now a mere servant of Saul is able to see the one among Jesse's sons upon whom YHWH's Spirit rests. YHWH's initial act of finding, choosing, and providing David among Jesse's sons is now being played out on the human stage, in the very court of the king. In the present context, David is found and chosen above Jesse's other sons and, indeed, the other sons of Israel, by Saul and his servant. Ultimately, however, YHWH providentially leads—that is, He inexplicably provides[43]—David to Saul by means of this discovery. Saul then sends to Jesse, commanding him, "Send me David your son [דָּוִד בִּנְךָ], who is with the sheep."[44] Once again, we should take care to note the increasing prominence of David among Jesse's sons as it is reflected in the references to him, not to mention in the narrative events taking place. David is introduced to Saul as בֵּן לְיִשַׁי, "a son of Jesse," a reference that at least acknowledges the existence of other sons. When Saul refers to David in his message to Jesse, however, David is called simply בִּנְךָ, "your son."

David's brothers have not yet entirely disappeared from the biblical account. Prior to David's victory over Goliath, "the three eldest sons of Jesse" (שְׁלֹשֶׁת בְּנֵי־יִשַׁי הַגְּדֹלִים) are named again in order of their birth; David, again, is characterized as "the least" (הַקָּטָן).[45] And yet, once again, it is David, the least (הַקָּטָן)—and not any among the eldest (הַגְּדֹלִים)—whom Saul, the army of Israel, and Israel's enemies see as YHWH's provision for Israel's deliverance. Apart from the general deliverance that David won for Israel, his accomplishment was also to have won freedom for his "father's house [בֵּית אָבִיו] . . . in Israel."[46] Whether or not the king made good on his promise is not clear. In either case, the freedom would have been short-lived, for David's family is soon driven into exile.[47] Nevertheless, it is significant that David takes on the role of the eldest son, if not the father, by doing what is required to win freedom for his father's house. Indeed, it is when

---

[42] See 1 Sam 16:7.

[43] Note the NRSV's and ESV's rendering of Saul's response (1 Sam 16:17) to his servants' proposal (16:16) as "Provide for me."

[44] 1 Sam 16:19.

[45] 1 Sam 17:13–14; also see 17:28.

[46] 1 Sam 17:25.

[47] See 1 Sam 22:1–4.

"Eliab, his eldest brother" (אֱלִיאָב אָחִיו הַגָּדוֹל), hears David inquiring of the men what the king would do for the victor over the Philistine that his anger flares up against David. Though Eliab says that David's coming down to see the battle is evidence of his "arrogance" (זְדֹנְךָ) and "the evil that is in [his] heart" (רֹעַ לְבָבֶךָ), it is likely that Eliab is offended by David's apparent arrogance that he might be the one to kill the Philistine and thus win the promised prize (one that is fit for an eldest son). Whatever the case, Eliab's chastisement of David for leaving "those few sheep" recalls the last time that David left the sheep to join his brothers, whereupon David eclipsed Eliab as the focus of the prophet's and everyone else's attention.[48] The coveted prize aside, David single-handedly wins the victory over Israel's enemies and, therefore, effectively delivers Saul's army (including his three eldest brothers), many of whom would have faced captivity or, as likely, death. At the end of the day, it is of David whom Saul inquires, "Whose son are you?" And it is David, not Eliab, who replies, "The son of your servant, Jesse the Bethlehemite" (בֶּן־עַבְדְּךָ יִשַׁי בֵּית הַלַּחְמִי).[49] From this point on, only David is known and referred to in the narrative, even if derogatively, as בֶּן־יִשַׁי, "the son of Jesse."[50]

Eliab and the rest of David's brothers, by contrast, are not named again in the narrative. Apart from the ruse in 1 Sam 20:29, the next and final time David's brothers are mentioned is when they go down to David at the cave of Adullam, where they hear that he has fled, to seek refuge with him there:

> And David left there and escaped to the cave of Adullam. And his brothers and all his father's house [אֶחָיו וְכָל־בֵּית אָבִיו] heard, and they came down to him there. And every man in distress, every man who had a debt-collector [after him], and every man whose life was bitter gathered to him. And he became commander over them [וַיְהִי עֲלֵיהֶם לְשָׂר], and with him there were around four hundred men. And David went from there to Mizpeh of Moab, and he said to the king of Moab, "Please let my father and mother come to you until I know what God will do for me." So he led them to the king of Moab, and they stayed with him all the days that David was in

---

[48] My discussion here, which points to only some of the verbal and thematic connections between 1 Samuel 16 and 17, suggests that source-critical delineations that would present these accounts for rather atomistic interpretation, such as reflected in McCarter's commentary on 1 Samuel, give up more than they gain.

[49] 1 Sam 17:55–58.

[50] 1 Sam 20:27, 30, 31; 22:7, 8, 9, 13; 25:10; 2 Sam 20:1; 23:1.

the stronghold.[51]

David, the least of Jesse's sons, now finds himself offering his protection not only to his brothers, but to his father and mother as well, among many others. Once again David eclipses his elder brothers and carries out duties that would have been expected of them, particularly in his caring for their parents.[52] The text does not state explicitly what becomes of his brothers when David places his father and mother under the Moabite king's care, but presumably his brothers follow him from this point as their commander and as part of the motley crew of "un-choice" men who followed him, until this son of Jesse is ultimately elevated to become the king that YHWH first saw among Jesse's sons.[53]

The Insignificance of David and His Father's House

Above, I discussed the surprise of YHWH's election and confirmation of "the least" of Jesse's sons among Jesse's other sons. This is all the more surprising when we step back and recognize how improbable and inexplicable is YHWH's choice of *any* "son of Jesse" to supersede Saul and his sons as Israel's king. As I demonstrated in chapter 2, David's emergence as the heir to Saul's throne has no natural basis, unlike Hattušili's claim to the Hittite throne. In this section, I shall focus my attention on the relative insignificance of David and his house, particularly vis-à-vis Saul and his house. This will prepare us better to appreciate the wonder of key moments in the narrative in which David is shown to be preferred or beloved by various figures above Jonathan, the natural heir to Saul's throne, and above the reigning king, Saul himself.[54] All this begins, as I have argued above, with YHWH's seeing (that is, finding, choosing, and providing) a king for Himself not among the sons

---

[51] 1 Sam 22:1–4.

[52] See, for example, Tsumura, "Family in the Historical Books," 59–79, at 75.

[53] 2 Sam 2:1–4; see also 2 Sam 5:1–3. It is also likely that at least his eldest three brothers, who were soldiers in Saul's army, served under David after Saul "placed him over his men of battle" (1 Sam 18:5; see also v. 13).

[54] As will become evident, there are a few instances when it is helpful to distinguish between Saul and his sons as the one or ones rejected in favor of David. In most instances, however, it is sufficient to treat together various figures' preference of David over Saul and, consequently (though not necessarily), over his sons, because one generally implies the other.

of Saul, whom He has rejected, but among Jesse's sons. YHWH's discovery, choice, and provision of David, then, are confirmed and embodied in the sight and actions of numerous human characters as the drama of David's gradual ascent to the throne unfolds.

The Responses of Samuel and the Bethlehemite Elders

In the previous chapter, I discussed how YHWH's statement "I have seen myself a king among his sons" (רָאִיתִי בְּבָנָיו לִי מֶלֶךְ) in 1 Sam 16:1 is an expression of His choice of the new king that He has seen (David) over against the one that He has rejected (Saul), as well as over against Jesse's other sons. One might extend the contrastive sense to include a distinction that is naturally implied, though not explicitly stated: YHWH has chosen or provided a king for himself from among Jesse's sons instead of from among Saul's sons, or, for that matter, from among any other sons of Israel. This is certainly borne out in the ensuing account, even if such an extended contrast is not readily obvious in 1 Sam 16:1. Let us consider, therefore, how the narrative—far from establishing any natural legitimacy for David's claim to the throne—presents YHWH's choice of this son of Jesse while depicting David and his father's house as relatively insignificant.

The opening of the account of David's anointing is important both for what it says and does not say:

> And YHWH said to Samuel, "How long will you mourn for Saul? I have rejected him from being king over Israel. Fill your horn with oil and go—I am sending you to Jesse the Bethlehemite because I have seen myself a king among his sons." And Samuel said, "How shall I go? Saul will hear, and he will kill me!" And YHWH said, "You shall take a heifer and say, 'I have come to sacrifice to YHWH.' And you shall call Jesse to the sacrifice. Now *I* will show you what you shall do, and you shall anoint for me the one whom I shall tell you." And Samuel did as YHWH told him, and he came to Bethlehem. And the elders of the city trembled upon meeting him, and they said, "Is your visit one of shalom?"[55]

YHWH's interruption of Samuel's mourning for Saul with the commission to go and anoint a new king among Jesse's sons is disconcerting if not bewildering to Samuel. But Samuel's fearful response—"How shall I

---

[55] 1 Sam 16:1–4. Verse 4's שָׁלֹם בּוֹאֶךָ is typically rendered in the versions and commentaries as "Do you come in peace?" "Do you come peaceably?" and the like.

go? Saul will hear, and he will kill me!"—has evoked no surprise among commentators. Walter Brueggemann's explanation is representative of many others:

> Samuel is commissioned to go to Jesse, to Bethlehem, outside the reach of Saul's northern kingdom and outside the Ramah-Bethel-Mizpah circuit familiar to Samuel. This is in every way a dispatch into new territory. Yahweh has recognized a new king . . . Samuel recognizes the ominous nature of the venture (v. 2a). It is hazardous to anoint a king when there already is a king! There is no vacancy in the office. Samuel by now is surely identified as a traitorous enemy of Saul, and he knows any overture toward a new king is high risk.[56]

Perhaps Brueggemann's assessment of Samuel's situation is the extent of it, and Samuel's reaction here might be considered entirely normal wherever YHWH might have sent him to anoint whomever He might have designated. Even so, Samuel's response is uncharacteristic of him in general, and in relation to Saul in particular, and therefore it is unsettling to the reading audience.

Samuel, after all, is known by "all Israel from Dan to Beersheba" as a bold and trustworthy prophet or seer of YHWH who judged Israel and led them in battle against the Philistines before anointing Saul as king.[57] And though Samuel appears to interpret the Israelites' request for a king as a rejection of him,[58] even after Saul is chosen as king, Samuel remains highly esteemed in the eyes of Israel and retains an important measure of authority. One clear indication of this, among others, is the elders' response to Samuel's visit in 1 Sam 16:4: "And the elders of the city trembled [וַיֶּחֶרְדוּ] upon meeting him, and they said, 'Is your visit one of shalom?'" Not only did Samuel discover and anoint the new king, but he also retains his authority to act as God's spokesperson to, and judge of, the king himself.[59] And most notably, on two occasions prior to YHWH's commission in 1 Samuel 16, Samuel

---

[56] Brueggemann, *First and Second Samuel*, 120–21.

[57] See, e.g., 1 Sam 3:20; 7:6, 15–16; 9:9; 12:7.

[58] 1 Sam 8:6–7. The request for a king was precipitated by the injustice of Samuel's sons, together with the elders' concern that Samuel was growing old (1 Sam 8:1–5).

[59] The narrative bears out the statement in 1 Sam 7:15 that "Samuel judged Israel all the days of his life," even if his leadership takes on a limited role after the institution of kingship is established.

stands before Saul and declares without any hint of fear for himself YHWH's judgment upon Saul for his disobedience:

> And Samuel said to Saul, "You have acted foolishly! You have not kept the commandment that YHWH your God commanded you. [But for that] surely now YHWH would have established your kingdom over Israel forever. But now, your kingdom will not stand. YHWH has sought for Himself a man according to His heart, and YHWH has appointed him ruler over His people, for you have not kept that which YHWH commanded you."[60]

And Samuel said, "Is YHWH's delight in burnt offerings and sacrifices [the same] as [that in] obeying YHWH's voice? See here! To obey is better than a sacrifice, and to pay close attention [to His word] is better than the fat of rams. For rebellion is [like] the sin of divination, and to defy [like] the iniquity of [serving] household gods.[61] Because you have rejected the word of YHWH, He has rejected you as king." . . . And Samuel said to Saul, "I will not return with you, because you have rejected the word of YHWH, and YHWH has rejected you from being king over Israel." . . . And

---

[60] 1 Sam 13:13–14.

[61] There are a number of difficulties in כִּי חַטַּאת־קֶסֶם מֶרִי וְאָוֶן וּתְרָפִים הַפְצַר, the MT's opening clause in 1 Sam 15:23. First, וְאָוֶן וּתְרָפִים by itself presents considerable difficulty. I understand אָוֶן as a corruption of עָוֹן—this is supported, in particular, by LXX[B]'s reading of πόνος—and, therefore, have rendered it as "iniquity" (so, too, NRS, NJPS, and ESV, among others). I read "iniquity," then, in construct with תְרָפִים (*teraphim*, or "household gods"), despite the conjunction separating the two terms in the MT (see, too, NJPS's "like the iniquity of teraphim"). My bracketed insertion ("serving") indicates my interpretation of תְרָפִים as an objective genitive; that is, it indicates my understanding that the iniquity lies with those who serve *teraphim* (similarly, see NRS and ESV, which render תְרָפִים in general terms as "idolatry," though both keep the conjunction and have, instead, "iniquity and idolatry"). My translation here, together with NJPS, has the advantage of standing in close parallel to the immediately preceding phrase "the sin of divination," both in form (nominative construct) and in meaning (a highly negative evaluation of forbidden worship or cultic practice). The meaning of הַפְצַר is also unclear. It is rendered variously in the English versions as "stubbornness" (NRS), "defiance" (NJPS), and "presumption" (ESV), to list but a few. In my view, the parallel term מֶרִי ("rebellion") may be the best indication of its general semantic range, thus I have rendered this infinitive form of פצר as "to defy." Finally, the Hebrew syntax leaves some question about the precise relationship between מרי and חטאת־קסם, and that between הפצר and תרפים [עון]. I interpret Sauls' rebellion and defiance as analogous to "the sin of divination" and "the iniquity of [serving] household gods," respectively, and not as equated with them. And while I agree with NRS, NJPS, and ESV here, in my own translation I have placed brackets around "like" to indicate the MT's ambiguity at this point.

Samuel said to him, "YHWH has torn the kingdom of Israel from you today, and He has given it to your neighbor, your better."[62]

Already, in Saul's presence, Samuel has all but taken the final step to transfer the kingdom to Saul's "neighbor." YHWH's commissioning of Samuel to go and anoint another is merely the next step that Samuel has already indicated would be taken. Why, then, does Samuel, who has stood fearlessly in Saul's presence and pronounced YHWH's rejection of him on more than one occasion, now fear for his life on this occasion, though in Saul's absence? As I have acknowledged, perhaps Samuel has simply grown fearful because of the increasing enmity between Saul and him. Or, perhaps there is no rational explanation for his fear of man above fear of God, especially for the prophet of God. Whereas the typical explanation for Samuel's fear seems to be based primarily on the principle of human analogy—that is, on how we might expect anyone to react in the face of such a command—I would like to suggest, rather, another possibility that has at least as much, if not more, basis in the biblical text.

There is no doubt, of course, that Samuel fears for his life: "How shall I go? Saul will hear, and he will kill me!" Biblical commentators, however, take into account only part of the demand by YHWH that evokes this cry from Samuel. Consider, for example, Brueggemann's comment once again: "It is hazardous to anoint a king when there already is a king! There is no vacancy in the office." The sole basis of Samuel's anguish, in Brueggemann's estimation, is the command to anoint a king, whoever that might be. But Samuel does not receive and respond in fear to a general command from YHWH to anoint a king; he receives and responds as he does to the specific command of YHWH to go to Jesse the Bethlehemite to anoint a king among his sons.

The narrative does not give us enough information to weigh the effect on Samuel of the general nature of the command (anoint a king) over against the effect of the specifics (anoint a king from among the sons of this man from this town). It is entirely conceivable, however, that it is the (intended) illocutionary force of this passage to communicate Samuel's lack of confidence in YHWH's choice—the son of a nobody from nowhere—as much as his general fear of Saul. It is deeply significant that the narrative fails to offer any pedigree for the king-elect or his father at this point, or anywhere else in the books of Samuel, a point to which I shall return below. Additionally, the relative

---

[62] 1 Sam 15:22–23, 26, 28.

insignificance of Bethlehem is reflected, intentionally or not, in the trembling elders' obvious alarm and fear over receiving a visit from Samuel; they are visibly shaken and dumbfounded by this visit from the man who speaks the pronouncements of YHWH and is known as a king-maker.[63] "Who are we, and what have we done, to merit a visit from YHWH's seer?" appears to be the question underlying their tremulous greeting. That the leaders of Jesse's hometown react this way to a visit from Samuel reflects, I suggest, their own estimation of their city's worthiness to receive visits—expected or unexpected—from the prophet Samuel. His visit is neither anticipated nor met with joy. It is notable that this smallish perception of Bethlehem is present elsewhere in the prophetic literature:

> And you, O Bethlehem of Ephrath,
> Least among the clans of Judah [צָעִיר לִהְיוֹת בְּאַלְפֵי יְהוּדָה],
> From you one shall come forth
> To rule Israel for Me—
> One whose origin is from of old,
> From ancient times.[64]

Is it possible that Samuel's perplexity and fear over what might happen to him reflect a similar sentiment regarding Bethlehem's, and Jesse's, insignificance? For if Samuel had reasonable grounds (or natural cause) to expect that someone fit to be king might come from Bethlehem, from Jesse's house, then it would have been reasonable for him to assume that he could find protection from him, as Abiathar the priest apparently did when he fled from Saul to David. Indeed, David then assured Abiathar: "Stay with me. Do not be afraid, because he who seeks your life seeks my life—you are safe with me."[65]

Whatever the intention behind the depiction of Samuel in 1 Sam 16:1–2, this response of the seer, a man who has never before flinched in the face

---

[63] 1 Sam 16:4–5. Brueggemann (*First and Second Samuel*, 121) argues that these "elders assume themselves to be in a no-win situation": "Either Samuel is Saul's man, come to forage in the unclaimed south, or he is not Saul's man, which puts them at risk with Saul." Also see Alter, *The David Story*, 96, where Alter writes regarding the elders, "Their reaction is another reflection of the dangerous political situation: the estrangement between Samuel and Saul appears to be generally known, and the elders are terrified at the idea that Samuel may have come to designate a new king, or otherwise subvert the reigning monarch, which could bring royal retribution down on Bethlehem."

[64] Mic 5:1 (NJPS; 5:2 in most English versions).

[65] 1 Sam 22:23; see vv. 20–22.

of potentially life-threatening situations, fails to engender any confidence in the ability of the man whom he will anoint to save and to protect, that is, to meet the most basic expectations of a king. This is remarkable for a text presumed to function as an exonerating apology for the historical David himself, or another of the Davidic line. As we have seen in chapter 1, many scholars include this account in the original History of David's Rise, though McCarter does not. But even in McCarter's case, he appears to assume that, if anything, this and other later additions to HDR strengthen the case for David. If so—and I would agree that it does—it strengthens it by emphasizing the intent of YHWH to elect whomsoever He wills, even the least among Israel's sons, and by de-emphasizing natural rights based on pedigree, merit, ability, and so forth. This stands in stark contrast to the Apology of Ḫattušili.

David, Son of a Nobody

I further suggest that the silence of the biblical text over the pedigree of David and his father, Jesse, should cause attentive readers to experience something of Samuel's unsettledness and perplexity over the choice or "seeing" of YHWH and, thus, the grounds of His command.[66] The narrative is uncharacteristically terse with regard to Jesse and the man whom Samuel is to anoint:

> And YHWH said to Samuel, "How long will you mourn for Saul? I have rejected him from being king over Israel. Fill your horn with oil and go—I am sending you to Jesse the Bethlehemite because I have seen myself a king among his sons."[67]

Jesse's pedigree is conspicuously absent not only here, but also elsewhere in the books of Samuel, as well as in the rest of the *Nebiim*, in all of which Jesse's son plays a deeply prominent role. To appreciate the weight of this argument from silence, it is necessary only to compare the introductions of other key figures in the book of 1 Samuel.

At the beginning of the prophet Samuel's birth narrative in 1 Samuel 1, the biblical text gives the genealogical record of Samuel's father, Elkanah, reaching back to the fourth generation:

---

[66] This presumes, of course, that the readers approach the narrative naively, that is, without drawing on their pre-existing or background knowledge of David's ancestry from later genealogical lists such as those in Ruth 4:18–22 and 1 Chr 2:1–15.

[67] 1 Sam 16:1.

> There was a man from Ramathaim of the Zuphites, from mountainous
> Ephraim, and his name was Elkanah, the son of Jeroham, the son of
> Elihu, the son of Tohu, the son of Zuph, an Ephraimite.[68]

Likewise, the introduction of Saul is preceded by the genealogical record of
his father, Kish, extending back to the fourth generation:

> There was a man from Benjamin, and his name was Kish, the son
> of Abiel, the son of Zeror, the son of Becorath, the son of Aphiah, a
> Benjaminite, a man of valor.[69]

The genealogy of Abiathar's father, Ahimelech, a key figure in the biblical
narrative together with Abiathar, can be worked out from two different
passages to the fourth generation as well:

> But there escaped one son of Ahimelech, son of Ahitub, whose name
> was Abiathar.[70]

---

[68] 1 Sam 1:1.

[69] 1 Sam 9:1. On the resolution of the textual problem in v. 1, see McCarter, *I Samuel*,
167–68. Verse 2, then, introduces Saul: "And he had an exceptionally fine son named Saul.
There was no man among the sons of Israel finer than he. From his shoulders up, [he was]
taller than any of the people." The NRS, NJPS, and ESV render בָּחוּר וָטוֹב as a substantival
hendiadys in which וָטוֹב is the subordinate modifier of בָּחוּר (i.e., "a handsome young
man"). I have treated בָּחוּר וָטוֹב, by contrast, as an adjectival hendiadys that modifies
בֵּן (i.e., "an exceptionally fine son"). In the first place, because טוֹב can be interpreted in
multiple senses (e.g., as referring to moral rectitude as well as physical appearance), "fine"
is preferable to "handsome," which is too restrictive in this case. Likewise, בָּחוּר can also
be interpreted in at least two senses. It often seems to mean simply "young man" or the like
(e.g., Deut 32:25; Eccl 11:9; Isa 62:5; Jer 15:8; 51:22; Ezek 9:6). As a participial passive
of בחר, however, it generally connotes some sense of "chosenness" or "excellence" (i.e.,
one who excels above others), as can be seen in the many references to Israel's soldiers
as אִישׁ בָּחוּר, i.e., "chosen/picked men" (e.g., Judg 20:15, 16, 34; 1 Sam 24:3 [2]; 2 Chr
13:3, 17; see also Ps 89:20; Jer 49:19; 50:44). Particularly with regard to Saul, Israel's first
king to be chosen by God and His people, therefore, it is important to reflect in English this
sense of בָּחוּר that may connote—significantly from the point of Saul's introduction into the
narrative—something of both his "outstanding" nature (see the rest of 1 Sam 9:2, and also
10:23–24) and his chosenness by God (see esp. 1 Sam 10:24: "Do you see the one whom
YHWH has chosen [הַרְאִיתֶם אֲשֶׁר בָּחַר־בּוֹ יְהוָה]").

[70] 1 Sam 22:20.

> And Ahijah—the son of Ahitub (the brother of Ichabod), the son of
> Phinehas, the son of Eli, the priest of YHWH in Shiloh—was bearing
> an ephod.[71]

Even Abner's introduction into the narrative is accompanied by the naming
of his father and his father's father:

> And Kish, the father of Saul, and Ner, the father of Abner, were
> sons of Abiel.[72]

` Read together with 1 Sam 9:1 (see above), therefore, the genealogy of Abner's
father, Ner, can also be traced back four generations. Including the sons, then,
five generations are recorded for the prophet Samuel, the king Saul, the priest
Abiathar, and the general Abner.

Because biblical genealogies have various functions according to their type
and literary context, it is difficult to make a statement about their function
that applies universally. In the case of isolated genealogical lists such as those
given in the books of Samuel, however, it is reasonable to conclude that they
have a certain legitimizing effect: they establish that the person in question has
a known history and thereby derives his significance and standing, whether
horizontally, vertically, or both.[73] The presence of a birth narrative carries
and conveys even greater significance for its subject. As Antony Campbell
comments regarding Samuel's birth narrative, "The principal point of a birth
story is to invest its hero with the distinction of being directly singled out
by God, even from before birth."[74] In view of the above introductions and
genealogical lists, and the birth narrative for Samuel, therefore, it cannot be
maintained, in any case, that for the editors of 1 Samuel such matters were
irrelevant.

How do we explain, then, the terse and abrupt introduction of Jesse, and
the failure of the biblical editors to identify David, genealogically speaking,
by anything more than the appellative "son of Jesse," which is even taken up
and used derogatively in the books of Samuel? This is particularly surprising

---

[71] 1 Sam 14:3.

[72] 1 Sam 14:51.

[73] On the types and functions of biblical genealogies in general, see Wilson, *Genealogy and History*; Flanagan, "Succession and Genealogy," 35–55; Wilson, "Genealogy, Genealogies," 2:929–32; Johnson, *The Purpose of the Biblical Genealogies*. I have found these to be mostly unhelpful, however, with regard to the short lists in the books of Samuel.

[74] Campbell, *1 Samuel*, 45.

in view of the probability, as many historical critics claim, that Jesse was in fact a prominent man,[75] not to mention the traditional material at the editors' disposal by which they might have established links between David and his "noble antecedents" from Judah, as I argued in chapter 2. This lacuna with regard to David, especially taken together with the presence of genealogical lists and even a birth narrative for others, would surely represent a missed opportunity of near colossal proportions for a document composed to legitimize David. Not only have the editors "missed" the most commonly used literary types (genealogical lists and birth narratives) and occasion (the introduction of a prominent figure) to prove that David is not an upstart, the son of a nobody; by their silence they have contributed to and cemented the very impression that he has no natural claim to Saul's throne. I submit, rather, that the authors/editors of the biblical text delight in this portrayal of David's lineage and background as insignificant and unknown next to that of Saul and others in the narrative. If one of the narrative's aims is to assert David's legitimacy, his lineage has nothing to do with it.

Other Effacements of David and His House

My argument that the biblical editors not only fail to build up David and his house (his בֵּית אָב) but also, in fact, depict them (particularly through the speech of various figures) as remarkably insignificant, rests on additional indicators in the narrative. This is all contrary to what one would expect from a document composed chiefly for the sake of political self-justification.

First, David's eldest brother, Eliab, effaces his own family in 1 Samuel 17. Eliab, upon hearing his younger brother David ask about the reward for the one who kills Goliath, becomes incensed and insults David:

> And Eliab, his eldest brother, heard him speaking to the men. And Eliab became incensed with David, and he said, "Why did you come down, and on whom did you unload those few sheep in the wilderness [מְעַט הַצֹּאן הָהֵנָּה בַּמִּדְבָּר]? *I* know your arrogance and the evil that is in your heart, that you came down in order to see the battle!"[76]

Eliab's intent, of course, is simply to insult David by implying that he is shirking his simple shepherding responsibilities and to insinuate that he has no place on the battlefield. But inasmuch as "those few sheep in the wilderness" belong

---

[75] E.g., Halpern, *David's Secret Demons*, 270–71.
[76] 1 Sam 17:28.

to David's father, as the reader is aware,[77] Eliab's insult falls inadvertently upon his own father's house.

Second, David himself essentially admits his family's and his own insignificance when Saul offers as a wife his eldest daughter, Merab, and again when Saul's servants encourage David to win as his wife Saul's younger daughter, Michal, through battle with the Philistines:

> And David said to Saul, "Who am I, and what is my life, [or] my father's family in Israel [מִי אָנֹכִי וּמִי חַיַּי מִשְׁפַּחַת אָבִי בְּיִשְׂרָאֵל], that I should become the king's son-in-law?"[78]

> And Saul's servants spoke these words to David. And David said, "Is it a small thing in your eyes to become the king's son-in-law? I am a poor man and of small repute [וְאָנֹכִי אִישׁ־רָשׁ וְנִקְלֶה]!"[79]

Unsurprisingly, many commentators take these words of David to be false self-deprecation.[80] They are consistent, however, with other characterizations of David in the biblical narrative, as we have seen above and will see further below. One might also note David's self-effacement when Saul pursues him in the wilderness:

> After whom [אַחֲרֵי מִי] has the king of Israel come out? After whom [אַחֲרֵי מִי] are you pursuing? After a dead dog [כֶּלֶב מֵת], after a single flea [פַּרְעֹשׁ אֶחָד]![81]

> Now let not my blood fall to the earth away from YHWH's presence. For the king of Israel has come out to seek a single flea [פַּרְעֹשׁ אֶחָד], [or] as one chases a partridge in the mountains [הַקֹּרֵא בֶּהָרִים].[82]

David might have asked Saul, "Who are *you*, O king rejected by YHWH, to pursue YHWH's newly anointed?" Instead, he displays humility and appeals to his own insignificance by comparing himself to the smallest of insects, a bird flitting about the mountains, and a dead dog.

---

[77] 1 Sam 17:15: "[B]ut David went back and forth from Saul in order to tend his father's sheep in Bethlehem."

[78] 1 Sam 18:18.

[79] 1 Sam 18:23.

[80] E.g., Alter, *The David Story*, 115.

[81] 1 Sam 24:15 (MT; v. 14 in most English versions).

[82] 1 Sam 26:20.

Third, David's enemies are allowed to voice their derision for David, and to question and mock him for his lack of status by way of invoking his father's name, that is, by referring to him as "the son of Jesse" (בֶּן־יִשַׁי).[83] The most striking example, perhaps, comes from the mouth of Nabal, when David's men go to him, at David's order, requesting food supplies:

> But Nabal answered the servants of David and said, "Who is David? And who is the son of Jesse [מִי דָוִד וּמִי בֶן־יִשָׁי]? Today there are many servants breaking loose from their masters. Shall I take my bread, my water, and my meat, which I slaughtered for my shearers, and give it to men who are from I do not know where [לַאֲנָשִׁים אֲשֶׁר לֹא יָדַעְתִּי אֵי מִזֶּה הֵמָּה]?"[84]

Likewise, Saul casts aspersion upon David by means of this patronymic epithet on multiple occasions,[85] as do others among David's enemies.[86] Each occurrence reminds the readers, together with the characters in the biblical narrative, of David's humble and—relative to Samuel, Saul, and others—insignificant, if not unknown, origins. The frequency with which this derogatory epithet is permitted—at least nine times in the books of Samuel in a derogatory sense—suggests that the biblical editors delighted in depicting David's lineage as unremarkable and insignificant.

Taken together, the above suggests that the biblical narrative does not aim to legitimize David in any natural sense at all. Rather, it aims to evoke a sense of wonder and mystery about the identity of YHWH's newly anointed, and to demonstrate dramatically how His finding, choosing, and providing Himself a new king for His people is grounded solely in His divine prerogative to choose whom He wills, and to take the small and insignificant and elevate him to a place of honor. The question that goes unanswered at the beginning of David's story proper—"Who is this son of Jesse?!"—remains a persistent one throughout much of the story[87] and, thus, functions to highlight the mystery and wonder surrounding YHWH's election and confirmation of him. James Kugel's remarks following upon his discussion of the election of David and

[83] So Halpern, *David's Secret Demons*, 271.

[84] 1 Sam 25:10–11.

[85] 1 Sam 20:27, 30, 31; 22:7, 8, 13.

[86] Besides Nabal's reference to David as "the son of Jesse" in 25:10, Doeg (22:9) and Sheba (2 Sam 20:1) also take up this epithet.

[87] See, for example, 1 Sam 17:58; 25:1.

several other figures in the Hebrew Bible are particularly apt in this context, and they serve as a fitting conclusion to my discussion above:

> That biblical authors show no hesitation in reporting on the rather dubious character or qualifications of these divinely chosen figures seems to be an important finding. Biblical narratives actually seem to highlight the fact that their heroes are far from the logical choice and, sometimes, far from pious or meritorious: these men and women have done nothing to deserve this sudden change in their status and they have certainly not sought it out on their own. Rather, it seems that they have been chosen for reasons that are inscrutable, or perhaps for no reason at all, and in this fact the biblical narratives seem to take some pleasure.[88]

David, Beloved Son of Saul

In the above section, I have focused on how YHWH's election of David and his house as the replacement of Saul and his house is particularly surprising in view of the former's relative insignificance. In the remainder of this chapter, I shall consider various moments in the narrative in which YHWH's election of David over Saul and his sons is confirmed. In particular, I shall contend that the words and preferences of various figures in the biblical narrative embody and confirm, and thereby mediate, YHWH's initial and immediate election of David.

First, I shall briefly discuss what might be characterized as David's gradual displacement of Jonathan as Saul's beloved son.[89] As will become evident, I mean this in a nuanced sense. In short, my characterization of David as the beloved son of Saul does not hinge upon Saul's affection for him, but rather upon various demonstrations by many figures in the narrative of a preference for David over Saul's sons (and Jonathan in particular). Because none of these demonstrations are more surprising and improbable than those by Jonathan himself, I shall treat them first.

---

[88] Kugel, *The God of Old*, 49–50. In the area of ethical and philosophical studies, Sekine (*Comparative Study of the Origins of Ethical Thought*) has argued that the concept or feeling of "wonder" is "the fountainhead" of Hebrew ethical thought (1). See, in particular, his introduction, chs. 8–14, and conclusion. Note, too, his citation of Heschel (*God in Search of Man*, p. 45) for demonstrating "that a 'wonder' comparable to Greek *thaumazein* lies at the root of Hebrew ethical thought" (2).

[89] Gary A. Anderson drew my attention to this theme in general, and to the familial language between David and Saul in 1 Samuel 24 and 26 in particular (personal communication).

Jonathan's Preference for David over Himself

The biblical depiction of Jonathan's attitude and disposition towards David, his natural enemy as far as his father Saul is concerned, is the most surprising of all. After David (in Jonathan's view) "took his life in his hand" to battle the Philistine and, thus, became the agent through whom "YHWH accomplished a great victory for all Israel,"[90] Jonathan does a remarkable thing. The narrator reports:

> When he finished speaking with Saul, Jonathan's soul became bound with the soul of David [וְנֶפֶשׁ יְהוֹנָתָן נִקְשְׁרָה בְּנֶפֶשׁ דָּוִד]. And Jonathan loved him as his [very] soul [וַיֶּאֱהָבוֹ יְהוֹנָתָן כְּנַפְשׁוֹ]. And Saul took him that day and did not give him leave to return to his father's house. And Jonathan made a covenant—[he] and David [וַיִּכְרֹת יְהוֹנָתָן וְדָוִד בְּרִית]—because he loved him as his [very] soul [בְּאַהֲבָתוֹ אֹתוֹ כְּנַפְשׁוֹ]. And Jonathan stripped himself [וַיִּתְפַּשֵּׁט יְהוֹנָתָן] of the robe that was upon him and gave it to David [וַיִּתְּנֵהוּ לְדָוִד], and also his outfit, including his sword, his bow, and his belt.[91]

Jonathan identifies David with himself, himself with David. Twice the narrator states that Jonathan loved David "as his [very] soul."[92] Jonathan's stripping himself of his prince's robe and giving it to David, along with his battle equipment, have significance at more than one level. At the surface level, with this gift Jonathan ratifies the covenant he has made with David. At another level, Jonathan's relinquishing of his battle equipment at this particular moment in the narrative marks the rise of a new champion in Israel as Jonathan, who acted essentially as Saul's champion before the introduction of David,[93] is already receding into the background. Perhaps Jonathan watched as Saul clothed David in his king's armor,[94] which, one might expect, would be better and more rightfully suited for Jonathan, but he is conspicuously absent in the narrative in 1 Samuel 17. Jonathan is not absent from the battlefield, however, for he witnessed, together with the men of Israel, David's unlikely victory over the Philistine. This is apparent from Jonathan's expression of covenant love for David immediately following David's encounter with the

---

[90] 1 Sam 19:5. These are Jonathan's words to Saul in his first (and successful) attempt to placate Saul's anger against David.

[91] 1 Sam 18:1–4.

[92] See, too, 1 Sam 20:17; 2 Sam 1:26.

[93] See esp. 1 Samuel 14.

[94] 1 Sam 17:38–39.

Philistine (and with Saul thereafter), and from Jonathan's mention of this battle in his appeal before Saul to spare David's life.[95]

From this point forward, it is David, and not Jonathan or any of the other sons of Saul, who is credited with leading Israel in battle against their enemies. And it is David, Saul's son by marriage, and not Jonathan or his brothers, Saul's sons by birth, whom the people love and name in the same breath as King Saul, and whose acclaim is published throughout Israel and even abroad.[96] At yet a higher level, Jonathan's act of stripping himself of his prince's robe (הַמְּעִיל) and giving it, together with his armor, sword, bow, and belt, prefigures the transferal of the kingdom to the house of David from the house of Saul.[97] As a manifestation of David's divine election, this symbolic act of Jonathan's works effectively both for the figures within the narrative and for the reading community. Within the world of the narrative, presumably, its significance as a portent of the inexorable will of YHWH—and, thus, a source of personal confirmation and assurance—would have loomed larger and larger for David, above all, with the passing of time. Saul, on the other hand, if privy to this exchange, would have likely viewed it ominously. The reading community, of course, can immediately see in this most remarkable and unlikely expression of Jonathan's love for David the mysterious hand of divine providence.

Saul, in fact, becomes jealously suspicious of David, and his murderous intents against him lead Jonathan, who "delighted in David very much,"[98] to warn David and intercede for him on two occasions, risking his own life in the process.[99] On the second of these occasions, just before Jonathan tests Saul to discern his true intents toward David, Jonathan makes a covenant "with the house of David," at which point he invokes YHWH's presence with David "as He has been with" Saul (וִיהִי יְהוָה עִמָּךְ כַּאֲשֶׁר הָיָה עִם־אָבִי).[100] At the same time, Jonathan's expectation that YHWH will "cut off every one of David's enemies [אֹיְבֵי דָוִד אִישׁ] from the face of the earth," followed by his covenantal invocation of vengeance—literally, "May YHWH seek [it] from the

[95] 1 Sam 18:1–4; 1 Sam 19:5.

[96] See, for example, 1 Sam 18:6–8, 16, 30; 21:12 [11]; 22:14; 29:5.

[97] For similar expressions of this view, see, in particular, McCarter, *I Samuel*, 305; Alter, *The David Story*, 112.

[98] 1 Sam 19:1; cf. 20:3.

[99] 1 Sam 19:1–7; ch. 20.

[100] 1 Sam 20:13b–17.

hand of David's enemies [וּבְקֵשׁ יְהוָה מִיַּד אֹיְבֵי דָוִד]"[101] — might be construed essentially as an imprecation against his father. Consider, for instance, that just prior to Jonathan's statement, the narrator has described Saul as "an enemy with David all the days [of his life]" (וַיְהִי שָׁאוּל אֹיֵב אֶת־דָּוִד כָּל־הַיָּמִים),[102] and Saul has openly spoken of David at least on one occasion, to Jonathan's sister, as "my enemy" (אֹיְבִי).[103] Note, too, Jonathan's later reference to the hand of David's declared enemy in his encouragement to David at Horesh, during David's ongoing flight from Saul: "Do not fear, because the hand of Saul, my father [יַד שָׁאוּל אָבִי], will not find you."[104] Saul is certainly aware that his son has chosen to honor David over him. In a burst of rage, Saul directly accuses Jonathan of as much: "Do I not know that you have chosen the son of Jesse [כִּי־בֹחֵר אַתָּה לְבֶן־יִשַׁי] to your shame?"[105] And in his paranoia, he even suspects Jonathan of conspiracy against him:

> And Saul said to his servants attending him, "Listen, you Benjaminites! Will the son of Jesse give fields and vineyards to each of you, and will he make each of you commanders over thousands and commanders over hundreds? For *that* have all of you conspired against me [קְשַׁרְתֶּם כֻּלְּכֶם עָלַי]! And none disclose to me when my son makes [a covenant] with the son of Jesse [בִּכְרָת־בְּנִי עִם־בֶּן־יִשַׁי]. And none of you worry over me, or disclose to me that my son has set up my servant to lie in ambush against me today [כִּי הֵקִים בְּנִי אֶת־עַבְדִּי עָלַי לְאֹרֵב כַּיּוֹם הַזֶּה]."[106]

The last time that Jonathan and David meet, when Jonathan goes out to David at Horesh where, the text reports, Jonathan "strengthened [David's] hand in God" (וַיְחַזֵּק אֶת־יָדוֹ בֵּאלֹהִים), once more the two make "a covenant before YHWH" (וַיִּכְרְתוּ שְׁנֵיהֶם בְּרִית לִפְנֵי יְהוָה). There, in fact, Jonathan openly and freely acknowledges that David, and not he, is destined to follow his father Saul as king: "And [Jonathan] said to [David], 'Do not fear, because the hand

[101] 1 Sam 20:15–16.

[102] 1 Sam 18:29.

[103] 1 Sam 19:17; also see 1 Sam 24:5 [4], 20 [19]; 26:8; 2 Sam 4:8; 22:1.

[104] 1 Sam 23:17. Consider how the threatening "hand" of Saul (among others) figures explicitly in the narrative at numerous points, both in reported speech (of Saul himself in 1 Sam 18:17 and 23:7; of David in 23:11, 12; 24:16 [15]; 27:1; of Jonathan here in 23:17; and see also 19:3; of the Ziphites in 23:20; and of Samuel in 28:17) and in the language of the narrator (1 Sam 18:10; 19:9; 22:6; 23:14).

[105] 1 Sam 20:30.

[106] 1 Sam 22:7–8.

of Saul, my father, will not find you. And you will reign over Israel, and I shall be second to you [וְאַתָּה תִּמְלֹךְ עַל־יִשְׂרָאֵל וְאָנֹכִי אֶהְיֶה־לְּךָ לְמִשְׁנֶה]; my father Saul also knows this.'"[107]

The improbability, based on the principle of human analogy,[108] that the reigning king's son would relinquish his legal claim to his father's throne and capitulate the kingdom to his father's enemy leads many contemporary scholars to treat these passages dismissively. McKenzie, for instance, asserts that "the picture of Jonathan in these verses is unrealistic. . . . The two may have been friends. But it is hard to believe that Jonathan would give up his future as king to someone he had just met."[109] In McKenzie's view, it appears, the author attempts to solidify David's right to the throne by basing it more steadily upon natural claims such as this—the prince essentially abdicated the throne to David, so it is his by right. This approach assumes the author's presumption of the readers' gullibility to believe an improbability such as this.

I submit, however, that these accounts and depictions of Jonathan's disposition toward David are not intended to legitimize David as the rightful heir based chiefly on the simple fact of Jonathan's status and the natural consequences of his actions (and as something to be gullibly accepted without pause). Rather, David's status as YHWH's elect is confirmed precisely by the inexplicability of Jonathan's choice of David over himself and his father, and by the wonder of Jonathan's intense love for and commitment to David, which is unparalleled even by David's own family. David himself declares how "marvelous" or "wondrous" was Jonathan's love—נִפְלְאַתָה אַהֲבָתְךָ לִי —and how it exceeded even "the love of women."[110] Much like the surprising election and confirmation of the least of Jesse's sons as the beloved son— surprising because improbable and near impossible—this unlikely account seems to be presented as a source of delight and wonder, and as one of several mysterious confirmations of YHWH's gracious election of David.

David, "Son of Saul"

Above, I have demonstrated David's identification with and gradual eclipse of Saul's son Jonathan, both in Jonathan's own sight and in that of the men

---

[107] 1 Sam 23:16–18.
[108] See p. 106, above.
[109] McKenzie, *King David*, 79–80.
[110] 2 Sam 1:26.

and women of Israel. Perhaps most importantly, however, in numerous and surprising ways David is characterized in the narrative, and treated by Saul himself, as a "son of Saul."[111] The king's adoption of "the least" son of a man with no reported family history is cause enough for wonder. This wonder is increased, however, by Saul's treatment of David as a son despite his deep antipathy for him. Unbeknownst to himself at first, and in spite of himself thereafter, Saul confirms or mediates in and through his adoption of David YHWH's initial and immediate election of David. Let us turn briefly, now, to see how this plays out in the narrative.

Saul's first words in the biblical narrative directly regarding the "son of Jesse the Bethlehemite," whom a servant has "seen," are addressed to Jesse: "Send me David your son" (שִׁלְחָה אֵלַי אֶת־דָּוִד בִּנְךָ).[112] On previous occasions Saul has chosen hundreds and thousands of other men to follow him into battle,[113] but Jesse is the first father named in the biblical narrative for whom Samuel's pronouncement that the reigning king "will take your sons" (אֶת־בְּנֵיכֶם יִקָּח)[114] hits home. King Saul's claim on David is reiterated after David's defeat of Goliath, when the narrative reports, "Saul took him [וַיִּקָּחֵהוּ] that day and did not give him leave to return to his father's house."[115] And later, at the feast in 1 Samuel 20, Saul demonstrates, by his violent reaction to Jonathan's reason for David's absence, the degree to which he expects David to renounce his "family" (מִשְׁפָּחָה) and his own brothers—curiously, Jonathan does not mention Jesse, David's father—in order to attend his table.[116] Of course, Saul's anger is provoked also because he has now missed another opportunity to kill David, but his expectations toward David are evident nonetheless. When the king first calls David, in 1 Samuel 16, Jesse obediently obliges and sends him "David his son" (דָּוִד בְּנוֹ).[117] This request of (or command to) Jesse for "your son," Jesse's obedient response, and Saul's ensuing instructions for Jesse to "let David remain in his station before

---

[111] For another treatment of the father-son relationship between Saul and David in 1 Samuel, see Pleins, "Son-slayers and Their Sons." This article compares father-son relationships in 1 Samuel with several in Genesis. On father-son relationships in Genesis, Levenson's *Death and Resurrection* is essential.

[112] 1 Sam 16:19.

[113] See 1 Sam 11:8; 13:2; 14:52.

[114] 1 Sam 8:11.

[115] 1 Sam 18:2.

[116] 1 Sam 20:27–30.

[117] 1 Sam 16:20.

me" seem highly significant, particularly in light of Saul's very last words concerning David in the biblical narrative, this time addressed directly to David himself: "Blessed be you, my son David [דָוִד בְּנִי אַתָּה בָּרוּךְ]! You will surely act and surely prevail!"[118] Saul's own words reflect a change in David's status from being "the son of Jesse" to becoming "the son of Saul." Let us survey in cursory fashion the key moments that transpire between these two utterances of Saul, and that function to confirm David's gradual displacement of Jonathan as King Saul's beloved son.

I have already mentioned Saul's clothing of David in his own armor before his contest with the Philistine champion in 1 Samuel 17, and how, from this point onward, David essentially replaces Jonathan in Saul's and everyone else's sight, including that of Israel's enemies, as Saul's champion warrior.[119] Saul, of course, grows jealous, suspicious, and fearful of David. The readers, at least, are privy to the knowledge that Saul's fear and, consequently, his actions are driven in part because YHWH had left Saul to be with David, and because, instead, "an evil spirit from God" (רָעָה אֱלֹהִים רוּחַ) came upon Saul.[120] Ironically, all this contributes to the further rise of David vis-à-vis Saul.

Saul initially promises to give his eldest daughter to David, asking him only to "be valiant [lit., "a son of valor"] for me" (חַיִל־לְבֶן־לִי הֱיֵה), in hopes that he will fall by "the hand of the Philistines." Against expectations, David, in fact, performs as Saul's "son of valor," that is, valiantly, but Saul gives Merab to another.[121] Then, when Saul hears that his younger daughter, Michal, "loved David" (דָוִד־אֶת שָׁאוּל־בַּת מִיכַל וַתֶּאֱהַב), he devises a plan to rid himself of David by offering his daughter—Saul tells David, "You shall become my son-in-law [בִּי תִּתְחַתֵּן] today"—as the reward for the impossible task of bringing Saul one hundred Philistine foreskins. By sending David into battle against the Philistines under these terms, Saul intends "to bring down David by the hand of the Philistines," that is, to make him a "son of death" (מָוֶת־בֶּן).[122] In a highly improbable and unanticipated turn of events, however, David brings back twice the number of foreskins, pays the brideprice for Saul's daughter, and thereby gains legal status as "the king's son-in-law"

---

[118] 1 Sam 26:25.

[119] See, e.g., 1 Sam 18:5–7, 13–16, 17, 25–30; 19:4–5, 8; 21:12 [11]; 29:5.

[120] 1 Sam 18:8–29; the quotation is from v. 10. The narrative explicitly identifies this cause and effect in 1 Sam 18:12, 28–29.

[121] 1 Sam 18:17–19.

[122] 1 Sam 18:20–25; also see 20:31.

and even higher acclaim to his name in Israel.[123] In a twist of deep irony, Saul's sending of Jonathan into battle against the Philistines in 1 Sam 31:1–7 consigns him to fall by "the hand of the Philistines," as Samuel had said,[124] and as a result, to become Saul's own "son of death." It was in the context of Jonathan's earlier battle against the Philistines, in 1 Samuel 14, that Saul essentially cursed his son to die. Similarly, it was in the context of David's first battle against the Philistines, in 1 Samuel 17, that Saul invoked YHWH to be with him. Both are fulfilled according to his word.

The narrative depicts by other means David's displacement of Jonathan as Saul's son and heir, as well as Saul's eclipse of Jesse as David's father, though the latter to a lesser degree. In the first place, both Jesse and Jonathan gradually recede into the background as the narrative progresses. I have already discussed above Jonathan's decreasing vis-à-vis David. The last time Jesse figures in the narrative by name—except as part of the commonly used "son of Jesse" epithet for David—is in 1 Samuel 17. As I have already noted, there is surprisingly no reference to him in David and Jonathan's ruse in 1 Sam 20:29. There is only one more reference to David's "father and mother" in 1 Sam 22:3, when David protects them by sending them to the king of Moab.

More significant and telling are the various ways and circumstances in which each of these figures speaks directly to and/or about the others. David directly addresses Saul but not Jesse as "my father" (אָבִי).[125] Jonathan, on the other hand, never addresses Saul in the second person as "my father" or the like, but only as "the king."[126] And though he speaks about Saul in the third person as "my father" on numerous occasions, the first time he does so, he declares to the people, "My father has troubled the land" (עָכַר אָבִי אֶת־הָאָרֶץ);[127] all the rest, then, occur within the context of his protecting and/or interceding for David against Saul.[128]

Similarly, Saul directly addresses David but not Jonathan as "my son" (בְּנִי דָוִד). When Saul learns that David could have easily killed him but instead has spared his life in the cave at Engedi, Saul cries out to him as "my

---

[123] 1 Sam 18:26–30.

[124] 1 Sam 28:19.

[125] 1 Sam 24:12 [11]. David calls Jesse "my father" on one occasion, but it is when he asks the king of Moab, "Please let my father and my mother stay with you" (1 Sam 22:3).

[126] E.g., 1 Sam 19:4; 20:29.

[127] 1 Sam 14:29.

[128] 1 Sam 19:2, 3; 20:2, 9, 12, 13; 23:17.

son David" (בְּנִי דָוִד). Weeping, Saul calls upon YHWH to reward David for his exceeding righteousness and the good he has done toward Saul.[129] At this time, Saul finally acknowledges that the kingdom will be David's—"Now, see, I know that you will surely be king, and that the kingdom of Israel will be established in your hand"[130]—and not Jonathan's, as he had hoped.[131] Later, when Saul learns that David has spared his life yet again, this time on the hill of Hachilah, Saul addresses David three times as "my son David" (בְּנִי דָוִד), adding his blessing on the third time: בָּרוּךְ אַתָּה בְּנִי דָוִד, "Blessed be you, my son David!"[132]

By contrast, quite surprisingly, Saul never addresses Jonathan directly (i.e., in the first person) as "my son." On one occasion, in direct speech to Jonathan, Saul calls him "son," but it is when he calls him "you son of a perverse, rebellious woman" (בֶּן־נַעֲוַת הַמַּרְדּוּת).[133] And though on two occasions Saul refers to Jonathan in speech to others as "my son," neither is auspicious for the son. The first occasion is when Jonathan ate honey after their battle with the Philistines, not knowing that Saul had made an oath. Saul suspects that someone among them has committed some grievous sin because God does not answer the priest, and so he utters yet another oath: "For as YHWH lives who saves Israel, even if it is in Jonathan my son [בְּיוֹנָתָן בְּנִי], he shall surely die."[134] The second occasion is when he essentially accuses Jonathan of conspiring against him, blaming his men for not telling him "when my son makes [a covenant] with the son of Jesse [בִּכְרָת־בְּנִי עִם־בֶּן־יִשַׁי]," or "that my son has set up my servant to lie in ambush against me today [הֵקִים בְּנִי אֶת־עַבְדִּי עָלַי לְאֹרֵב]."[135] As for Jesse, he never addresses David directly in familial terms, and the only time he speaks about him is when he refers to him as "the least" (הַקָּטָן).[136] The one time that Jesse speaks directly

[129] 1 Sam 24:17–20 (MT; vv. 16–19 in most English versions).

[130] 1 Sam 24:21 (MT; v. 20 in most English versions).

[131] 1 Sam 20:31.

[132] 1 Sam 26:17, 21, 25. As I noted earlier, this third address and blessing marks Saul's final words to David in the biblical narrative.

[133] 1 Sam 20:30. נעות reads as נערות ("young women") in 4QSam[b] and is reflected in the LXX, reading, therefore, "Son of rebelling young women." See McCarter, I Samuel, 339.

[134] 1 Sam 14:39. Saul calls him "Jonathan my son" in this same context two more times in vv. 40 and 42.

[135] 1 Sam 22:8.

[136] 1 Sam 16:11.

to David in the narrative, in fact, his expressed concern is not for David but for the well-being of David's three elder brothers at battle.[137]

Furthermore, in and through other language of the narrative, Saul shows greater esteem for David than his own son, and Jonathan esteems David above his own father. First, it is notable that Saul's and Jonathan's positive responses to David are characterized in highly similar language. When Saul first meets David, the text reports that he "loved him very much" (וַיֶּאֱהָבֵהוּ מְאֹד).[138] Likewise, upon the first reported meeting between Jonathan and David, it is twice reported by the narrator that Jonathan "loved him as his [very] soul" (וַיֶּאֱהָבֵהוּ יְהוֹנָתָן כְּנַפְשׁוֹ; בְּאַהֲבָתוֹ אֹתוֹ כְּנַפְשׁוֹ).[139] Also, both Saul and Jonathan are reported to "delight" (חָפֵץ) in David.[140] And finally, whereas Saul declares that David has "found favor in my eyes" (מָצָא חֵן בְּעֵינָי),[141] David later recognizes that he has "found favor in the eyes" of Jonathan (מָצָאתִי חֵן בְּעֵינֶיךָ).[142]

Second, both the father and son extend benedictions to David at several critical points in the narrative. Saul invokes YHWH's presence with David in battle against the Philistine (לֵךְ וַיהוָה יִהְיֶה עִמָּךְ; "Go, and may YHWH be with you"),[143] YHWH's reward to him for David's mercy toward Saul (וַיהוָה יְשַׁלֶּמְךָ טוֹבָה; "May YHWH reward you with good"),[144] and a blessing upon him as "my son" for once again sparing Saul's life (בָּרוּךְ אַתָּה בְּנִי דָוִד; "Blessed be you, my son David").[145] Similarly, Jonathan invokes YHWH's presence with David "as He has been with my father" (וִיהִי יְהוָה עִמָּךְ כַּאֲשֶׁר הָיָה עִם־אָבִי) and sends him away "in peace" (לֵךְ לְשָׁלוֹם)[146] when he confirms that Saul intends to kill David.

---

[137] 1 Sam 17:17–18.

[138] 1 Sam 16:21. The MT does not specify the subject of וַיֶּאֱהָבֵהוּ. Most translations, therefore, insert at least "Saul" as the subject in order to avoid any ambiguity about who loves whom. LXX[L] goes even further and names "Saul" as the subject and "David" as the object.

[139] 1 Sam 18:1, 3. See the similar statements about Jonathan's love for David in 1 Sam 20:17 and 2 Sam 1:26.

[140] 1 Sam 18:22 (Saul) and 19:1 (Jonathan). Saul's expression of delight, of course, is part of his strategy to send David to his death in battle.

[141] 1 Sam 16:22.

[142] 1 Sam 20:3; also see v. 29.

[143] 1 Sam 17:37.

[144] 1 Sam 24:20 (MT; v. 19 in most English versions).

[145] 1 Sam 26:25.

[146] 1 Sam 20:13, 42.

Third, by contrast, Saul's and Jonathan's language toward and treatment of each other are starkly different, as we have seen above. On the one hand, the two fail to use anything resembling the covenantal and "affectionate" language with regard to one another that they employ toward David. Even more significantly, however, Saul essentially curses Jonathan on two occasions (and attempts to slay him on the second),[147] and Jonathan, likewise, essentially curses his father,[148] and he continuously sides with David against his father.[149]

David, Beloved Son of YHWH and His People Israel

In the previous section, my central aim was to demonstrate how YHWH's election of David was mediated and confirmed in and through David's wondrous and entirely improbable elevation above Saul's intended heir, Jonathan, in the eyes of the people, Saul, and Jonathan himself. David survives "my brother Jonathan" (אָחִי יְהוֹנָתָן)[150] and thus becomes the beloved son and heir of King Saul. This discussion naturally led us to consider, as well, David's gradual eclipse of King Saul in Jonathan's eyes. I shall not rehearse this again in the present context but, instead, simply refer the reader to review above the numerous ways in which Jonathan honors and prefers David above and over against his own father, even to the point of being accused as a co-conspirator with David. Besides this, there are a number of other signals in the biblical narrative of David's gradual displacement of Saul as the beloved son of Israel, thus further confirming his belovedness in YHWH's sight. We can best appreciate this, perhaps, by considering David's displacement of Saul in the eyes of various constituents of Israel, beginning with Samuel and including the house of Jesse, the elders of Bethlehem, the men of Israel (especially

---

[147] 1 Sam 14:24, 27–30, 39–44; see, too, 20:30–34. Pleins ("Son-slayers and Their Sons," esp. 32–33, 37) argues that Saul's attempt on Jonathan's life marks a key moment in the development of the relationships between Saul, Jonathan, and David. Saul's attempt to kill his own heir drives Jonathan to support David even more strongly, and plays a role in closing off succession to Jonathan and opening the way for Saul's "son" David to succeed him.

[148] In 1 Sam 20:16, Jonathan calls for YHWH to "seek [it] from the hand of David's enemies," that is, to requite them; together with my discussion on pp. 171–72, above, see the following passages where Saul is presented as David's "enemy": 1 Sam 18:29; 19:17; 24:5 [4], 20 [19]; 26:8; 2 Sam 4:8; 22:1.

[149] See 1 Sam 19:1–7; ch. 20; 22:8; and 23:16–18.

[150] 2 Sam 1:26.

Saul's army), the women of Israel,[151] Saul's attendants and servants, Saul's own children, and even Saul himself.

The Public Confirmation of David Through His Anointing

David's anointing by Samuel is the first public demonstration, or confirmation, of YHWH's election of David as Saul's replacement. I have already discussed in considerable detail, above, the shocking revelation to Samuel—matched, perhaps, by dreaded suspicion among the elders of Bethlehem—that YHWH had elected His new king from among the sons of an unknown Bethlehemite, an insignificant man from an insignificant town. I also discussed the surprising discovery—for the prophet and everyone else present—that YHWH's eyes had fallen not on the eldest and most Saul-like of the family, but on the least. I have not yet directly addressed, however, an ambiguity in this account that appears to be irresolvable. In short, the problem might be expressed in this question: How public is YHWH's rejection of Eliab, Abinadab, Shammah, and the next four sons; and how public is YHWH's confirmation that "[David] is he," YHWH's newly elected king to replace Saul? I do not mean to ask merely how many people are assumed to be watching as the prophet examines Jesse's sons one by one and, at the end, shows some special interest in the youngest. The question has to do with the degree, rather, to which those present understood the significance of what was occurring, as well as the makeup of the crowd of witnesses. Let me address the last part of this question first.

Jesse and his sons, at least, witness the anointing of David "in the midst of his brothers," though whether or not they understood its significance is another question that I shall address below. But were the elders, and perhaps their families, also present when Samuel anointed David? Readers are left to infer the answer—for there is no mention of them after Samuel tells them in 1 Sam 16:5, "Consecrate yourselves and come with me to the sacrifice"—based on where they conclude that the anointing occurred.

One possibility is that the anointing ceremony took place at the time of the sacrifice, apparently just prior to the sacrificial meal. There are two bases for this conclusion. First, from the end of verse 5 ("And he consecrated Jesse and his sons, and he called them to the sacrifice") to the beginning of verse 6 ("When they came"), the most natural reading of the narrative flow of events

---

[151] Partly because of the women's elevation of David above Saul (even if unintended), outside the constituency of Israel the Philistines also come to perceive David as Israel's most beloved son, as we shall see below.

is that "to the sacrifice" is assumed but elided in verse 6 (that is, "When they came to the sacrifice"). Second, Samuel's statement in verse 11 — "we will not sit down [around the table] until his arrival here" (לֹא־נָסֹב עַד־בֹּאוֹ פֹה) — might indicate that Samuel and the rest are to be conceived here as preparing to partake of the sacrificial feast. McCarter translates סבב as "sit down to eat," noting that the term "had this sense at least in later Hebrew (Sir 32:1), and LXX^B (*kataklithōmen*) seems to have understood *nsb* this way in the present case."[152] If so, one might assume that the elders, who were invited to the sacrifice, are presumed to be standing nearby.

According to another view, however, it is also possible to conceive of the events depicted in verses 6–13 as taking place when Samuel went (presumably to Jesse's home) to consecrate Jesse and his sons. The language of verses 5 and 6 is not precise enough to preclude this possibility, and the text's mention of the brothers but not the elders in verses 6–13 (especially in verse 13) offers some support to this view. This would account for Robert Alter's determination, expressed in his comments on verse 13, that "[t]he anointment takes place within the family circle and is a clandestine act."[153] The case for the first possible reading — that the elders, and perhaps their families, also stood as witnesses to David's anointing — is the stronger of the two, but because ambiguity remains, one cannot conclude definitively either way.

The degree to which we should credit the various figures in the narrative (including David) with an awareness or correct assessment of the significance of Samuel's visit and anointing of David is also unclear. A significant problem for readers of this account centers around the identification of the speaker, the intended or direct recipient of the speech, and any others who overhear the speech in each verse. First, let us view the progression of dialogue in verses 6–10 (note that capitalized pronouns refer to YHWH):

> When they came, he saw Eliab. And he said, "Surely before YHWH is His anointed!" (v. 6)

> But YHWH said to Samuel, "Do not look to his appearance or to the height of his standing, because I have rejected him. For it is not that

---

[152] McCarter, *I Samuel*, 275. The NJPS, too, renders נסב as "sit down to eat," though a textual note states uncertainty about the Hebrew meaning. Hertzberg offers an alternative explanation that, nevertheless, presumes the sacrificial context: " 'Closing the circle' (*sābab*) presupposes the company assembled for the sacrifice" (*I & II Samuel: A Commentary*, 138).

[153] Alter, *The David Story*, 97.

which man sees, because man sees the outward appearance. YHWH, however, sees the heart." (v. 7)

So Jesse called to Abinadab, and he paraded him before Samuel. But he [He?] said, "YHWH has not chosen this one either." (v. 8)

And Jesse paraded Shammah. But he [He?] said, "YHWH has not chosen this one either." (v. 9)

And Jesse paraded seven of his sons before Samuel. But Samuel said to Jesse, "YHWH has not chosen these." (v. 10)

Samuel is the speaker in verse 6, but is he directing his discovery to YHWH, to those present at the ceremony, or is he merely musing to himself? Nearly all of the modern versions—the NRSV, NIV, NJPS, and ESV, for example—render וַיֹּאמֶר in verse 6 as "thought," but this is conjecture, reflecting the general assumption that Samuel offers few if any clues to the true intent of his visit. The only thing we can say for certain is that YHWH, at least, hears and responds to Samuel in verse 7. But this raises another question.

How exactly does YHWH speak in the narrative? Is it by any means perceivable to others besides Samuel? McCarter, for example, assumes that YHWH speaks to Samuel in this account by means of some oracular device: "If Samuel is not using the lots in the examination of Jesse's sons, he is using something similar which gives 'yes' and 'no' answers."[154] The use of some oracular device is certainly conceivable for the decisions reflected in verses 8–10, 12, but the nature of the content of YHWH's speech in verses 1–3, 7, in particular, mitigates against this assumption, for these are far from "yes" and "no" questions and answers.[155] If that is the case, it would appear that YHWH is conceived as speaking or revealing His will directly to Samuel, at least initially, without the means of some oracular device that might be heard (or, as the came may be, seen) by witnesses. And if we are to conceive of YHWH as speaking directly to Samuel in verses 1–3, 7 (that is, unmediated by any oracular device), it seems unnecessary to conceive of Him as switching to communication by means of an oracular device midway through the occasion. In that case, only Samuel's audible statements would

[154] McCarter, *I Samuel*, 277.

[155] Once again, see p. 134 n. 14, above, for Alter's explanation of the different character of divine speech in 1 Sam 16:1–13, particularly in the early verses.

be accessible to them. Of course, even if we are to conceive of Samuel as seeking YHWH's will by means of an oracular device throughout the account, it does not necessarily follow that the witnesses hear and understand Samuel's questions (for example, perhaps they are unspoken), nor YHWH's answers (if they are unable to read the lots).

Furthermore, the identities of the speaker and the intended recipient of the speech recorded in verses 8 and 9 are not clear. Reading forward, from verse 7, one might easily assume that YHWH continues as the subject of אמר in verses 8 and 9, revealing His will to Samuel. Because YHWH speaks of Himself in the third person in verse 7 ("For it is not that which man sees [that YHWH sees] . . . YHWH, however, sees the heart"), the third-person references in verses 8 and 9 ("YHWH has not chosen this one either") do not pose any problem for construing these statements as YHWH's speech. In verse 10, however, after the text reports that "Jesse paraded seven of his sons before Samuel" (in language nearly identical to verses 8 and 9), Samuel is identified as the speaker, and Jesse as the direct recipient, of the announcement that "YHWH has not chosen these" (also in language nearly identical to that in the previous two verses). In light of this, in retrospect, it is also possible that the same scenario is conceived of in verses 8 and 9, as well as for sons four through seven: Jesse parades a son before Samuel, and Samuel reports to Jesse that "YHWH has not chosen him either." The point is that the identification of the subject of אמר, and of all who hear these statements, influences the degree to which one attributes to Jesse, his sons, and any other bystanders cognizance of what is taking place before their eyes.

In the end, with regard to who hears Samuel's statements—not to mention YHWH's—and the degree to which they understand their significance, the only thing we can determine with certainty is that Jesse hears directly from Samuel in verse 10 that "YHWH has not chosen these." There is no indication either way whether Jesse's sons, or any other bystanders, hear this as well. The text, then, allows the conception of at least five different scenarios with regard to the identity of the witnesses and the degree to which they are aware of the day's significance:

1) Jesse alone is minimally aware that something of importance is happening to David, for Samuel dismisses Jesse's first seven sons, telling him that "YHWH has not chosen these"; the prophet

is impatient to see the remaining son, who is "tending the sheep"; and upon examining him, he anoints only David "in the midst of his brothers."

2) In addition to Jesse, Jesse's sons are also minimally aware that something of importance is happening to David for the same reasons as above (i.e., they hear and witness as much as Jesse).

3) In addition to Jesse and his sons, the elders and perhaps their families are also present and have some sense of David's newfound importance.

4) Jesse and his sons realize the full significance of Samuel's visit, even if only when YHWH's Spirit comes upon David.

5) In addition to the scenario depicted in 4), the elders and perhaps their families are present and also realize that Samuel has come to anoint a new king in their midst.

I suggest that it is reasonable to presume some significant degree of awareness on the part of Jesse, and anyone else who overhears Samuel's words, about what is taking place given that a) Samuel follows his statement to Jesse in verse 10, at least, with his command to have the eighth son brought to him; b) Samuel experiences a moment of recognition—though it is unclear whether YHWH's declaration that "this is he" is somehow discernible to the others, perhaps by some oracular device and procedure visible to them, or perhaps in Samuel's reaction to David in contrast to the others; c) Samuel then proceeds to anoint David; and d) something discernible happens to David, for YHWH's Spirit comes upon him with some force (וַתִּצְלַח רוּחַ־יְהוָה אֶל־דָּוִד).

Whatever the case, that is, to whatever degree Jesse and the other attendees were aware of the significance of David's anointing at the time, I cannot agree with the view that characterizes them as more or less extraneous to the narrative. Hertzberg, for examples, argues thus:

> Samuel uses the word 'anointed' only in his verdict on Eliab. But we are hardly to suppose that it was said out loud. It is, like the Lord's 'word' to Samuel, something which takes place between the Lord and Samuel, without other witnesses. In this way it accords generally with the rest of this section; the other people are really

only supernumeraries, mentioned as far as is necessary for the circumstances, the divine action of the choosing and anointing of the king. Even David appears only in order to be anointed. The whole narrative is completely theocentric; it does not therefore ask how the details are to be understood, whether historically or psychologically.[156]

Hertzberg's assertion that Samuel is not speaking aloud lacks any solid basis, but this is not the chief problem with this statement; it is his view of the narrative as "completely theocentric," to the extent that everyone's presence, even David's, is almost superfluous. As I have argued at length in chapter 4, "the divine action of the choosing . . . of the king," at least, is completed before Samuel steps foot in Bethelehem, and so Hertzberg misses and undermines at least one of the main points of the anointing of David: YHWH sends Samuel to anoint David to make manifest and to confirm visibly the heretofore hidden will of YHWH to human witnesses. And even if we allow the possibility that none besides Samuel, not even David, perhaps, realize the full significance of Samuel's actions at that time, the event of David's anointing, in that case, would still stand as a testimony to YHWH's election of him that would grow in significance as events leading David to the throne took their course.

Finally, however, I suggest that there is significance in the fact that David is not introduced with the fanfare surrounding Samuel's presentation of Saul to the people of Israel:

> [Saul] stood among the people. And he was taller than any of the people from his shoulders up. And Samuel said to all the people, "Do you see the one whom YHWH has chosen [הַרְאִיתֶם אֲשֶׁר בָּחַר־בּוֹ יְהוָה]? There is no one like him among all the people." And all the people shouted, "Long live the king!"[157]

Even after David's anointing, it is not clear whether the witnesses in Bethlehem have truly seen, as YHWH has seen, the one whom YHWH has chosen. Instead, the considerable ambiguity over the question of precisely who knows how much about David's new status as YHWH's anointed king, if recognized, evokes in the readers some sense of the mystery and surprise that gradually unfolds through the course of the narrative as David is revealed

---

[156] Hertzberg, *I & II Samuel*, 138.
[157] 1 Sam 10:23b–24.

and confirmed as YHWH's, and therefore Israel's, beloved son, whom YHWH has found, chosen, and provided to replace Saul.

David's Elevation over Saul in the Eyes of His Family and "All Israel"

Soon enough, David begins to displace Saul as the one to whom his family and "all Israel," including Saul himself, look to fulfill the essential duties of a king by offering them protection and deliverance from their enemies. In the chapter following the account of David's anointing, the Philistines are gathered at Socoh, "which belongs to Judah," and arrayed against "Saul and the men of Israel."[158] Israel faces what appears to be an undefeatable foe in the Philistine champion, Goliath of Gath, as the narrative's description of him implies, who comes out and issues this challenge "to the battle lines of Israel":

> "Why have you come out to take battle formation? Am I not a Philistine, and you, servants of Saul? Choose yourselves a man and let him come down to me! If he prevails in the fight with me and defeats me, we shall be your servants. But if I prevail against him and defeat him, then you shall be our servants, and you shall serve us!" And the Philistine said, "I defy the battle lines of Israel today. Give me a man that we might fight together!" And Saul and all Israel heard these words of the Philistine, and they were terrified and very much afraid.[159]

The Philistine calls upon Israel to "choose yourselves a man" (בְּרוּ־לָכֶם אִישׁ)— that is, to select a representative for themselves—and to "give me a man" (תְּנוּ־לִי אִישׁ) from among their battle lines. It is no small irony that the man whom Israel has already chosen as their chief representative,[160] after they asked Samuel to "give us a king" (תְּנָה־לָּנוּ מֶלֶךְ),[161] is reduced to dismay and great fear, together with "all Israel," upon hearing these words.[162] "But David

---

[158] 1 Sam 17:1–3.

[159] 1 Sam 17:8b–11.

[160] 1 Sam 12:13: "And now see [וְעַתָּה הִנֵּה] the king whom you have chosen [בְּחַרְתֶּם], whom you requested. See here [וְהִנֵּה], YHWH has set over you a king."

[161] 1 Sam 8:6.

[162] 1 Sam 17:11.

. . ." (וְדָוִד).[163] With this disjunctive, the account shifts to introduce the one whom they will "choose" and "give" to fight the Philistine.

In a remarkable moment of upheaval in the unfolding drama, as if in partial fulfillment of Hannah's prayer,[164] Saul becomes David and David becomes Saul. Saul invokes YHWH, who has left him, to be with David: "Go, and may YHWH be with you!" (לֵךְ וַיהוָה יִהְיֶה עִמָּךְ).[165] Saul then acts as David's armor-bearer by bringing forth the armor and weapons of war for YHWH's king, the people's deliverer. Saul equips David as a king, to represent him and his people in battle.[166] David, however, rejects and "removes" (וַיְסִרֵם) Saul's armor,[167] "for he had not tested [the gear]" (כִּי לֹא־נִסָּה).[168] Rather than go forth into battle clothed as Saul, he prefers the shepherding tools—a staff, a sling and stones, and his shepherd's pouch—with and by which YHWH had equipped and prepared him for battle. These he had tested,[169] and by these he will now be tested and proven before the eyes of all Israel as a shepherd better equipped and suited than Saul to lead and protect YHWH's people. As their representative, therefore, David takes the place of his three elder brothers[170] and all Israel, including Saul himself, and goes out to fight "YHWH's battle" against the Philistine.

---

[163] So begins 1 Sam 17:12. Of course, the more natural rendering in English within the context of v. 12 is something like "Now David . . ." because the disjunctive marks a break in the narrative flow in order to introduce new background information. Following immediately upon v. 11, however, וְדָוִד also marks a contrast between "Saul and all Israel," who "were terrified and very much afraid," and David, who will rise up to defeat the Philistine.

[164] See 1 Sam 2:4–9, where Hannah communicates, in various ways, how YHWH exalts the weak and humble, and humbles the strong and exalted.

[165] 1 Sam 17:37; see 16:13–14, 18.

[166] 1 Sam 17:38–39; cf. 16:21.

[167] It is of small consequence, perhaps, but interesting, nevertheless, to note that David "removes" Israel's reproach (הֵסִיר חֶרְפָּה מֵעַל יִשְׂרָאֵל; 1 Sam 17:26) this day by "taking off" the Philistine's head (וַהֲסִרֹתִי אֶת־רֹאשְׁךָ מֵעָלֶיךָ; 17:46). This becomes the first demonstration or confirmation to "all Israel," even if only in retrospect, that YHWH has "rejected" and will "remove" Saul to make way for David as His king.

[168] 1 Sam 17:39; that is, he was not experienced with them.

[169] 1 Sam 17:40; also see 17:34–37.

[170] As I have noted above, beyond the general deliverance that he won for Israel, David's victory over the Philistine champion was to have special significance for his "father's house," i.e., to "make his father's house free in Israel" (1 Sam 17:25).

This "test" proves in dramatic fashion the claims thus far that YHWH is or shall be with David,[171] and David's claim that "to YHWH [belongs] the battle" (לַיהוָה הַמִּלְחָמָה),[172] even apart from the near miraculous nature of the shepherd boy's victory over a seasoned warrior.[173] At the conclusion of the battle, the Philistine, who had "cursed David by his gods" (וַיְקַלֵּל הַפְּלִשְׁתִּי אֶת־דָּוִד בֵּאלֹהָיו),[174] "fell on his face to the ground" (וַיִּפֹּל עַל־פָּנָיו אָרְצָה) before David in much the same manner that his god Dagon was twice found to be "fallen on his face to the ground before the ark of YHWH" (וְהִנֵּה דָגוֹן נֹפֵל לְפָנָיו אַרְצָה לִפְנֵי אֲרוֹן יְהוָה), and subsequently, the head of the Philistine warrior was "cut off" like that of his god Dagon before the ark of YHWH.[175] Not only does this show or make known to "all the earth that there is a God in Israel" (וְיֵדְעוּ כָּל־הָאָרֶץ כִּי יֵשׁ אֱלֹהִים לְיִשְׂרָאֵל), as David declares,[176] but also that this God's presence is concentrated in and with David in demonstrable force for the purpose of securing His people's freedom from servitude.[177]

In other contexts, I have already made reference to the various markers in 1 Samuel 18–19, in particular, of David's increasing prominence and belovedness in the people's eyes vis-à-vis Jonathan, and in Jonathan's eyes vis-à-vis his father. That which I have argued, above, pertaining to David's gradual displacement of Jonathan applies *mutatis mutandis* to David's gradual displacement of Saul. Because of David's successes, he is named alongside Saul in the songs of the women of Israel, who sing that "Saul defeated his thousands, and David, his tens of thousands."[178] Commentators typically note that herein is reflected a poetical device in Hebrew intended to say, simply, that Saul and David together have defeated thousands upon thousands.[179] Saul, however, takes this literally, and he jealously fears that

---

[171] I.e., by the narrator in 1 Sam 16:13, by Saul's servant in 16:18, and by Saul himself in 17:37.

[172] 1 Sam 17:47; also see vv. 37, 46.

[173] 1 Sam 17:33, 49–50.

[174] 1 Sam 17:43.

[175] 1 Sam 17:49, 51; 5:3–4.

[176] 1 Sam 17:46.

[177] See 1 Sam 17:9, where Goliath cries out to Israel's army: "If he prevails in the fight with me and defeats me, we shall be your servants. But if I prevail against him and defeat him, then you shall be our servants, and you shall serve us [וְהָיִיתֶם לָנוּ לַעֲבָדִים וַעֲבַדְתֶּם אֹתָנוּ]!"

[178] 1 Sam 18:7.

[179] E.g., McCarter, *I Samuel*, 311–12.

David is superseding him in the eyes of the people, so he "eyes" (עוֹיֵן) him from then on, but for evil intent.[180] In fact, as is later confirmed, David's successes and subsequent fame cause Israel's enemies, at least, to assume that David has superseded Saul:

> And the servants of Achish said to him, "Is this not David, king of the land [מֶלֶךְ הָאָרֶץ]? Was it not for him that they sang while dancing, 'Saul defeated his thousands, and David, his tens of thousands'?"[181]

The people of Israel do not go to this extreme, of course, but the text takes numerous opportunities to emphasize how pleased they are in David and, in particular, how they loved him.[182] Besides Jonathan, Saul's younger daughter, too, loves David such that it adds to Saul's fear of David.[183] Her devotion to David above her father is confirmed when she abets David in his escape from Saul and his messengers, when they plot to kill him, just as Jonathan's allegiance to David over Saul is confirmed when he refuses to submit to Saul's command to have David brought for execution and, instead, helps David to escape "in peace."[184] Ahimelech the priest, too, lends his assistance to David, even if unwittingly, and testifies before Saul and his men of David's exalted position in Saul's house: "Who among all your servants is as faithful as David, the king's son-in-law [כְדָוִד נֶאֱמָן וַחֲתַן הַמֶּלֶךְ], commander of your guard, and honored in your house [וְנִכְבָּד בְּבֵיתֶךָ]?"[185]

The people's love and honor for David, from the women of Israel to Saul's children, are indirect reasons why David must flee not only from Saul, but even from the court of Achish: a man this greatly esteemed must be the true king of Israel (so assume the Philistines), or but one step from the throne (so assumes Saul). After escaping from Saul to Gath, then from Gath to Adullam,

---

[180] 1 Sam 18:5–9.

[181] 1 Sam 21:12 (MT; v. 11 in most English versions); also see 29:5.

[182] 1 Sam 18:5, 16, 22, 30; 19:5. In his moving lament over Saul and Jonathan, David cries: "Saul and Jonathan—Beloved and dear [הַנֶּאֱהָבִים וְהַנְּעִימִם]" (2 Sam 1:23). It is striking to note, however, that apart from this dirge, only David, and not Saul and Jonathan, is characterized in the biblical narrative as the object of the people's love, including that of Jonathan and Saul (see the many references in my discussion and notes above).

[183] 1 Sam 18:20, 28–29.

[184] 1 Sam 19:11–17; 20:30–34, 42.

[185] 1 Sam 22:14. For "commander of your guard," I read סר as שׂר, with LXX (ἄρχων). Alternatively, see NJPS: ". . . and obedient to your bidding."

for the first time David takes a sizeable population under his protection and leadership not merely as a commander (שׂר) representing King Saul, as he was before,[186] but as their commander (שׂר) entirely independent of Saul.[187] More than before, even, David is equipped and increasingly suited to serve as the next shepherd-king of Israel. For David's father's house, a growing group of discontents, debtors, otherwise troubled men (and, by extension, their families), and Abiathar the priest, David fully replaces Saul as the one who provides them refuge and protection.[188]

Even more remarkable than leading these hundreds who "gathered to him" (וַיִּתְקַבְּצוּ אֵלָיו), David fights "YHWH's enemies" for those who have not. First, he does this at risk of death while in flight from Saul, who is more preoccupied with unjustly pursuing David, as even Saul later recognizes,[189] than with coming to save his people. When David hears that the Philistines have attacked Keilah, he, not Saul, rushes to deliver them. These are people who have not followed David, and who would even betray him given the opportunity. Yet, David carries out the responsibility of the king and "saves" (וַיֹּשַׁע) the people of Keilah.[190] David continues fighting YHWH's battles while living in exile among the Philistines, again at great risk, and he enriches the people of Judah by sending them gifts "from the plunder of YHWH's enemies."[191] Later, when "all the tribes of Israel" come to Hebron to anoint David, the people recognize how David essentially functioned as their king even during Saul's lifetime: "Even in times past, when Saul was king over us, you were the one leading out and bringing in Israel [to and from battle]."[192] David is still no picture of moral perfection—it is surprising how much David resembles Saul in certain aspects of his character, and in some respects appears even worse.[193] Nevertheless, his loyalty to God, king, and his people is increasingly demonstrated and confirmed in the eyes of the people.

---

[186] 1 Sam 18:13.

[187] 1 Sam 22:2.

[188] See, especially, 1 Sam 22:1–5, 20–23; 27:2.

[189] See, e.g., 1 Sam 24:18 [17]; 26:21.

[190] 1 Sam 23:1–13.

[191] 1 Sam 27:8–12; 30:26–31.

[192] 2 Sam 5:2a.

[193] On this, see my discussion on pp. 75–76, 78–84, above: "(3) Historical Survey of the Unworthy Predecessor."

David's Elevation over Saul in Saul's Own Eyes

Finally, David is confirmed and acknowledged as the beloved son of YHWH and His people by Saul himself. Many of my observations above are relevant here, especially Saul's honoring and elevation of David above his own son, and his choice and provision of David as his representative to fight YHWH's battles and bring deliverance from His enemies. There is no clearer demonstration of this, however, than in the two instances when David spares Saul's life. In moments of lucidity, Saul recognizes, perhaps for the first time in 1 Samuel 24, and then again in 1 Samuel 26, that YHWH "delivered" him into David's hand (סִגַּרְנִי יְהוָה בְּיָדְךָ).[194] There is no longer any doubt for him that David—as "my son" and not "the son of Jesse" in these moments—"will surely be king, and that the kingdom of Israel will be established in [his] hand."[195] This is an amazing admission, as is Saul's following petition: "Now swear to me by YHWH that you will not cut off my offspring after me, and that you will not destroy my name from my father's house."[196] The tables have turned once again. Earlier, it was Saul who was in the position of power and authority to "make [David's] father's house free in Israel" or cut them off.[197] Now, Saul not only acknowledges that David will be king in his place, but he pleads to David as if before the king, the one who holds the fate of his father's house in his hand.

Conclusion

If one hopes to understand the significance of David's rise and replacement of Saul as king of Israel within the context of the biblical narrative, it is necessary to begin and end the discussion with YHWH's election of David consequent to His rejection of Saul. In the previous chapter, therefore, I discussed YHWH's initial and immediate election of David in terms of His finding, choosing, and providing Himself a king in the person of David. This initial and immediate act of YHWH, together with the eternal covenant that He establishes with David in 2 Samuel 7, sets or frames the meta-context within which every human act and utterance in the narrative derives and

---

[194] 1 Sam 24:19 (MT; v. 18 in most English versions); see 26:23.

[195] 1 Sam 24:21 (MT; v. 20 in most English versions); see 26:25.

[196] 1 Sam 24:22 (MT; v. 21 in most English versions). See also Jonathan's similar plea in 1 Sam 20:14–15.

[197] 1 Sam 17:25; 22:1–4.

carries significance. "YHWH was with David/him" is not simply a leitmotif that sounds every now and then, but it is the warp and woof through which the thread of David's story is woven.

In light of this, I have attempted to demonstrate how David's gradual elevation above the sons of Jesse, the sons of Saul, and Saul himself is not presented in the biblical narrative as the natural grounds upon which to legitimize David and thus uphold his natural right to the throne. It is with surprise and wonder, rather, that David's belovedness vis-à-vis each of these—that is, Jesse's sons, Saul's sons, and Saul himself—unfolds in the sight and through the actions of nearly all of the characters in the narrative. At the point of David's zenith under Saul's command, the narrative reports that "David had greater success than all of Saul's servants, and his name was honored greatly [וַיֵּיקַר שְׁמוֹ מְאֹד]."[198] Sometimes intentionally, but more often unwittingly (and thus adding to the readers' awe over the hidden but ever-present hand of divine providence),[199] the many figures surrounding David—from lowly maidservants to kings, from prophets to priests, from family and friends to enemies—confirm and embody in and through their preferences and actions that "for as is his name, so is he":[200] דָּוִד, "beloved"[201] among the sons of Jesse, Saul, all Israel, and YHWH Himself.

---

[198] 1 Sam 18:30.

[199] Consider the etymological and semantic connections to "provide," which I have discussed on p. 140, above.

[200] This phrase—כִּי כִשְׁמוֹ כֶּן־הוּא—is from 1 Sam 25:25, regarding Nabal. Besides this, there are several other indications within the books of Samuel that the narrator delights in the significance of names: e.g., Samuel in 1 Sam 1:20; Ichabod in 4:21; and Jedidiah in 2 Sam 12:25. See Garsiel, *Biblical Names*.

[201] The debate surrounding the meaning of David's name is well known. See, for example, Halpern, *David's Secret Demons*, 266–69. My reading of דָּוִד as "beloved" is not based on historical so much as it is on literary and theological grounds. That is, whatever the original meaning of this name or title, "David" in the present biblical narrative is the personal name of YHWH's chosen servant who is loved by all Israel, as the text states at several points. In biblical literature and theology, then, it is most natural to interpret the meaning of David's name as I have done—beloved.

Conclusion

Thoughtful designations of biblical accounts tend not only to describe their contents, but also to reflect and inform certain fundamental assumptions and conclusions about their nature and meaning. Few such designations are as undisputed and entrenched in scholarly and popular literature on the Bible as "the History of David's Rise" and, increasingly, "the Apology of David" (or some slight variation on either of these). As I noted in chapter 1, these designations—originally formulated as titles of the original source underlying the biblical account of 1 Samuel 16–2 Samuel 5—are often used quite indiscriminately for the present shape of the biblical narrative as well as its putative source by scholars who think that HDR was transmitted from its original composition through numerous redactional stages with only light revision, which, if anything, only strengthened the *Tendenz* of the apology for David in this extended account. In this view, the primary functions of the biblical narrative and its original source are practically one and the same: to exonerate the historical David of all charges against him and to legitimize his replacement of Saul, thus proving David to be the rightful and lawful occupant of Israel's throne. Michael Dick's interest "solely . . . in the content of the apology in HDR defending the Davidic claim to legitimate succession of Saul's kingship" irrespective of "whether the HDR is a discrete literary unit, where it begins or ends, or even when it may have been written" exemplifies the reading of the present biblical text in terms of this particular set of presumptions about its historical meaning.[1]

---

[1] Dick, "David's Rise to Power," 4. See my discussion and quotation, pp. 16–17, above.

In chapter 1, through sustained attention to the work of Kyle McCarter, in particular, I demonstrated how some scholars have arrived at and determined this particular meaning of the account. We saw how the more closely these scholars approach the historical David by means of their source-critical, form-critical, and ideological-critical analyses, the more they root their interpretation of the text's true meaning, or illocutionary force, in the mundane exigencies of an ancient Near Eastern king who would go to almost any measure to retain power. Also in chapter 1, and extending on into chapters 2 and 3, I discussed problems with the hypothetical reconstruction of an originally independent and unified "History of David's Rise"; the determination that it functioned as "an apology in the sense defined by Harry Hoffner," that is, "a document composed for a king who had usurped the throne, composed in order to defend or justify his assumption of the kingship by force";[2] and that this personal apology was composed chiefly to refute various underlying charges against David. In sum, we saw how this reading of the biblical account as David's personal self-justification, and this reimagination of David, by some, as a calculating "terrorist" and "Middle Eastern tyrant,"[3] are based heavily on assumptions about the historical agenda of David and his author(s) according to "what we know of ancient Middle Eastern rulers [and this would include, among other things, the sorts of propagandistic texts they commission to shore up their bases of power] and of human nature in general."[4]

Uriel Simon offers a penetrating criticism of this sort of approach—which he terms "the scientific *peshat*"—to the biblical text and its sources reflected above:

> The shunning of apologetics, which is characteristic of the contemporary *peshat* exegete, and the intensification of the realistic outlook through numerous scientific discoveries, place us today before the opposite danger [that is, the danger opposite to religious apologetics, which often lead to "contamination of the *peshat* enterprise"]: hyper-realism. For as much as realism is able to give life to Biblical personalities and events, it also tends to reduce them to our own dimensions. In his caution against idealization the exegete is liable to be caught in standardization, to blur the one-time greatness of a marvelous

---

[2] McCarter, "The Apology of David," 495–96, at 499, citing Hoffner, "Propaganda and Political Justification," 49.

[3] See McKenzie's characterization of David in these terms on p. 1, above, and on the same page, Halpern's concluding characterization of David in *David's Secret Demons*, 479–80.

[4] McKenzie, *King David*, 186.

person or a sublime situation. By eschewing otherworldly spirituality too much, he is apt to cling to complete banality, forcing on the Bible a level of expectation that is derived from his own secular existence.[5]

"The History of David's Rise," "the Apology of David," and similar designations commonly employed for the biblical narrative, whatever the literary stage in question, reflect the embracing of a "realism" that is derivative from one's individual "secular existence." In these titles of the biblical account, "David" is a genitive of origin, or a subjective genitive,[6] which reflects scholars' conception of him as the principal source of the personal self-justification of his rise to, and usurpation of, Saul's throne. "YHWH" is absent from these designations, as He is, for example, from McKenzie's "plausible tale" of "what actually happened in David's lifetime," when McKenzie "replace[s] the authors' explanations of David's motives with others that are more in line with what we know of ancient Middle Eastern rulers and of human nature in general."[7] When YHWH is mentioned in these scholars' expositions, it is typically as one of several legitimizers—even if a *leitmotif*—in service to David and his personal needs for legitimacy in the face of charges that he rose to Saul's throne illegitimately.

I have argued that HDR—a hypothetical source that scholars reconstruct variously in accordance with their personal interests in what really happened in David's own lifetime and, consequently, what the account really means—cannot be so easily characterized as the sort of personal self-justification that some scholars have taken it to be. Questions of exoneration and/or legitimacy are certainly not givens, and there is not sufficient justification for disregarding even the truncated account's literary and theological particularities in favor of an overly individualistic and against-the-grain formulation of its true secular meaning (even if acknowledging its obvious

---

[5] Simon, "The Religious Significance of the *Peshat*," 48–49.

[6] See, e.g., the online edition of Wilson, *The Columbia Guide to Standard American English* (New York: Columbia University Press, 1993). Online: http://www.bartleby.com/68/. The genitive of origin (http://www.bartleby.com/68/40/2740.html) "is the name some grammarians give genitive cases that indicate by genitive inflection the originator or source of a modified noun: *Hawthorne's novels, his grades, the minister's sermon.*" The subjective genitive (http://www.bartleby.com/68/95/5795.html) "is a kind of *genitive* in which the thing 'possessed' is a noun naming an action performed by the word in the *genitive* case . . . Some of these are also called *genitives of origin.*" Cited 28 April 2008.

[7] McKenzie, *King David*, 186–88.

religious nature), not according to its own language and conceptual categories, but according, for example, to "what we know of ancient Middle Eastern rulers and of human nature in general." If this is the case for the hypothetically reconstructed HDR, it is all the more so with interpretations of the present biblical account's significance along the above lines.

If not for the sake of exonerating and/or legitimizing an individual king before a community of skeptics and critics, then for what purpose was the story of David's rise composed and transmitted? I suggest that it was composed and transmitted for the sake of shaping and reflecting the identity of YHWH's, and Israel's, beloved son—the figure of David and each of his "sons" to inherit his throne—and, consequently, that of YHWH's people, whom David embodies. McCarter himself takes a similar position vis-à-vis selected texts, as we have seen in his interpretation of the story of David's battle with the Philistine champion in 1 Samuel 17:

> Here is David, small, apparently defenseless, with none of the bearing or equipment of a trained soldier—the perfect personification of the tiny nation of Judah. And against him stands the gigantic enemy, heavily armed and evidently irresistible, as the enemies of Judah so often seemed. David has no real hope in force of arms, and despite his courage and wit he finally must rely on the one good hope that Judah, too, had in times of danger. . . . The theological implications are clear: it is Yahweh who gives victory, and he may give it to the weak (Israel) in order that his power might be known to all.[8]

It is highly conceivable, and probable, that the entire account of David's election and confirmation—and not simply isolated narratives—served the overarching aim of depicting for YHWH's people something about the nature of YHWH and their own elect status as His beloved son. Indeed, I suggest that a close reading of the narrative, such as I have presented in the preceding chapters, naturally leads us to this assumption, which in turn enables us to make the best sense of the biblical account.

Viewing the narrative as intentionally crafted to shape the identity of YHWH's people, and not chiefly for the sake of exonerating an individual king, presents obvious difficulties for making any confident pronouncement about the historical context of the account's composition. The very nature of its purpose to inform the identity of the people as a whole has a departicularizing

---

[8] McCarter, *I Samuel*, 297. See an extended quotation and my discussion on p. 29, above.

effect that makes it impossible, without more data than are currently available, to date the account and locate it in a singular Davidic context or period. Whether finally published in David's or Solomon's day, or in Hezekiah's or Josiah's, the account would have served its intended purpose effectively even if the perlocutionary aims one might attribute to it would have varied somewhat according to the period. This is not as precise as we would prefer, but neither is it ahistorical; it assumes, at least, the particular cultural milieu of Iron Age Israel. Certitude beyond that, however, is unattainable based on the available evidence.

In chapters 4 and 5, then, I focused my attention on the present biblical narrative and demonstrated that YHWH's election of David is more than a *leitmotif*: It is the very basis of and essential means by which David is thrust onto the scene; is confirmed as YHWH's beloved son in and through his surprising elevation above the sons of Jesse, the sons of Saul, and the sons of all Israel (including Saul himself); endures the indignities heaped upon him by Saul and others; and eventually secures his position as king of Israel for YHWH. Ultimately in the biblical account, therefore, it is YHWH's election of David, and not David's military successes, his winning the people's acclaim, his covenants with Saul's children, and so on, that is the grounds upon which David's kingship rises and stands.

Of course, various figures in the biblical narrative take David's successes in Saul's court and on the battlefield, for example, as manifestations that YHWH is with him. Within the narrative world, therefore, it might be said that David's successes, coupled with Saul's demise, have an apologetic function of sorts: In and through them, YHWH publicly confirms His election of David. But the function of these accounts is not precisely the same for the readers of the narrative. They (we) already have privileged information prior to and upon the introduction of David in the narrative that YHWH has elected David and will make him king.

Reading the narrative in this light, we can appreciate features that frustrate construals of the account as individual self-justification. For instance, we can attain a reasonable explanation for why the authors and/or editors of the account passed over a wealth of traditional and historical resources that were almost certainly available to them for aggrandizing their depiction of David. Even more notably, we can gain better purchase on the ambivalent portrayal of David whereby they complicate the readers' estimation of David's worthiness to receive YHWH's special favor. And we can make much better sense of the inordinate amount of space devoted by the narrator to David's life as a fugitive in exile. There is no real evidence supporting theories that this account stood as an unavoidable embarrassment to the king and his people.[9] What we find, instead, is inner-biblical evidence that the people of ancient Israel were meant to identify with this story of YHWH's election and confirmation of His elect as he suffered unjust persecutions and survived many imminent threats from within and without the people of YHWH.

There are important indicators that at some early point this narrative functioned to shape and inform Israel's corporate identity. Eight of the Masoretic Text's fourteen psalms carrying a Davidic historical superscription—a heading that associates the psalm with some specific episode in the life of David—identify the people of YHWH with David and his experience during his days as a fugitive from Saul.[10] Is it possible that the editors who affixed the superscriptions to these psalms were competent readers of the Samuel narratives, that they understood its intended purpose? Before too easily dismissing this evidence on the grounds that many of these psalms were composed and/or received their superscriptions much later than the composition in Samuel, one should note that they follow a trajectory set by the editors of Samuel itself.

Embedded in the books of Samuel, there is an unmistakable indication that the story of David's rise was intentionally edited and transmitted in such a way that its readers would corporately identify with the figure of David. I am referring to 2 Samuel 22, the song that, according to verse 1, "David spoke to YHWH . . . on the day that YHWH delivered him from the hand of all his enemies and from the hand of Saul." Even if this song were not included in the book of Psalms—it is essentially the same as Psalm 18—one could only conclude that it, too, was edited and published together with the rest of Samuel as a song to be sung by the people of YHWH as if they were the ones that "YHWH delivered . . . from the hand of all [their] enemies and from the hand of Saul." David's song is their song because David's story is also their story.

David's story begins with YHWH's choice of him as the new king who will replace Saul. This act of divine provision should inform one's reading

---

[9] See the discussion on pp. 115–17, above.

[10] Pss 18, 34, 52, 54, 56, 57, 59, 142. Pss 7 and 63 may also be linked to this account, but the reference in each superscription is ambiguous. The superscriptions of Pss 3, 30, 51, and 60 associate these psalms with David's life after becoming king.

of every narrative event thereafter. The readers do not look for exoneration, and the primary response that the narrative evokes from the reading community that God's people constitute is not the nodding of heads along the way to acknowledge and validate the legality or legitimacy of David's rise to kingship. The narrative is framed in such a way that, especially from the readers' perspective, the accounts of people and events contributing to, and impeding, David's rise to the throne are not protestations of, or apology for, David's innocence vis-à-vis Saul and the like. Rather, they depict for YHWH's people, whom David represents and embodies, the mercies, burdens, obligations, privileges, and sufferings that are constitutive parts of David's divine election, and thus of theirs. This narrative represents to God's covenant-community the story of YHWH's surprising election and confirmation of David as His beloved son. In the biblical account—unlike in "the History of David's Rise" or "the Apology of David"—"David" has become the objective genitive, acted upon by "YHWH," the subjective genitive of origin. To YHWH's people, the implied readers of the narrative, there is no need to offer an apology for David's replacement of Saul as the beloved son of YHWH.

Bibliography

Alt, Albrecht. *Die Staatenbildung der Israeliten in Palästina. Verfassungs-geschichtliche Studien.* Zur Feier des Reformationsfestes. Leipzig: Edelmann, 1930.

Alter, Robert. *The David Story: A Translation with Commentary of 1 and 2 Samuel.* New York: W. W. Norton, 1999.

————. *The Art of Biblical Narrative.* New York: Basic Books, 1981.

Anderson, Arnold A. *2 Samuel.* Word Biblical Commentary 11. Dallas, Tex.: Word Books, 1989.

Anderson, Gary A. "Joseph and the Passion of Our Lord." Pages 198–215 in *The Art of Reading Scripture.* Edited by Ellen F. Davis and Richard B. Hays. Grand Rapids, Mich.: Eerdmans, 2003.

Armington, Shawn Aaron. "Recurrent Narratives in 1 Samuel: Art and Intention in the Redaction Process." Ph.D. diss., Princeton Theological Seminary, 2000.

Arnold, Bill T. *1 and 2 Samuel.* The NIV Application Commentary. Grand Rapids, Mich.: Zondervan, 2003.

Aschkenasy, Nehama. "Biblical Substructures in the Tragic Form: Hardy, The Mayor of Casterbridge; Agnon, and the Crooked Shall Be Made Straight." Pages 85–94 in *Biblical Patterns in Modern Literature.* Edited by David H. Hirsch and Nehama Aschkenasy. Chico, Calif.: Scholars Press, 1984.

Auld, A. Graeme. *Kings without Privilege: David and Moses in the Story of the Bible's Kings.* Edinburgh, Scotland: T&T Clark, 1994.

Austin, John L. *How to Do Things with Words.* Cambridge, Mass.: Harvard University Press, 1962.

Barrick, W. Boyd. "Saul's Demise, David's Lament, and Custer's Last Stand." *Journal for the Study of the Old Testament* 73 (1997) 25–41.

Barthelemy, Dominique, et al. *The Story of David and Goliath: Textual and Literary Criticism: Papers of a Joint Research Venture.* Orbis biblicus et orientalis 73. Fribourg, Suisse: Editions universitaires; Göttingen: Vandenhoeck & Ruprecht, 1986.

Beck, Astrid B. "Introduction to the Leningrad Codex." Pages ix–xx in *The Leningrad Codex: A Facsimile Edition*. Edited by David Noel Freedman. Grand Rapids, Mich.: Eerdmans; Leiden: Brill Academic Publishers, 1998.

Beckman, Gary. "The Hittite Assembly." *Journal of the American Oriental Society* 102 (1982) 435–42.

Bentzen, Aage. *Introduction to the Old Testament*. 2d ed. Copenhagen: G.E.C. Gad, 1952.

Bergen, Robert D. *1, 2 Samuel*, The New American Commentary. Nashville, Tenn.: Broadman & Holman, 1996.

Bic, Milos. "La folie de David." *Revue d'histoire et de philosophie religieuses* 37 (1957) 156–62.

Biddle, Mark E. "Ancestral Motifs in 1 Samuel 25: Intertextuality and Characterization." *Journal of Biblical Literature* 121 (2002) 617–38.

Birch, Bruce C. *The Rise of the Israelite Monarchy: The Growth and Development of I Samuel 7–15*. Society of Biblical Literature Dissertation Series 27. Missoula, Mont.: Scholars Press, 1976.

Bodner, Keith. "Eliab and the Deuteronomist." *Journal for the Study of the Old Testament* 28 (2003) 55–71.

Bosworth, David A. "Evaluating King David: Old Problems and Recent Scholarship." *Catholic Biblical Quarterly* 68 (2006) 191–210.

Brettler, Marc Zvi. *The Creation of History in Ancient Israel*. London: Routledge, 1995.

Briggs, Richard. *Words in Action: Speech Act Theory and Biblical Interpretation: Toward a Hermeneutic of Self-Involvement*. Edinburgh, Scotland: T&T Clark, 2001.

Brooks, Byron A. *King Saul: A Tragedy*. New York: Nelson & Phillips, 1876.

Brown, Francis, S. R. Driver, Charles A. Briggs, James Strong, and Wilhelm Gesenius. *The Brown-Driver-Briggs Hebrew and English Lexicon: With an Appendix Containing the Biblical Aramaic: Coded with the Numbering System from Strong's Exhaustive Concordance of the Bible*. Peabody, Mass.: Hendrickson, 1996.

Brueggemann, Walter. *David's Truth in Israel's Imagination and Memory*. 2d ed. Minneapolis, Minn.: Fortress Press, 2002.

———. "Narrative Coherence and Theological Intentionality in 1 Samuel 18." *Catholic Biblical Quarterly* 55 (1993) 225–43.

———. *First and Second Samuel*. Louisville, Ky.: Westminster John Knox Press, 1990.

Brueggemann, Walter. "David and His Theologian." *Catholic Biblical Quarterly* 30 (1968) 156–81.

Bryce, Trevor. *The Kingdom of the Hittites*. 2d ed. Oxford: Oxford University Press, 2005.

Budde, Karl. *Die Bücher Samuel*. Kurzer Hand-Commentar zum Alten Testament, Abt. 8. Tübingen: J.C.B. Mohr, 1902.

———. *Die Bücher Richter und Samuel. Ihre Quellen und ihr Aufbau*. Giessen: J. Ricker, 1890.

Campbell, Antony F. *1 Samuel*. The Forms of the Old Testament Literature 7. Grand Rapids, Mich.: Eerdmans, 2003.

———. *Of Prophets and Kings: A Late Ninth Century Document (1 Samuel 1–2 Kings 10)*. Washington, D.C.: Catholic Biblical Association of America, 1986.

Campbell, Antony F., and Mark A. O'Brien. *Unfolding the Deuteronomistic History: Origins, Upgrades, Present Text*. Minneapolis, Minn.: Fortress Press, 2000.

Carlson, Rolf August. *David, the Chosen King: A Traditio-Historical Approach to the Second Book of Samuel*. Stockholm: Almquist & Wiksell, 1964.

Carr, David McClain. *Reading the Fractures of Genesis: Historical and Literary Approaches*. Louisville, Ky.: Westminster John Knox Press, 1996.

Cartledge, Tony W. *1 & 2 Samuel*. Macon, Ga.: Smyth & Helwys, 2001.

Chavalas, Mark. "Genealogical History as 'Charter': A Study of Old Babylonian Period Historiography and the Old Testament." Pages 103–28 in *Faith, Tradition, and History: Old Testament Historiography in its Near Eastern Context*. Edited by A. R. Millard, James Karl Hoffmeier, and David W. Baker. Winona Lake, Ind.: Eisenbrauns, 1994.

Childs, Brevard S. *Introduction to the Old Testament as Scripture*. Philadelphia: Fortress Press, 1979.

Clements, Ronald E. *Abraham and David: Genesis XV and its Meaning for Israelite Tradition*. Studies in Biblical Theology, 2nd series, 5. London: S.C.M. Press, 1967.

Conrad, Joachim. "Zum geschichtlichen Hintergrund der Darstellung von Davids Aufstieg." *Theologische Literaturzeitung* 97 (1972) 321–32.

Coogan, Michael D. *The Old Testament: A Historical and Literary Introduction to the Hebrew Scriptures*. New York: Oxford University Press, 2006.

Cooper, Howard. "'Too Tall by Half' — King Saul and Tragedy in the Hebrew Bible." *Journal of Progressive Judaism* 9 (1997) 5–22.

Couffignal, Robert. *Saül, héros tragique de la Bible*. *Étude littéraire du récit de son règne d'après les Livres de Samuel (1 S 9–31 et 2 S 1)*. Thèmes et mythes 19. Paris: Lettres modernes Minard, 1999.

Cross, Frank Moore. *Canaanite Myth and Hebrew Epic: Essays in the History of the Religion of Israel*. Cambridge, Mass.: Harvard University Press, 1973.

Cross, Frank Moore, Donald W. Parry, Richard J. Saley, and Eugene C. Ulrich, eds. *Qumran Cave 4: XII: 1–2 Samuel*. Discoveries in the Judaean Desert XVII. Edited by Emanuel Tov. Oxford: Oxford University Press, 2005.

Crüsemann, Frank. "Zwei alttestamentliche Witze. I Sam 21:11–15 und II Sam 6:16, 20–23 als Beispiele einer biblischen Gattung." *Zeitschrift für die alttestamentliche Wissenschaft* 80 (1980) 215–27.

Cryer, Frederick H. "David's Rise to Power and the Death of Abner: An Analysis of 1 Samuel 26:14–16 and its Redaction-Critical Implications." *Vetus Testamentum* 35 (1985) 385–94.

Davies, Philip R. *First Person: Essays in Biblical Autobiography*. Biblical Seminar 81. London: Sheffield Academic Press, 2002.

———. *In Search of 'Ancient Israel.'* Journal for the Study of the Old Testament. Supplement Series 148. Sheffield: JSOT Press, 1992.

Day, John. *In Search of Pre-Exilic Israel: Proceedings of the Oxford Old Testament Seminar*. Journal for the Study of the Old Testament Supplement Series 406. London: T&T Clark, 2004.

De Vries, Simon J. "Moses and David as Cult Founders in Chronicles." *Journal of Biblical Literature* 107 (1988) 619–39.

———. "David's Victory over the Philistine as Saga and as Legend." *Journal of Biblical Literature* 92 (1973) 23–36.

Desrousseaux, Louis, and Jacques Vermeylen, eds. *Figures de David a travers la Bible: XVIIe congres de l'ACFEB, Lille, 1er–5 septembre 1997*. Lectio divina 177. Paris: Cerf, 1999.

Dick, Michael B. "The 'History of David's Rise to Power' and the Neo-Babylonian Succession Apologies." Pages 3–19 in *David and Zion: Biblical Studies in Honor of J. J. M. Roberts*. Edited by Kathryn L. Roberts and Bernard Frank Batto. Winona Lake, Ind.: Eisenbrauns, 2004.

Dietrich, Walter. *David und Saul im Widerstreit. Diachronie und Synchronie im Wettstreit. Beiträge zur Auslegung des ersten Samuelbuches.* Orbis biblicus et orientalis 206. Fribourg: Academic Press; Göttingen: Vandenhoeck & Ruprecht, 2004.

————. "Der historische David—Sein oder Schein?" *Biblica* 84 (2003) 108–17.

————. *Von David zu den Deuteronomisten. Studien zu den Geschichtsüberlieferungen des Alten Testaments.* Stuttgart: W. Kohlhammer, 2002.

————. "Die David-Abraham-Typologie im Alten Testament." Pages 41–55 in *Verbindungslinien. Festschrift für Werner H. Schmidt zum 65. Geburtstag.* Edited by Axel Graupner, Holger Delkurt, Alexander B. Ernst and Lutz Aupperle. Neukirchen-Vluyn: Neukirchener, 2000.

Dietrich, Walter, and Thomas Naumann. "The David-Saul Narrative." Pages 276–318 in *Reconsidering Israel and Judah: Recent Studies on the Deuteronomistic History.* Edited by Gary N. Knoppers and J. Gordon McConville. Winona Lake, Ind.: Eisenbrauns, 2000.

————. *Die Samuelbücher.* Erträge der Forschung 287. Darmstadt: Wissenschaftliche Buchgesellschaft, 1995.

Dotan, Aron, ed. *Torah, Nevi'im u-Khetuvim: Biblia Hebraica Leningradensia.* Peabody, Mass.: Hendrickson, 2001.

Driver, Samuel R. *An Introduction to the Literature of the Old Testament.* Gloucester, Mass.: P. Smith, 1972.

Edelman, Diana Vikander. *King Saul in the Historiography of Judah.* Journal for the Study of the Old Testament Supplement Series 121. Sheffield, England: Sheffield Academic Press, 1991.

————. "Tel Masos, Geshur, and David." *Journal of Near Eastern Studies* 47 (1988) 253–58.

Edenburg, Cynthia. "How (Not) to Murder a King: Variations on a Theme in 1 Sam 24; 26." *Scandinavian Journal of the Old Testament* 12 (1998) 64–85.

Eissfeldt, Otto. *Die Komposition der Samuelisbücher.* Leipzig: J. C. Hinrich, 1931.

Elliger, Karl, Wilhelm Rudolph, et al., eds. *Torah, Nevi'im u-Khetuvim: Biblia Hebraica Stuttgartensia.* 5th ed. Stuttgart: Deutsche Bibelgesellschaft, 1997.

Eslinger, Lyle M. "Inner-Biblical Exegesis and Inner-Biblical Allusion: The Question of Category." *Vetus Testamentum* 42 (1992) 47–58.

Evans, Craig A., Shemaryahu Talmon, and James A. Sanders, eds. *The Quest for Context and Meaning: Studies in Biblical Intertextuality in Honor of James A. Sanders*. Biblical Interpretation Series 28. Leiden: Brill, 1997.

Exum, J. Cheryl. *Tragedy and Biblical Narrative: Arrows of the Almighty*. Cambridge; New York: Cambridge University Press, 1992.

Exum, J. Cheryl, and J. William Whedbee. "Isaac, Samson, and Saul: Reflections on the Comic and Tragic Visions." *Semeia* 32 (1984) 5–40.

Feldman, Louis H. "Josephus' Portrait of Saul." *Hebrew Union College Annual* 53 (1982) 45–99.

Fensham, Frank C. "Father and Son as Terminology for Treaty and Covenant." Pages 121–35 in *Near Eastern Studies in Honor of William Foxwell Albright*. Edited by Hans Goedicke. Baltimore: Johns Hopkins Press, 1971.

Fewell, Danna Nolan. *Reading between Texts: Intertextuality and the Hebrew Bible*. Literary Currents in Biblical Interpretation. Louisville, Ky.: Westminster John Knox Press, 1992.

Finkelstein, Israel, and Neil Asher Silberman. *David and Solomon: In Search of the Bible's Sacred Kings and the Roots of Western Civilization*. New York: Free Press, 2006.

Finlay, Timothy D. *The Birth Report Genre in the Hebrew Bible*. Tübingen: Mohr Siebeck, 2005.

Fishbane, Michael. "Inner-Biblical Exegesis." Pages 33–48 in *From the Beginnings to the Middle Ages (Until 1300)*. Edited by Magne Sæbø. Vol. 1 of *Hebrew Bible/Old Testament: The History of Its Interpretation*. Edited by Magne Sæbø. Göttingen: Vandenhoeck & Ruprecht, 1996.

Flanagan, James W. *David's Social Drama: A Hologram of Israel's Early Iron Age*. The Social World of Biblical Antiquity 7. Sheffield: Almond Press, 1988.

————."Succession and Genealogy in the Davidic Dynasty." Pages 35–55 in *The Quest for the Kingdom of God: Studies in Honor of George E. Mendenhall*. Edited by Herbert B. Huffmon, Frank A. Spina, and Alberto Ravinell Whitney Green. Winona Lake, Ind.: Eisenbrauns, 1983.

————. "Chiefs in Israel." *Journal for the Study of the Old Testament* 20 (1981) 47–73.

Fokkelman, Jan P. *King David*. Vol. 1 of *Narrative Art and Poetry in the Books of Samuel: A Full Interpretation Based on Stylistic and Structural Analyses*. Studia Semitica Neerlandica 20. Assen, Netherlands: Van Gorcum, 1981.

Foresti, Fabrizio. *The Rejection of Saul in the Perspective of the Deuteronomistic School: A Study of 1 Sm 15 and Related Texts.* Studia Theologica-Teresianum 5. Roma: Edizioni del Teresianum, 1984.

Fowler, Alastair. *Kinds of Literature: An Introduction to the Theory of Genres and Modes.* Cambridge, Mass.: Harvard University Press, 1982.

Freedman, David Noel. "Early Israelite History in the Light of Early Israelite Poetry." Pages 3–35 in *Unity and Diversity: Essays in the History, Literature, and Religion of the Ancient Near East.* Edited by Hans Goedicke and J. J. M. Roberts. Baltimore: Johns Hopkins University Press, 1975.

————, ed. *The Leningrad Codex: A Facsimile Edition.* Grand Rapids, Mich.: Eerdmans; Leiden: Brill Academic Publishers, 1998.

Freedman, H., and Maurice Simon. *Midrash Rabbah: Exodus.* Translated by S. M. Lehrman. 3d ed. London; New York: Soncino Press, 1983.

Freedman, Russell. *Lincoln: A Photobiography.* New York: Clarion Books, 1987.

Frei, Hans W. *The Eclipse of Biblical Narrative: A Study in Eighteenth and Nineteenth Century Hermeneutics.* New Haven: Yale University Press, 1974.

Fretheim, Terence E. "Divine Foreknowledge, Divine Constancy, and the Rejection of Saul's Kingship." *Catholic Biblical Quarterly* 47 (1985) 595–602.

Friedman, Richard Elliott. *The Hidden Book in the Bible.* San Francisco: Harper, 1998.

Frolov, Serge. "Succession Narrative: A 'Document' or a Phantom?" *Journal of Biblical Literature* 121 (2002) 81–104.

Gakuru, Griphus. *An Inner-Biblical Exegetical Study of the Davidic Covenant and the Dynastic Oracle*, Mellen Biblical Press Series 58. Lewiston, N.Y.: Mellen Press, 2000.

Garsiel, Moshe. *Biblical Names: A Literary Study of Midrashic Derivations and Puns.* Ramat Gan: Bar-Ilan University, 1991.

————. *The First Book of Samuel: A Literary Study of Comparative Structures, Analogies and Parallels.* Ramat-Gan, Israel: Revivim Publishing House, 1985.

George, Mark K. "Yhwh's Own Heart." *Catholic Biblical Quarterly* 64 (2002) 442–59.

Goetschel, Roland. "Le Messie fils de David et le Messie fils de Joseph dans la littérature rabbinique ancienne." Pages 265–75 in *Figures de David à travers la Bible*. Edited by Louis Desrousseaux and Jacques Vermeylen. Paris: Cerf, 1999.

Gordon, Robert P. "In Search of David: The David Tradition in Recent Study." Pages 285–98 in *Faith, Tradition, and History: Old Testament Historiography in its Near Eastern Context*. Edited by A. R. Millard, James Karl Hoffmeier, and David W. Baker. Winona Lake, Ind.: Eisenbrauns, 1994.

————. *I & II Samuel: A Commentary*. Grand Rapids, Mich.: Regency Reference Library, 1988.

————. *1 & 2 Samuel*, Old Testament Guides. Sheffield: JSOT Press, 1987.

————. "David's Rise and Saul's Demise—Narrative Analogy in 1 Samuel 24–26." *Tyndale Bulletin* 31 (1979) 37–64. Repr., pages 319–39 in *Reconsidering Israel and Judah: Recent Studies on the Deuteronomistic History*. Edited by Gary N. Knoppers and J. Gordon McConville. Winona Lake, Ind.: Eisenbrauns, 2000.

Goshen-Gottstein, Moshe H., ed. *The Aleppo Codex*. Jerusalem: Magnes, 1976.

————, ed. *The Hebrew University Bible, The Book of Isaiah*. Jerusalem: Magnes, 1995.

Goshen-Gottstein, Moshe H., and Shemaryahu Talmon, eds. *The Hebrew University Bible: The Book of Ezekiel*. Jerusalem: Magnes, 2004.

Götze, Albrecht. *Hattušiliš. Der Bericht über seine Thronbesteigung nebst den Paralleltexten*. Darmstadt: Wissenschaftliche Buchgesellschaft, 1967.

Green, Barbara. *How are the mighty fallen? A Dialogical Study of King Saul in 1 Samuel*. Journal for the Study of the Old Testament Supplement Series 365. London: Sheffield Academic Press, 2003.

Greenberg, Gary. *The Sins of King David: A New History*. Naperville, Ill.: Sourcebooks, 2002.

Greenspahn, Frederick E. *When Brothers Dwell Together: The Preeminence of Younger Siblings in the Hebrew Bible*. New York: Oxford University Press, 1994.

Grillet, Bernard, and Michel Lestienne. *Premier livre des règnes*. Paris: Cerf, 1997.

Grønbæk, Jakob H. *Die Geschichte vom Aufstieg Davids (1. Sam. 15–2. Sam. 5)*. *Tradition und Komposition.* Copenhagen: Prostant Apud Munksgaard, 1971.

Gunn, David M. *The Fate of King Saul: An Interpretation of a Biblical Story.* Journal for the Study of the Old Testament Supplement Series 14. Sheffield, England: Department of Biblical Studies, University of Sheffield, 1980.

———. *The Story of King David: Genre and Interpretation.* Journal for the Study of the Old Testament Supplement Series 6. Sheffield, England: Department of Biblical Studies, University of Sheffield, 1978.

Gunn, David M., Wilhelm Caspari, Bernhard Luther, and Alfons Schulz. *Narrative and Novella in Samuel: Studies by Hugo Gressmann and Other Scholars, 1906–1923.* Journal for the Study of the Old Testament Supplement Series 116. Sheffield: Almond Press, 1991.

Hackett, Jo Ann. "1 and 2 Samuel." Pages 85–95 in *The Women's Bible Commentary.* Edited by Carol A. Newsom and Sharon H. Ringe. London: SPCK, 1992.

Halpern, Baruch. *David's Secret Demons: Messiah, Murderer, Traitor, King.* The Bible in its World. Grand Rapids, Mich.: Eerdmans, 2001.

———. "Text and Artifact: Two Monologues?" Pages 311–41 in *The Archaeology of Israel: Constructing the Past, Interpreting the Present.* Edited by Neil Asher Silberman and David B. Small. Sheffield, U. K.: Sheffield Academic Press, 1997.

———. *The First Historians: The Hebrew Bible and History.* San Francisco: Harper & Row, 1988.

———. *The Constitution of the Monarchy in Israel.* Harvard Semitic Monograph Series 25. Chico, Calif.: Scholars Press, 1981.

Hamilton, Mark W. *The Body Royal: The Social Poetics of Kingship in Ancient Israel.* Biblical Interpretation Series 78. Leiden: Brill, 2005.

Haroutunian, Hripsime. "A Complete Bibliography of Harry A. Hoffner Jr., 1963–2003." Pages xiii–xxiii in *Hittite Studies in Honor of Harry A. Hoffner Jr.* Edited by Gary Beckman, Richard Beal, and Gregory McMahon. Winona Lake, Ind.: Eisenbrauns, 2003.

Hawk, L. Daniel. "Saul as Sacrifice: The Tragedy of Israel's First Monarch." *Bible Review* 12 (1996) 20–25, 56.

Hentschel, Georg. *Saul. Schuld, Reue und Tragik eines Gesalbten*, Biblische Gestalten, Bd. 7. Leipzig: Evangelische Verlagsanstalt, 2003.

Hertzberg, Hans Wilhelm. *Die Samuelbücher*. Göttingen: Vandenhoeck & Ruprecht, 1956. Translated by John S. Bowden. Reprinted as *I & II Samuel: A Commentary*. Old Testament Library. Philadelphia: Westminster Press, 1964.

Heschel, Abraham. *God in Search of Man: A Philosophy of Judaism*. New York: Farrar, Straus & Cudahy, 1955.

Heym, Stefan. *Der König David Bericht. Roman*. Frankfurt am Main: Fischer-Taschenbuch, 1972.

Hill, Andrew E., and John H. Walton. *A Survey of the Old Testament*. 2d ed. Grand Rapids, Mich.: Zondervan, 2000.

Ho, Craig Y. S. "The Stories of the Family Troubles of Judah and David: A Study of Their Literary Links." *Vetus Testamentum* 49 (1999) 514–31.

Hoffmann, Inge. *Der Erlass Telipinus*. Texte der Hethiter, Heft 11. Heidelberg: C. Winter, 1984.

Hoffner, Harry A., Jr. "Ancient Israel's Literary Heritage Compared with Hittite Textual Data." Pages 176–92 in *The Future of Biblical Archaeology: Reassessing Methodologies and Assumptions*. Edited by James K. Hoffmeier and Alan Millard. Grand Rapids, Mich.: Eerdmans, 2004.

———. "Propaganda and Political Justification in Hittite Historiography." Pages 49–62 in *Unity and Diversity: Essays in the History, Literature, and Religion of the Ancient Near East*. Edited by Hans Goedicke and J. J. M. Roberts. Baltimore: Johns Hopkins University Press, 1975.

———. "Some Contributions of Hittitology to Old Testament Study." *Tyndale Bulletin* 20 (1969) 27–55.

———. "Hittite Analogue to the David and Goliath Contest of Champions." *Catholic Biblical Quarterly* 30 (1968) 220–25.

Hölscher, Gustav. *Geschichtsschreibung in Israel. Untersuchungen zum Jahvisten und Elohisten*. Lund: C.W.K. Gleerup, 1952.

Hughes, Paul Edward. "Compositional History: Source, Form, and Redaction Criticism." Pages 221–44 in *Interpreting the Old Testament: A Guide for Exegesis*. Edited by Craig C. Broyles. Grand Rapids, Mich.: Baker Academic, 2001.

Humphreys, W. Lee. "From Tragic Hero to Villain: A Study of the Figure of Saul and the Development of 1 Samuel." *Journal for the Study of the Old Testament* 22 (1982) 95–117.

Humphreys, W. Lee. "The Rise and Fall of King Saul: A Study of an Ancient Narrative Stratum in 1 Samuel." *Journal for the Study of the Old Testament* 18 (1980) 74–90.

———. "The Tragedy of King Saul: A Study of the Structure of 1 Samuel 9–31." *Journal for the Study of the Old Testament* 6 (1978) 18–27.

———. *The Tragic Vision and the Hebrew Tradition.* Overtures to Biblical Theology 18. Philadelphia: Fortress Press, 1985.

Hurvitz, Avi. "Can Biblical Texts be Dated Linguistically? Chronological Perspectives in the Historical Study of Biblical Hebrew." Pages 143–60 in *Congress Volume: Oslo 1998.* Edited by André Lemaire and Magne Sæbø. Leiden: Brill, 2000.

Hutton, Jeremy Michael. "The Transjordanian Palimpsest: The Overwritten Texts of Personal Exile and Transformation in the Deuteronomistic History." Ph.D. diss., Harvard University, 2005.

Ishida, Tomoo. *History and Historical Writing in Ancient Israel: Studies in Biblical Historiography.* Studies in the History and Culture of the Ancient Near East 16. Leiden: Brill, 1999.

———. "The Story of Abner's Murder: A Problem Posed by the Solomonic Apologist." *Eretz-Israel* 24 (1993) 109–13.

———. "The Succession Narrative and Esarhaddon's Apology: A Comparison." Pages 166–73 in *Ah, Assyria— : Studies in Assyrian History and Ancient Near Eastern Historiography Presented to Hayim Tadmor.* Edited by Mordechai Cogan and Israel Ephal. Jerusalem: Magnes Press, 1991.

———. *The Royal Dynasties in Ancient Israel: A Study on the Formation and Development of Royal-Dynastic Ideology.* Beihefte zur Zeitschrift für die alttestamentliche Wissenschaft 142. Berlin: de Gruyter, 1976.

Isser, Stanley Jerome. *The Sword of Goliath: David in Heroic Literature.* Atlanta: Society of Biblical Literature, 2003.

Jobling, David. *1 Samuel.* Berit Olam: Studies in Hebrew Narrative and Poetry. Collegeville, Minn.: Liturgical Press, 1998.

———. "Saul's Fall and Jonathan's Rise: Tradition and Redaction in 1 Sam 14:1–46." *Journal of Biblical Literature* 95 (1976) 367–76.

Johnson, Marshall D. *The Purpose of the Biblical Genealogies: With Special Reference to the Setting of the Genealogies of Jesus.* 2d ed. Eugene, Ore.: Wipf and Stock, 2002.

Kaiser, Otto. "David und Jonathan. Tradition, Redaktion und Geschichte in I Sam 16–20: Ein Versuch." *Ephemerides Theologicae Lovanienses* 66 (1990) 281–96.

Kalluveettil, Paul. *Declaration and Covenant: A Comprehensive Review of Covenant Formulae from the Old Testament and the Ancient Near East.* Analecta Biblica 88. Rome: Biblical Institute Press, 1982.

Kang, Sa-Moon. *Divine War in the Old Testament and in the Ancient Near East.* Berlin: de Gruyter, 1989.

Kirsch, Jonathan. *King David: The Real Life of the Man Who Ruled Israel.* New York: Ballantine Books, 2000.

Kittel, R., and P. Kahle, eds. *Torah, Nevi'im u-Khetuvim: Biblia Hebraica.* 3d ed. Stuttgart: Württembergische Bibelanstalt, 1937.

Klein, Johannes. *David versus Saul. Ein Beitrag zum Erzählsystem der Samuelbücher.* Stuttgart: Kohlhammer, 2002.

Klein, Ralph W. *1 Samuel.* Word Biblical Commentary 10. Waco, Tex.: Word Books, 1983.

Klengel, Horst. "Problems in Hittite History, Solved and Unsolved." Pages 101–9 in *Recent Developments in Hittite Archaeology and History: Papers in Memory of Hans G. Güterbock.* Edited by K. Aslihan Yener, Harry A. Hoffner Jr., and Simrit Dhesi. Winona Lake, Ind.: Eisenbrauns, 2002.

Knierim, Rolf. "The Messianic Concept in the First Book of Samuel." Pages 20–51 in *Jesus and the Historian: Written in Honor of Ernest Cadman Colwell.* Edited by F. Thomas Trotter. Philadelphia: Westminster Press, 1968.

Knoppers, Gary N. "David's Relation to Moses: The Contexts, Content and Conditions of the Davidic Promises." Pages 91–118 in *King and Messiah in Israel and the Ancient Near East: Proceedings of the Oxford Old Testament Seminar.* Edited by John Day. Sheffield, U. K.: Sheffield Academic Press, 1998.

Knoppers, Gary N., and J. Gordon McConville, eds. *Reconsidering Israel and Judah: Recent Studies on the Deuteronomistic History,* Sources for Biblical and Theological Study 8. Winona Lake, Ind.: Eisenbrauns, 2000.

Koch, Klaus. *Was ist Formgeschichte? Neue Wege der Bibelexegese*. [Neu-kirchen-Vluyn]: Neukirchener Verlag des Erziehungsvereins, 1964. Translated by S. M. Cupitt as *The Growth of the Biblical Tradition: The Form-Critical Method*, Scribner Studies in Biblical Interpretation. New York: Scribner, 1969.

Kratz, Reinhard Gregor. *Die Komposition der erzählenden Bücher des Alten Testaments. Grundwissen der Bibelkritik* Göttingen: Vandenhoeck & Ruprecht, 2000. Translated by John Bowden as *The Composition of the Narrative Books of the Old Testament*. London: T&T Clark, 2005.

Kugel, James L. *The God of Old: Inside the Lost World of the Bible*. New York: Free Press, 2003.

Langlamet, Francois. "'David—Jonathan—Saul' ou le 'Livre de Jonathan' 1 Sam 16,14–2 Sam 1,27." *Revue Biblique* 101 (1994) 326–54.

————. "De 'David, fils de Jesse' au 'Livre de Jonathan.' Deux editions divergentes de l 'Ascension de David' en 1 Sam 16–2 Sam 1?" *Revue Biblique* 100 (1993) 321–57.

Lawton, Robert B. "Saul, Jonathan and the 'Son of Jesse'." *Journal for the Study of the Old Testament* 58 (1993) 35–46.

Lebedev, Victor V. "The Oldest Complete Codex of the Hebrew Bible." Pages xxi–xxviii in *The Leningrad Codex: A Facsimile Edition*. Edited by David Noel Freedman. Grand Rapids, Mich.: Eerdmans; Leiden: Brill Academic Publishers, 1998.

Lemche, Niels P. "David's Rise." *Journal for the Study of the Old Testament* 10 (1978) 2–25.

The Israelites in History and Tradition. Louisville, Ky.: Westminster John Knox Press, 1998.

Levenson, Jon D. *The Death and Resurrection of the Beloved Son: The Transformation of Child Sacrifice in Judaism and Christianity*. New Haven: Yale University Press, 1993.

————. *The Hebrew Bible, the Old Testament, and Historical Criticism: Jews and Christians in Biblical Studies*. Louisville, Ky.: Westminster John Knox Press, 1993.

————. *Sinai and Zion: An Entry into the Jewish Bible*. New Voices in Biblical Studies. Minneapolis, Minn.: Winston Press, 1985.

————."1 Samuel 25 as Literature and as History." *Catholic Biblical Quarterly* 40 (1978) 11–28.

Levenson, Jon D., and Baruch Halpern. "The Political Import of David's Marriages." *Journal of Biblical Literature* 99 (1980) 507–18.

Levinson, Bernard M. "The Right Chorale: From the Poetics to the Hermeneutics of the Hebrew Bible." Pages 129–53 in *Not in Heaven: Coherence and Complexity in Biblical Narrative*. Edited by Jason Philip Rosenblatt and Joseph C. Sitterson. Bloomington, Ind.: Indiana University Press, 1991.

Long, V. Philips. *The Reign and Rejection of King Saul: A Case for Literary and Theological Coherence*. Society of Biblical Literature Dissertation Series 118. Atlanta, Ga.: Scholars Press, 1989.

————, ed. *Israel's Past in Present Research: Essays on Ancient Israelite Historiography*. Sources for Biblical and Theological Study 7. Winona Lake, Ind.: Eisenbrauns, 1999.

Longman, Tremper. *Fictional Akkadian Autobiography: A Generic and Comparative Study*. Winona Lake, Ind.: Eisenbrauns, 1991.

Machinist, Peter. "Literature as Politics: The Tukulti-Ninurta Epic and the Bible." *Catholic Biblical Quarterly* 38 (1976) 455–82.

Malul, Meir. "Was David Involved in the Death of Saul on the Gilboa Mountain? Testing an Hypothesis Regarding Tribal Complicity in the Davidic Rise to Power According to Biblical Tradition." *Revue Biblique* 103 (1996) 517–45.

Mason, Rex. *Propaganda and Subversion in the Old Testament*. London: SPCK, 1997.

Matthews, Victor H. *A Brief History of Ancient Israel*. Louisville, Ky.: Westminster John Knox Press, 2002.

Matthews, Victor H., and James C. Moyer. *The Old Testament: Text and Context*. 2d ed. Peabody, Mass.: Hendrickson, 2005.

Mazar, Amihai. *Archaeology of the Land of the Bible 10,000–586 B.C.E.* New York: Doubleday, 1990.

McCarter, P. Kyle. "The Apology of David." *Journal of Biblical Literature* 99 (1980) 489–504. Repr., pages 260–75 in *Reconsidering Israel and Judah: Recent Studies on the Deuteronomistic History*. Edited by Gary N. Knoppers and J. Gordon McConville. Winona Lake, Ind.: Eisenbrauns, 2000.

————. "The Historical David." *Interpretation* 40 (1986) 117–29.

————. *I Samuel: A New Translation with Introduction, Notes, and Commentary*. The Anchor Bible 8. Garden City, N.Y.: Doubleday, 1980.

————. *II Samuel: A New Translation with Introduction, Notes, and Commentary*. The Anchor Bible 9. Garden City, N.Y.: Doubleday, 1984.

McGinnis, Claire M. "Swimming with the Divine Tide: An Ignatian Reading of 1 Samuel." Pages 240–70 in *Theological Exegesis: Essays in Honor of Brevard S. Childs*. Edited by Christopher R. Seitz and Kathryn Greene-McCreight. Grand Rapids, Mich.: Eerdmans, 1999.

McKenzie, Steven L. *King David: A Biography*. Oxford: Oxford University Press, 2000.

Mettinger, Tryggve N. D. *King and Messiah: The Civil and Sacral Legitimation of the Israelite Kings*. Old Testament Series 8. Lund: LiberLäromedel/Gleerup, 1976.

Meyers, Carol. "Kinship and Kingship: The Early Monarchy." Pages 221–71 in *The Oxford History of the Biblical World*. Edited by Michael David Coogan. New York: Oxford University Press, 1998.

Mildenberger, Friedrich. "Die vordeuteronomistische Saul-Davidüberlieferung." Ph.D. diss., University of Tübingen, 1962.

Miller, J. Maxwell. "Saul's Rise to Power: Some Observations Concerning I Sam 9:1–10:16; 10:26–11:15 and 13:2–14:46." *Catholic Biblical Quarterly* 36 (1974) 157–74.

Miscall, Peter D. *1 Samuel: A Literary Reading*. Indiana Studies in Biblical Literature. Bloomington, Ind.: Indiana University Press, 1986.

———. *The Workings of Old Testament Narrative*. Semeia Studies. Philadelphia, Pa.: Fortress Press, 1983.

Moberly, R. W. L. *The Bible, Theology, and Faith: A Study of Abraham and Jesus*. Cambridge Studies in Christian Doctrine. Cambridge, U.K.: Cambridge University Press, 2000.

Moor, Johannes Cornelis de. *Synchronic or diachronic? A Debate on Method in Old Testament Exegesis*. Oudtestamentische studiën d. 34. Leiden: Brill, 1995.

Moran, William L. "The Ancient Near Eastern Background of the Love of God in Deuteronomy." *Catholic Biblical Quarterly* 25 (1963) 77–87.

Morgenstern, Julian. "David and Jonathan." *Journal of Biblical Literature* 78 (1959) 322–25.

Mulder, Martin Jan. "The Transmission of the Biblical Text." Pages 87–135 in *Mikra: Text, Translation, Reading and Interpretation of the Hebrew Bible in Ancient Judaism and Early Christianity*. Edited by Martin Jan Mulder. Assen: Van Gorcum; Philadelphia: Fortress Press, 1988.

Murray, Donald F. *Divine Prerogative and Royal Pretension: Pragmatics, Poetics, and Polemics in a Narrative Sequence about David (2 Samuel 5.17–7.29)*. Journal for the Study of the Old Testament Supplement Series 264. Sheffield, U. K.: Sheffield Academic Press, 1998.

Na'aman, Nadav. "Sources and Composition in the History of David." Pages 170–86 in *The Origins of the Ancient Israelite States*. Edited by Volkmar Fritz and Philip R. Davies. Sheffield, U. K.: Sheffield Academic Press, 1996.

Nicholson, Sarah. *Three Faces of Saul: An Intertextual Approach to Biblical Tragedy*. Journal for the Study of the Old Testament Supplement Series 339. London: Sheffield Academic Press, 2002.

Nicol, George G. "David, Abigail and Bathsheba, Nabal and Uriah: Transformations within a Triangle." *Scandinavian Journal of Old Testament* 12 (1998) 130–45.

Noll, Kgurt L. *The Faces of David*. Journal for the Study of the Old Testament Supplement Series 242. Sheffield, U. K.: Sheffield Academic Press, 1997.

North, Robert. "David's Rise: Sacral, Military, or Psychiatric." *Biblica* 63 (1982) 524–44.

Nübel, H.-U. "Davids Aufstieg in der frühe israelitischer Geschichtsschreibung." Ph.D. diss., Bonn: Rheinische Friedrich-Wilhelms-Universität, 1959.

Olyan, Saul M. *Rites and Rank: Hierarchy in Biblical Representations of Cult*. Princeton, N.J.: Princeton University Press, 2000.

Otten, Heinrich. *Die Apologie Hattušilis III. Das Bild der Überlieferung, Studien zu den Bogasköy-Texten*. Wiesbaden: Harrassowitz, 1981.

Payne, David F. "Apologetic Motifs in the Books of Samuel." *Vox Evangelica* 23 (1993) 57–66.

———. "Estimates of the Character of David." *Irish Biblical Studies* 6 (1984) 54–70.

Penkower, Jordan S. "The Development of the Masoretic Bible." Pages 2077–84 in *The Jewish Study Bible*. Edited by Adele Berlin and Marc Z. Brettler. New York: Oxford University Press, 2004.

Perdue, Leo G. " 'Is There Anyone Left of the House of Saul . . .?' Ambiguity and the Characterization of David in the Succession Narrative." *Journal for the Study of the Old Testament* 30 (1984) 67–84.

Perdue, Leo G. "The Testament of David and Egyptian Royal Instructions." Pages 79–96 in *Scripture in Context II: More Essays on the Comparative Method*. Edited by William W. Hallo, James C. Moyer, and Leo G. Perdue. Winona Lake, Ind.: Eisenbrauns, 1983.

Petersen, David L. "Portraits of David—Canonical and Otherwise." *Interpretation* 40 (1980) 130–42.

Peterson, Eugene H. *The Message: The Bible in Contemporary Language*. Colorado Springs, Colo.: NavPress, 2002.

Peterson, Merrill D. *Lincoln in American Memory*. New York: Oxford University Press, 1994.

Pisano, Stephen. "2 Samuel 5–8 and the Deuteronomist: Textual Criticism or Literary Criticism?" Pages 258–83 in *Israel Constructs Its History: Deuteronomistic Historiography in Recent Research*. Edited by Albert de Pury, Thomas Römer, and Jean-Daniel Macchi. Sheffield, U. K.: Sheffield Academic Press, 2000.

Pleins, J. David. "Son-slayers and Their Sons." *Catholic Biblical Quarterly* 54 (1992) 29–38.

Polzin, Robert. *David and the Deuteronomist: 2 Samuel*. Indiana Studies in Biblical Literature. Bloomington, Ind.: Indiana University Press, 1993.

———. *Samuel and the Deuteronomist: 1 Samuel. A Literary Study of the Deuteronomic History 2*. San Francisco: Harper & Row, 1989.

Provan, Iain W., V. Philips Long, and Tremper Longman. *A Biblical History of Israel*. Louisville, Ky.: Westminster John Knox Press, 2003.

Pury, Albert de, Thomas Römer, and Jean-Daniel Macchi, eds. *Israel Constructs Its History: Deuteronomistic Historiography in Recent Research*. Journal for the Study of the Old Testament Supplement Series 306. Sheffield, U. K.: Sheffield Academic Press, 2000.

Rabin, Chaim, Shemaryahu Talmon, and Emanuel Tov, eds. *The Hebrew University Bible, The Book of Jeremiah*. Jerusalem: Magnes, 1997.

Rad, Gerhard von. *Old Testament Theology, Vol. 1: The Theology of Israel's Historical Traditions*. New York: Harper, 1962.

Reis, Pamela Tamarkin. "Collusion at Nob: A New Reading of 1 Samuel 21–22." *Journal for the Study of the Old Testament* 61 (1994) 59–73.

Rendsburg, Gary A. "David and His Circle in Genesis 38." *Vetus Testamentum* 36 (1986) 438–46.

Rendtorff, Rolf. "Beobachtungen zur altisraelitischen Geschichtsschreibung anhand der Geschichte vom Aufstieg Davids." Pages 428–39 in *Probleme biblischer Theologie. Gerhard von Rad zum 70. Geburtstag.* Edited by Hans Walter Wolff. Munich: C. Kaiser, 1971.

Revell, E. J. "The Interpretive Value of the Massoretic Punctuation." Pages 64–73 in *From the Beginnings to the Middle Ages (Until 1300)*. Edited by Magne Sæbø. Volume 1 of *Hebrew Bible/Old Testament: The History of its Interpretation*. Edited by Magne Sæbø. Göttingen: Vandenhoeck & Ruprecht, 2000.

———. "The Leningrad Codex as a Representative of the Masoretic Text." Pages xxix–xlvi in *The Leningrad Codex: A Facsimile Edition*. Edited by David Noel Freedman. Grand Rapids, Mich.: Eerdmans and Leiden: Brill, 1998.

Robert, Philippe de. "Saül, héros tragique dans un prophète incertain." Pages 99–111 in *Héros et l'héroïne bibliques dans la culture*. Montpellier, France: Université Paul-Valéry de Montpellier, 1997.

Römer, Thomas, and Albert de Pury. "Deuteronomistic Historiography (DH): History of Research and Debated Issues." Pages 24–141 in *Israel Constructs its History: Deuteronomistic Historiography in Recent Research*. Edited by Albert de Pury, Thomas Römer and Jean-Daniel Macchi. Sheffield, U. K.: Sheffield Academic Press, 2000.

Rosenberg, David. *The Book of David: A New Story of the Spiritual Warrior and Leader Who Shaped Our Inner Consciousness*. New York: Harmony Books, 1997.

Rosenberg, Joel. *King and Kin: Political Allegory in the Hebrew Bible*, Indiana Studies in Biblical Literature. Bloomington, Ind.: Indiana University Press, 1986.

Rost, Leonhard. *Die Überlieferung von der Thronnachfolge Davids*. Stuttgart: Kohlhammer, 1926.

———. *The Succession to the Throne of David*, Historic Texts and Interpreters in Biblical Scholarship 1. Sheffield, U. K.: Almond Press, 1982.

Rudman, Dominic. "The Patriarchal Narratives in the Books of Samuel." *Vetus Testamentum* 54 (2004) 239–49.

Sáenz-Badillos, Angel. *A History of the Hebrew Language*. Cambridge: Cambridge University Press, 1993.

Sanders, James A. *From Sacred Story to Sacred Text: Canon as Paradigm*. Philadelphia: Fortress Press, 1987.

Sanford, John A. *King Saul, The Tragic Hero: A Study in Individuation.* New York: Paulist Press, 1985.

Schicklberger, Franz. "Die Davididen und das Nordreich. Beobachtungen zur sog. Geschichte vom Aufstieg Davids." *Biblische Zeitschrift* 18 (1974) 255–63.

Schulte, Hannelis. *Die Entstehung der Geschichtsschreibung im Alten Israel.* Beihefte zur Zeitschrift für die alttestamentliche Wissenschaft 128. Berlin: De Gruyter, 1972.

Seidl, Theodor. "David statt Saul. Gottliche Legitimation und menschliche Kompetenz des Konigs als Motive der Redaktion von 1 Sam 16–18." *Zeitschrift für die alttestamentliche Wissenschaft* 98 (1986) 39–55.

Sekine, Seizō. *A Comparative Study of the Origins of Ethical Thought: Hellenism and Hebraism.* Translated by Judy Wakabayashi. Lanham, Md.: Rowman & Littlefield, 2005.

Simon, Uriel. "The Religious Significance of the *Peshat.*" *Tradition* 23 (1988) 41–63.

Smith, Henry Preserved. *A Critical and Exegetical Commentary on the Books of Samuel.* New York: Scribner, 1904.

Smith, Morton. "The So-Called-'Biography of David' in the Books of Samuel and Kings." *Harvard Theological Review* 44 (1951) 167–69.

Sperling, S. David. *The Original Torah: The Political Intent of the Bible's Writers.* Reappraisals in Jewish Social and Intellectual History. New York: New York University Press, 1998.

Stein, Peter. "'Und man berichtete Saul...' Text- und literarkritische Untersuchungen zu 1 Samuels 24 und 26." *Biblische Notizen* 90 (1997) 46–66.

Sternberg, Meir. *The Poetics of Biblical Narrative: Ideological Literature and the Drama of Reading.* Indiana Literary Biblical Series. Bloomington, Ind.: Indiana University Press, 1985.

Steussy, Marti J. *David: Biblical Portraits of Power.* Columbia, S.C.: University of South Carolina Press, 1999.

Stoebe, Hans Joachim. *Das erste Buch Samuelis.* Kommentar zum Alten Testament Bd. 8, Hft. 1. Gütersloh: Mohn, 1973.

Stolz, Fritz. *Das erste und zweite Buch Samuel.* Zürcher Bibelkommentare. AT 9. Zürich: Theologischer Verlag, 1981.

Stott, Katherine. "Herodotus and the Old Testament: A Comparative Reading of the Ascendancy Stories of King Cyrus and David." *Scandinavian Journal of the Old Testament* 16 (2002) 52–78.

Sturtevant, Edgar Howard, and George Bechtel. *A Hittite Chrestomathy*. Philadelphia: Linguistic Society of America University of Pennsylvania, 1935.

Tadmor, Hayim. "Autobiographical Apology in the Royal Assyrian Literature." Pages 36–57 in *History, Historiography and Interpretation: Studies in Biblical and Cuneiform Literatures*. Edited by Hayim Tadmor and Moshe Weinfeld. Jerusalem: Magnes, 1983.

Taggar-Cohen, Ada. "Political Loyalty in the Biblical Account of 1 Samuel XX–XXII in the Light of Hittite Texts." *Vetus Testamentum* 55 (2005) 251–68.

Thompson, Thomas L. *The Messiah Myth: The Near Eastern Roots of Jesus and David*. New York: Basic Books, 2005.

———. *The Mythic Past: Biblical Archaeology and the Myth of Israel*. New York: Basic Books, 1999.

Tigay, Jeffrey H. "The Stylistic Criterion of Source Criticism in the Light of Ancient Near Eastern and Postbiblical Literature." Pages 149–73 in *Empirical Models for Biblical Criticism*. Edited by Jeffrey H. Tigay. Philadelphia: University of Pennsylvania Press, 1985.

Tov, Emanuel. "The Status of the Masoretic Text in Modern Text Editions of the Hebrew Bible: The Relevance of Canon." Pages 234–51 in *The Canon Debate*. Edited by Lee Martin McDonald and James A. Sanders. Peabody, Mass.: Hendrickson, 2002.

———. *Textual Criticism of the Hebrew Bible*. 2d ed. Minneapolis: Fortress Press; Assen: Van Gorcum, 2001.

Tsumura, David T. *The First Book of Samuel*, New International Commentary on the Old Testament. Grand Rapids, Mich.: Eerdmans, 2007.

———. "Family in the Historical Books." Pages 59–79 in *Family in the Bible: Exploring Customs, Culture, and Context*. Edited by Richard S. Hess and M. Daniel Carroll R. Grand Rapids, Mich.: Baker Academic, 2003.

Tull, Patricia. "Intertextuality and the Hebrew Scriptures." *Currents in Research: Biblical Studies* 8 (2000) 59–90.

Ünal, Ahmet. *Hattušili III. Hattušili bis zu seiner Thronbesteigung 1: Historischer Abriß*. Texte der Hethiter, Heft 3–4. Heidelberg: Winter, 1974.

van den Hout, Th. P. J. "The Proclamation of Telipinu." Pages 194–198 in *The Context of Scripture, Vol. 1: Canonical Compositions from the Biblical World*. Edited by William W. Hallo and K. Lawson Younger, Jr. Leiden: Brill, 1997.

van den Hout, Th. P. J. "Apology of Ḫattušili III." Pages 199–204 in *The Context of Scripture, Vol. 1: Canonical Compositions from the Biblical World*. Edited by William W. Hallo and K. Lawson Younger, Jr. Leiden: Brill, 1997.

Van Seters, John. *In Search of History: Historiography in the Ancient World and the Origins of Biblical History*. New Haven: Yale University Press, 1983. Repr., Winona Lake, Ind.: Eisenbrauns, 1997.

———. "Problems in the Literary Analysis of the Court History of David." *Journal for the Study of the Old Testament* 1 (1976) 22–29.

VanderKam, James C. "Davidic Complicity in the Deaths of Abner and Eshbaal: A Historical and Redactional Study." *Journal of Biblical Literature* 99 (1980) 521–39.

Vaughn, Andrew G. " 'And Lot Went with Him': Abraham's Disobedience in Genesis 12:1–4a." Pages 111–23 in *David and Zion: Biblical Studies in Honor of J. J. M. Roberts*. Edited by Kathryn L. Roberts and Bernard Frank Batto. Winona Lake, Ind.: Eisenbrauns, 2004.

Vaux, Roland de. *Ancient Israel: Its Life and Institutions*. New York: McGraw-Hill, 1965.

———. "Le roi d'Israël, vassal de Yahvé." Pages 119–33 in *Melanges Eugène Tisserant*. Città del Vaticano: Biblioteca Apostolica Vaticana, 1964.

Veijola, Timo. *David. Gesammelte Studien zu den Davidüberlieferungen des Alten Testaments*. Helsinki: Finnische Exegetische Gesellschaft, 1990.

———. "David in Keila. Tradition und Interpretation in 1 Sam 23:1–13." *Revue Biblique* 91 (1984) 51–87.

———. *Die ewige Dynastie. David und die Entstehung seiner Dynastie nach der deuteronomistischen Darstellung*. Helsinki: Suomalainen Tiedeakatemia, 1975.

Vermeylen, Jacques. *La loi du plus fort. Histoire de la rédaction des récits davidiques de 1 Samuel 8 à 1 Rois 2*. Bibliotheca Ephemeridum theologicarum Lovaniensium 154. Leuven: Leuven University Press, 2000.

———. "La maison de Saul et la maison de David. Un ecrit de propagande theologico-politique, de 1 S 11 a 2 S 7." Pages 35–74 in *Figures de David a travers la Bible. XVIIe congres de l'ACFEB, Lille, 1er–5 septembre 1997*. Edited by Louis Desrousseaux and Jacques Vermeylen. Paris: Cerf, 1999.

Viviano, Pauline A. "Source Criticism." Pages 29–51 in *To Each its Own Meaning: An Introduction to Biblical Criticisms and their Application*. Edited by Stephen R. Haynes and Steven L. McKenzie. Louisville, Ky.: Westminster John Knox Press, 1993.

Vorster, Willem S. "Readings, Readers, and the Succession Narrative: An Essay on Reception." Pages 395–407 in *Beyond Form Criticism: Essays in Old Testament Literary Criticism*. Edited by Paul R. House. Winona Lake, Ind.: Eisenbrauns, 1992.

Ward, Roger Lemuel. "The Story of David's Rise: A Traditio-Historical Study of 1 Samuel XVI 14–II Samuel V." Ph.D. diss., Vanderbilt University, 1967.

Watts, Rikk E. "Echoes from the Past: Israel's Ancient Traditions and the Destiny of the Nations in Isaiah 40–55." *Journal for the Study of the Old Testament* 28 (2004) 481–508.

Weinfeld, Moshe. "The Roots of the Messianic Idea." Pages 279–87 in *Mythology and Mythologies: Methodological Approaches to Intercultural Influences. Proceedings of the Second Annual Symposium of the Assyrian and Babylonian Intellectual Heritage Project held in Paris, France, Oct. 4–7, 1999*. Edited by Robert M. Whiting. Helsinki: Neo-Assyrian Text Corpus Project, 2001.

————. *Deuteronomy and the Deuteronomic School*. Oxford: Clarendon Press, 1972.

————. "The Covenant of Grant in the Old Testament and in the Ancient Near East." *Journal of the American Oriental Society* 90 (1970) 184–203.

Weiser, Artur. "Die Legitimation des Königs David. Zur Eigenart und Entstehung der sogenannten Geschichte von Davids Aufstieg." *Vetus Testamentum* 16 (1966) 325–54.

Wellhausen, Julius. *Prolegomena to the History of Israel*, Scholars Press Reprints and Translations Series 17. Atlanta, Ga.: Scholars Press, 1994.

Wenin, André. "With Lyre and Slingshot: David's Rise to Kingship." *Revue Theologique de Louvain* 28 (1997) 260–61.

White, Marsha C. "Saul and Jonathan in 1 Samuel 1 and 14." Pages 119–38 in *Saul in Story and Tradition*. Edited by Carl S. Ehrlich and Marsha C. White. Tübingen: Mohr Siebeck, 2006.

Whitelam, Keith W. "The Defence of David." *Journal for the Study of the Old Testament* 29 (1984) 61–87.

Willis, John T. "Function of Comprehensive Anticipatory Redactional Joints in 1 Samuel 16–18." *Zeitschrift für die alttestamentliche Wissenschaft* 85 (1973) 294–314.

Wilson, Kenneth G., ed. *The Columbia Guide to Standard American English.* New York: Columbia University Press, 1993.

Wilson, Robert R. "Genealogy, Genealogies." Pages 929–32 in vol. 2 of *The Anchor Bible Dictionary*. Edited by David Noel Freedman. 6 vols. New York: Doubleday, 1992.

———. *Genealogy and History in the Biblical World.* New Haven: Yale University Press, 1977.

Wolf, Herbert M. "The Apology of Hattušiliš Compared with Other Ancient Near Eastern Political Self-Justifications." Ph.D. diss., Brandeis University, 1967.

Wolterstorff, Nicholas. *Divine Discourse: Philosophical Reflections on the Claim that God Speaks.* Cambridge: Cambridge University Press, 1995.

Yonick, Stephen. *Rejection of Saul as King of Israel According to 1 Sm 15: Stylistic Study in Theology.* Jerusalem: Franciscan Print Press, 1970.

Zakovitch, Yair. *David, me-ro'eh le-mashiah.* Yerushalayim: Yad Ben-Tsevi, 1995.

———. "Through the Looking Glass: Reflections/Inversions of Genesis Stories in the Bible." *Biblical Interpretation* 1 (1993) 139–52.

Zapf, David L. "How Are the Mighty Fallen: A Study of 2 Samuel 1:17–27." *Grace Theological Journal* 5 (1984) 95–126.

Zwickel, Wolfgang. "David als Vorbild fur den Glauben. Die Veranderung des Davidbildes im Verlauf der alttestamentlichen Geschichte, dargestellt an 2 Sam 6." *Biblische Notizen* 79 (1995) 88–101.

Index of Primary Sources

Biblical Texts (according to BHS)

Index of Subjects

Index of Modern Authors

Harvard Theological Studies

64. Nasrallah, Laura, Charalambos Bakirtzis, and Steven J. Friesen, eds. *From Roman to Early Christian Thessalonikē: Studies in Religion and Archaeology*, 2010.

63. Short, J. Randall. *The Surprising Election and Confirmation of King David*, 2010.

61. Schifferdecker, Kathryn. *Out of the Whirlwind: Creation Theology in the Book of Job*, 2008.

60. Luijendijk, AnneMarie. *Greetings in the Lord: Early Christians and the Oxyrhynchus Papyri*, 2008.

59. Yip, Francis Ching-Wah. *Capitalism As Religion? A Study of Paul Tillich's Interpretation of Modernity*, 2010.

58. Pearson, Lori. *Beyond Essence: Ernst Troeltsch as Historian and Theorist of Christianity*, 2008.

57. Hills, Julian V. *Tradition and Composition in the* Epistula Apostolorum, 2008.

56. Nickelsburg, George W. E. *Resurrection, Immortality, and Eternal Life in Intertestamental Judaism and Early Christianity*. Expanded Edition, 2006.

55. Johnson-DeBaufre, Melanie. *Jesus Among Her Children: Q, Eschatology, and the Construction of Christian Origins*, 2005.

54. Hall, David D. *The Faithful Shepherd: A History of the New England Ministry in the Seventeenth Century*, 2006.

53. Schowalter, Daniel N., and Steven J. Friesen, eds. *Urban Religion in Roman Corinth: Interdisciplinary Approaches*, 2004.

52. Nasrallah, Laura. *"An Ecstasy of Folly": Prophecy and Authority in Early Christianity*, 2003.

51. Brock, Ann Graham. *Mary Magdalene, The First Apostle: The Struggle for Authority*, 2003.

50. Trost, Theodore Louis. *Douglas Horton and the Ecumenical Impulse in American Religion*, 2002.

49. Huang, Yong. *Religious Goodness and Political Rightness: Beyond the Liberal-Communitarian Debate*, 2001.

48. Rossing, Barbara R. *The Choice between Two Cities: Whore, Bride, and Empire in the Apocalypse*, 1999.

47. Skedros, James Constantine. *Saint Demetrios of Thessaloniki: Civic Patron and Divine Protector, 4th–7th Centuries C.E.*, 1999.

46. Koester, Helmut, ed. *Pergamon, Citadel of the Gods: Archaeological Record, Literary Description, and Religious Development*, 1998.

45. Kittredge, Cynthia Briggs. *Community and Authority: The Rhetoric of Obedience in the Pauline Tradition*, 1998.

44. Lesses, Rebecca Macy. *Ritual Practices to Gain Power: Angels, Incantations, and Revelation in Early Jewish Mysticism*, 1998.

43. Guenther-Gleason, Patricia E. *On Schleiermacher and Gender Politics*, 1997.

42. White, L. Michael. *The Social Origins of Christian Architecture* (2 vols.), 1997.

41. Koester, Helmut, ed. *Ephesos, Metropolis of Asia: An Interdisciplinary Approach to its Archaeology, Religion, and Culture*, 1995.

40. Guider, Margaret Eletta. *Daughters of Rahab: Prostitution and the Church of Liberation in Brazil*, 1995.

39. Schenkel, Albert F. *The Rich Man and the Kingdom: John D. Rockefeller, Jr., and the Protestant Establishment*, 1995.

38. Hutchison, William R. and Hartmut Lehmann, eds. *Many Are Chosen: Divine Election and Western Nationalism*, 1994.

37. Lubieniecki, Stanislas. *History of the Polish Reformation and Nine Related Documents*. Translated and interpreted by George Huntston Williams, 1995.

– Davidovich, Adina. *Religion as a Province of Meaning: The Kantian Foundations of Modern Theology*, 1993.

36. Thiemann, Ronald F., ed. *The Legacy of H. Richard Niebuhr*, 1991.

35. Hobbs, Edward C., ed. *Bultmann, Retrospect and Prospect: The Centenary Symposium at Wellesley*, 1985.

34. Cameron, Ron. *Sayings Traditions in the Apocryphon of James*, 1984. Reprinted, 2004.

33. Blackwell, Albert L. *Schleiermacher's Early Philosophy of Life: Determinism, Freedom, and Phantasy*, 1982.

32. Gibson, Elsa. *The "Christians for Christians" Inscriptions of Phrygia: Greek Texts, Translation and Commentary*, 1978.

31. Bynum, Caroline Walker. Docere Verbo et Exemplo: *An Aspect of Twelfth-Century Spirituality*, 1979.

30. Williams, George Huntston, ed. *The Polish Brethren: Documentation of the History and Thought of Unitarianism in the Polish-Lithuanian Commonwealth and in the Diaspora 1601–1685*, 1980.

29. Attridge, Harold W. *First-Century Cynicism in the Epistles of Heraclitus*, 1976.

28. Williams, George Huntston, Norman Pettit, Winfried Herget, and Sargent Bush, Jr., eds. *Thomas Hooker: Writings in England and Holland, 1626–1633*, 1975.

27. Preus, James Samuel. *Carlstadt's* Ordinaciones *and Luther's Liberty: A Study of the Wittenberg Movement, 1521–22*, 1974.

26. Nickelsburg, George W. E. *Resurrection, Immortality, and Eternal Life in Intertestamental Judaism*, 1972.

25. Worthley, Harold Field. *An Inventory of the Records of the Particular (Congregational) Churches of Massachusetts Gathered 1620–1805*, 1970.

24. Yamauchi, Edwin M. *Gnostic Ethics and Mandaean Origins*, 1970.

23. Yizhar, Michael. *Bibliography of Hebrew Publications on the Dead Sea Scrolls 1948–1964*, 1967.

22. Albright, William Foxwell. *The Proto-Sinaitic Inscriptions and Their Decipherment*, 1966.

21. Dow, Sterling, and Robert F. Healey. *A Sacred Calendar of Eleusis*, 1965.

20. Sundberg, Jr., Albert C. *The Old Testament of the Early Church*, 1964.

19. Cranz, Ferdinand Edward. *An Essay on the Development of Luther's Thought on Justice, Law, and Society*, 1959.

18. Williams, George Huntston, ed. *The Norman Anonymous of 1100 A.D.: Towards the Identification and Evaluation of the So-Called Anonymous of York*, 1951.

17. Lake, Kirsopp, and Silva New, eds. *Six Collations of New Testament Manuscripts*, 1932.

16. Wilbur, Earl Morse, trans. *The Two Treatises of Servetus on the Trinity: On the Errors of the Trinity, 7 Books, A.D. 1531. Dialogues on the Trinity, 2 Books. On the Righteousness of Christ's Kingdom, 4 Chapters, A.D. 1532*, 1932.

15. Casey, Robert Pierce, ed. Serapion of Thmuis's *Against the Manichees*, 1931.

14. Ropes, James Hardy. *The Singular Problem of the Epistles to the Galatians*, 1929.

13. Smith, Preserved. *A Key to the Colloquies of Erasmus*, 1927.

12. Spyridon of the Laura and Sophronios Eustratiades. *Catalogue of the Greek Manuscripts in the Library of the Laura on Mount Athos*, 1925.

11. Sophronios Eustratiades and Arcadios of Vatopedi. *Catalogue of the Greek Manuscripts in the Library of the Monastery of Vatopedi on Mt. Athos*, 1924.

10. Conybeare, Frederick C. *Russian Dissenters*, 1921.

9. Burrage, Champlin, ed. *An Answer to John Robinson of Leyden by a Puritan Friend: Now First Published from a Manuscript of A.D. 1609*, 1920.

8. Emerton, Ephraim. *The* Defensor pacis *of Marsiglio of Padua: A Critical Study*, 1920,

7. Bacon, Benjamin W. *Is Mark a Roman Gospel?* 1919.

6. Cadbury, Henry Joel. 2 vols. *The Style and Literary Method of Luke*, 1920.

5. Marriott, G. L., ed. Macarii Anecdota: *Seven Unpublished Homilies of Macarius*, 1918.

4. Edmunds, Charles Carroll and William Henry Paine Hatch. *The Gospel Manuscripts of the General Theological Seminary*, 1918.

3. Arnold, William Rosenzweig. *Ephod and Ark: A Study in the Records and Religion of the Ancient Hebrews*, 1917.

2. Hatch, William Henry Paine. *The Pauline Idea of Faith in its Relation to Jewish and Hellenistic Religion*, 1917.

1. Torrey, Charles Cutler. *The Composition and Date of Acts*, 1916.

Harvard Dissertations in Religion

In 1993, Harvard Theological Studies absorbed
the Harvard Dissertations in Religion series.

31. Baker-Fletcher, Garth. *Somebodyness: Martin Luther King, Jr. and the Theory of Dignity*, 1993.

30. Soneson, Jerome Paul. *Pragmatism and Pluralism: John Dewey's Significance for Theology*, 1993.

29. Crabtree, Harriet. *The Christian Life: The Traditional Metaphors and Contemporary Theologies*, 1991.

28. Schowalter, Daniel N. *The Emperor and the Gods: Images from the Time of Trajan*, 1993.

27. Valantasis, Richard. *Spiritual Guides of the Third Century: A Semiotic Study of the Guide-Disciple Relationship in Christianity, Neoplatonism, Hermetism, and Gnosticism*, 1991.

26. Wills, Lawrence Mitchell. *The Jews in the Court of the Foreign King: Ancient Jewish Court Legends*, 1990.

25. Massa, Mark Stephen. *Charles Augustus Briggs and the Crisis of Historical Criticism*, 1990.

24. Hills, Julian Victor. *Tradition and Composition in the* Epistula apostolorum, 1990. Reprinted, 2008.

23. Bowe, Barbara Ellen. *A Church in Crisis: Ecclesiology and Paraenesis in Clement of Rome*, 1988.

22. Bisbee, Gary A. *Pre-Decian Acts of Martyrs and* Commentarii, 1988.

21. Ray, Stephen Alan. *The Modern Soul: Michel Foucault and the Theological Discourse of Gordon Kaufman and David Tracy*, 1987.

20. MacDonald, Dennis Ronald. *There Is No Male and Female: The Fate of a Dominical Saying in Paul and Gnosticism*, 1987.

19. Davaney, Sheila Greeve. *Divine Power: A Study of Karl Barth and Charles Hartshorne*, 1986.

18. LaFargue, J. Michael. *Language and Gnosis: The Opening Scenes of the Acts of Thomas*, 1985.

12. Layton, Bentley, ed. *The Gnostic Treatise on Resurrection from Nag Hammadi*, 1979.

11. Ryan, Patrick J. *Imale: Yoruba Participation in the Muslim Tradition: A Study of Clerical Piety*, 1977.

10. Neevel, Jr., Walter G. *Yāmuna's* Vedānta *and* Pāñcarātra: *Integrating the Classical and the Popular*, 1977.

9. Yarbro Collins, Adela. *The Combat Myth in the Book of Revelation*, 1976.

8. Veatch, Robert M. *Value-Freedom in Science and Technology: A Study of the Importance of the Religious, Ethical, and Other Socio-Cultural Factors in Selected Medical Decisions Regarding Birth Control*, 1976.

7. Attridge, Harold W. *The Interpretation of Biblical History in the* Antiquitates judaicae *of Flavius Josephus*, 1976.

6. Trakatellis, Demetrios C. *The Pre-Existence of Christ in the Writings of Justin Martyr*, 1976.

5. Green, Ronald Michael. *Population Growth and Justice: An Examination of Moral Issues Raised by Rapid Population Growth*, 1975.

4. Schrader, Robert W. *The Nature of Theological Argument: A Study of Paul Tillich*, 1976.

3. Christensen, Duane L. *Transformations of the War Oracle in Old Testament Prophecy: Studies in the Oracles Against the Nations*, 1975.

2. Williams, Sam K. *Jesus' Death as Saving Event: The Background and Origin of a Concept*, 1972.

1. Smith, Jane I. *An Historical and Semantic Study of the Term "Islām" as Seen in a Sequence of Qur'an Commentaries*, 1970.